" Jon Bunn's fine memoir is a rarity among the burgeoning tide of unimaginative, formulaic, self-serving autobiographies, diaries, and apologias of politicians, five-minutes-of-fame entertainers, and self-aggrandizing CEOs and 'finance bros.'

Bunn provides, instead, a candid, self-written (and well-written) account of an uncommon common man who, in the course of seven decades, has literally raised himself, and (driven by insatiable curiosity) mastered the art of stained glass, skydived at county fairs, developed a hands-on knowledge of the natural world (particularly in the swamps and bayous of East Texas, Acadian Louisiana, and the strip mines and quarries of Central Indiana). He also earned a master's degree in theater at Indiana University, wrote a couple of novels, wrote a number of poems and song lyrics, and survived a planned triple-bypass heart surgery that went to a quad-bypass in the operating room. Apparently, he's also a fine freshwater and saltwater fisherman!

My favorite portion of Bunn's memoir comes about midway through and deals with his admission into Indiana University, where he went on to capitalize on every educational opportunity that adequately funded education policies provided for at the time. **"**

Shaun O'L. Higgins
Media executive, film curator, and author/co-author of
Leadership Secrets of Elizabeth I (2000)
Vachel Lindsay: Troubadour in the Wildflower City (1999)
The Newspaper in Art (1997)
Press Gallery: The Newspaper in Modern and Postmodern Art (2005)
Fellow alumni, BHS Class of 1966

"I was so touched by your memoir. The main takeaway for me is that you have opened up your soul to present a very honest authentic view of your life. My belief is that everyone has a story to tell, but most people either cannot or don't want to tell it, usually because it is too painful, but as Socrates said, 'the unexamined life is not worth living.' Not sure I totally agree with that sentiment, but hey, he was Socrates, I'm not.

Some of your initial musings bring back memories of a bygone era, because of course we were born around the same time. Eating paste (I never did, but knew kids who did), building things (I constructed an alligator bath for the alligator I was going to order by email), making things with a lead mold (I almost electrocuted myself doing that as a child), picking up pop bottles to get some small change—the things that kids will do when left to their own devices, which we frequently were in our generation.

Your portrayal of abuse brought tears to my eyes. What comes through in your book is that you are a survivor. I feel a kinship with that, and I suspect there are legions of your readers who can relate to that. You must look back and marvel at all of the things you have accomplished in life despite the obstacles in your way. I know I do the same. I guess I attribute my own trajectory to stubbornness, perseverance, the support of a few key people, and a lot of pure luck. Sometimes it is just getting up and putting one foot in front of the other.

In sum, I think you have produced a raw and true book that will touch so many people. It was an honor to read it."

Judy Stephens Morrow, PhD
Retired Faculty / Research Associate
University of North Carolina at Chapel Hill
Fellow alumni, BHS Class of 1966

"Our paths crossed at a class reunion, after not having seen each other for decades. We struck up a conversation, and the next thing I know you're asking me to read a manuscript of yours. I had been working as an editor for many years at that point and had gradually begun to specialize in working with first-time authors, and writers who wanted to self-publish, so my interest was piqued.

And then the *next* thing I know, we were working on the manuscript to your first novel. And despite the fact that you have an almost alarming proclivity for switching back and forth between past and present tense, it was obvious to me from the very first that you are a great storyteller—in writing, as well as in person.

It has been my absolute pleasure to work with you on both of your novels to date. Editing *The West Bluff*, I got to know about your years growing up in East Texas, and how your immersion in the arts of hunting, fishing, and trapping in the swamps and bayous had left an indelible impression. Working on *Shoals Bluff*, I got to know more about your experiences in Indiana, and how the terrain there also shaped you, as did the people whose lives intersected with yours. I also began to understand how the main character of that book embodied some of the lasting terrors of your childhood.

And now in this book, I've finally begun to get a clearer picture of where you're coming from, geographically and psychically and historically. As an editor, I marvel at your ability to tell your story in both first and third person, which creates a bit of objectivity in the narrative at times, and to tell your stories occasionally in the form of poetry or lyrics, as well as prose. I am certain your memoir will be inspirational to many readers, and to other writers as well."

Margaret (Peg) Flaten Daisley
Editor, BlueHorizonBooks.com
Fellow alumni, BHS Class of 1966

Books by Jon Bunn

IT WAS JUST STORIES …
and then everything changed.
A Memoir, 2024
A collection of 44 short stories, poems and lyrics

SHOALS BLUFF
Historical Fiction Novel, 2020

THE WEST BLUFF
Historical Fiction Novel, 2018

IT WAS JUST STORIES…

and then everything changed.

a memoir

Jon Bunn

IT WAS JUST STORIES...
and then everything changed.

Jon Bunn c/o Mayhaw Press
22212 Rock Wren
Spicewood, TX 78669
JonBunn.com

Published by:
Mayhaw Press

Cover & Book Design:
Dawn Daisley
MorningLiteBookDesign.com

Printed in the United States of America

Publisher's Cataloging-in-Publication data:
Bunn, Jon
It Was Just Stories... and then everything changed. / Jon Bunn / Memoir
ISBN: 979-8-3305-2676-5

ABOUT THE COVER
The author's great grandfather John Bone (Bee) Paine is pictured sitting on a wagon of 85 bushels of corn at the Paine home in Douglas, Texas, where he was born November 13, 1853. Britton (Brit) Tucker, a ranch hand, is on a horse. The person astride the oxen is unidentified. John Paine's daughter is the author's grandmother, Bina Electra Paine Bunn. All the farm animals had names. Oxen from L to R and back to front are Ball, Ben, Lip, Charlie, Buck, Jeff, Curly, and Tom. In 1936, the town of Douglas had one dwelling and four buildings, as well as a cemetery. In the 1970's, the town was essentially abandoned.

Dedication of The Spurs

Spurs. I wore them for the jingle. I had no interest or desire to use them on an animal and bring hurt to anyone. I just liked their sound. It was nice dress-up to wear them in the rodeos, trail rides, parades, and in the arenas. Me and all the horses I ever rode had this understanding once I mounted up. Riding bareback, I would get the feel of the horse and understanding of their temperament. When you're riding bareback, you are more as one with them.

However, I kept those spurs around me, even when the leather straps and buckles became stiff, dry-rotted, and fell off in the rodeo arena. They were, to me, a symbol that reminded me of my two daughters and that's why I gave the spurs to them.

The spur is to symbolize to them the idea of going forward, even if times are rough and tough after I'm gone. The spurs are, for me, the perfect metaphor that connects me to them. That's why the Lord only gave me two children—because I only had two spurs.

Three spurs would be absurd! I can't even visualize what that would look like.

Introduction

The "story" of a person is told or observed differently, depending upon who is doing the telling. Simply put, when one is asked to share something about themself, it may be something simple or complex, plain or embellished. It may just be factual or fantastical and it could change *after* the telling or changed *during* the telling. It depends upon the author!

When someone says, "I didn't know that about you," it is seldom greeted by silence, but instead with additional commentary. All it takes is for someone to write it down and they, then, become a historian.

History becomes that gathering activity that captures, perhaps, that essence. In pre-history, the time I like to think of that predates writing, it must have been a mighty effort to "get the word out," using massive labor forces to move stones and other heavy objects about, striking chisels with hammers and such. Those were some heavy words, for sure.

As heavy tools became lighter and turned into pencils, the stories could be more complete and interesting. It no longer took decades to carve out a sentence. The accoutrement of capture is still changing, from cave walls to clay tablets, to papyrus, to paper, and now the computer.

Such a grand harvest, as such, will always take place, as long as there are people to gather. As such, the rolling forth of the past into the present and beyond has left a rich stream of artifacts that can be gleaned and savored anew.

The few examples in beginning this story seek to illustrate the weaving of a newer tapestry that is seen, revealed, and living within a common man.

The survivors and the ancestors go forth …

Contents

~ PART ONE ~

What You Didn't Learn, You Learned

When Jonny was a youngster (that's me), growing up in southeastern Texas, there was always a need to fill in a gap or two when seeking something else to do, after the usual mischiefs and mishaps. Since we lived on a ranch in the country, we could just go about and do what we wanted, as we didn't see the parents much. Sorta free range and all.

Just to know that our culprit (me) would find mischiefs is to illuminate that bygone wastrel's curiosity with firecrackers and things that go "bang." Having unfettered access to rifles, shotguns, pistols, and the like was not a curiosity to be of much interest to me, to want to go out and blast away, except for the empty beer cans, tossed in and floating by on the Sabine River.

The emerging and growing interest was whetted on the Fourth of July and the few weeks before and after the celebration of our Independence Day festivities. The firecracker stands would spring up and begin to sell a variety of my favorites—regular firecrackers, cracker balls, bottle rockets, and cherry bombs. Always in hand were a few parental contributions, and I doubled my efforts to make money, usually by walking the ditches along the sides of the roads and finding discarded Coke bottles to turn in for the deposits. Another gold mine was the construction sites where we would pick up bottles after the workers discarded them.

The soft drink companies were offering 1 cent or 2 cents for each bottle brought back into the store that first sold them. It was spending money for me and the other neighborhood kids. Some kids even had their parents buy them wire baskets for their bikes, so they could really make a haul back to the store. Red Flyer wagons could be pulled along, and they would hold lots of bottles. A heavy-duty rig in those days was to have your Schwinn bike pulling your wagon down the road. I could out-pick most of the others and we got the lion's share of the booty. That was the big choice, to pull your rig or walk it. Some stores, like the 7-11's would buy bottles, six of them in a folding cardboard carton, at six bottles for 15 cents, a bloody goldmine!

Most of the returns to the stores came from empties of Coke, 7-Up, Grapette, RC Cola (Royal Crown had bigger servings), Orange Aid, and Big Red, with a few Root Beer bottles. Squirt was in there, too. If you found Squirt bottles, it was as likely as not that there was hard liquor being mixed with it. It was too sour to just drink it, like you normally would. It was usually mixed with vodka. I was lucky. I had parents who drank, sometimes they drank a lot, at least one did, a lot. And so, when the neighbors began popping firecrackers, I could pressure the parents to give me a dollar, and on a rare occasion, two dollars, to go get firecrackers.

What to buy, what to buy? Regular firecrackers were 1½ inches long and I could get them in packs of 20, 50, and on up. The neighbors would sometimes set off a whole package of 100 all at once.

Jealousy did not work. I was not going to shoot off even two at a time. It made lots of noise, but it was over in less than a minute. So, me and my sister Kelly set them off one at a time.

We were always looking to find something to blow up. Having three dollars or more, when we pooled our coins, gave us lots of packs, and some punks to light them with, and even got us some bottle rockets, too.

A good sharp eye spotted something that looked like shotgun barrels sticking out of a trash can that turned out to be just that, old shotguns that were thrown away with broken wooden stocks. The guns were quite old, and nobody wanted them, so we grabbed them and hauled them home to use them to shoot firecrackers out of. Light a firecracker and drop it down the barrel and shoot it just like it was a real shotgun. That was the idea.

What made it extra neat was the idea that a firecracker could be dropped into the barrel and then you'd drop in a marble to see if that would work. Of course, it would work. And it did! They went out so fast one had to really watch close to see the marble go flying away. Better than a slingshot, that was. It only held a momentary interest, however, as you could lose your marbles when you did it, so to speak.

The fuses were really too short to shoot marbles safely, as you could hardly get it to the shoulder and aim it before it flew off, so interest in doing it faded and then interest was lost.

Ant hills were favorite places to blow up. After all, the fire ants were always getting on us and stinging us on our bare feet, so war was always declared. It was payback time. When unusually heavy rains occurred, the ants would float out over the top of the anthill, and all gather in a floating red mat. When anyone walked to the store to get groceries, cigarettes, or something like milk and white bread, wet legs let the ants cling to us, and someone would get badly stung in a heartbeat. It was almost unavoidable, especially during hurricanes when the winds blew them off the water and they flew through the air and hit you like blowing sand would and they would stick on you, on your clothing and then bite your arms and legs.

Again, it was payback time!

The next farm over, neighbors on the other side of the fence had three or four 55-gallon drums with one end cut out. They would use this drum for burning. Lots of trash on the ground and other things that would not burn were tossed around. Bottles and cans and other things. We especially prized one-pound coffee cans with twist keys to open them with. Fixing a shooter can was done by making a small hole in the center of the can to fit a firecracker in. The coffee can would shoot high into the air.

Another great target was putting a firecracker in a crawfish hole and blowing up the mud castle on top. Any hole in a log, or glass bottle, or a pipe was good amusement in those days. It was better than playing with a sock, which was one of our "toys" at the time. We added old shotguns from the garbage cans to shoot bottle rockets through. Sometimes it was fun to twist two or three fuses together and light those. Three firecrackers at once, what a bang!

During one day of shooting off firecrackers, I noticed I had silver flash powder on my hand from opening and separating lots of firecrackers into my paper sack. I reached into my bag for another firecracker, and unbeknownst to me, a spark had fallen in and lit the one I picked up. My hand just cleared the bag when it went off in my closed hand. It felt like a car door slamming shut on my hand.

I was really yelling—wailing would be a more apt description. Upon inspection, the hand was a bit swollen, nothing was bleeding or missing and so the remedy was to pour vinegar over it and go back outside and play.

After praying to God to make the throbbing pain stop, swearing on my mother's grave (and all the relatives I could think of who might hold sway), swearing I would never do it again, I slowly realized my sister would get my sack of firecrackers if I didn't pop them, so, I resumed the ant wars and popped my own damned firecrackers.

❋ ❋ ❋

The drinkers and drunks seemed to always be hanging around our place on weekends. When the BBQ pit was smoking, they all showed up. Beer and whiskey came out. Once it got late, we went to bed, as nobody told us to go to bed or not. One night really late, my mother came home in a strange car with this man.

That never happens.

I watched them from my upstairs window. She's falling down drunk and is trying to get out of the car and get away from that man. They struggle and he fights with her and drags her back into his car, and he gets out of there, tearing down the gravel road to the asphalt and drives into the night going away from town. My sister and I scream at them.

She gets on the phone to get Dad, and we just have to wait. Can't do anything, standing in the dark, and we are horribly terrified, just waiting. Dad gets to the house and Kelly is told to stay by the phone, and I get in our station wagon with him and we tear out down the road in pitch dark.

Questions, questions, just questions and yelling. "I don't know who it was, Dad. Maybe from the BBQ the other day."

In the distance, we see the lights from that car that has stopped on the side of the road. The door is open, engine running, the overhead dome light shines, and we don't see anybody—till we go around to the passenger side and there is my mom with her clothes pulled off her. She is almost unconscious, and that man is not around.

Just then, another car comes up really fast and screeches to a halt behind our car, and a man gets out who I recognize, and he and my dad start off into the night. And then the man turns around and takes me away from the scene to his car and drives me back to our ranch. My dad disappeared into the night, yelling for that man.

I know about cows and horses, and I know what's happened. I felt a wretched stomachache and I felt hollow. Felt like I had been run over by a car. My mind removed most of my memories and I have deeply suppressed the ordeal, until now. I was 8 or 9 years old.

Running wild or near to it seemed like fun and the only thing that would get me and my sister away from the hazards and dangers that came with life in those days was to be away or far away as we could from my dad. We always had to gauge his moods and temperament when he came home. Once we heard the gravel popping in the driveway from his car wheels. I knew we probably should get ready for anything, depending on his mood and drink consumption.

I learned later in life that he was a Rage-o-holic, the description given him by counselors in Alcoholics Anonymous. I was given an additional descriptive as an ACA—Adult Child of an Alcoholic.

In an instant, his moods would swing, and I was usually the first victim that suffered. It was spread out over years and years of abuse to all of us, me in particular. That was my role. If he knocked me around, at least he would possibly not hurt my sister or my mom, depending. Gauge the booze, gauge the torment. The severity of his rage went from angry words to threats, to hits, slaps, kicks, punches, and so on. Switches when we were little moved up to sticks or other objects, such as belts, pieces of rope, leather harness, then to fists. At one of the weekend BBQ get-togethers with several of his drinking friends, I was taken into the tack room, slung around on full display, and half-dragged in front of all of them, and I was whipped with my bullwhip, for all to see and hear.

At another related time, I watched a man leave our house, following my sister out, and she was clearly not happy about the man following her. She later said to me that he had promised to pay her money for something disgusting. My sister was only in the fifth grade, one grade ahead of me.

Unrelated or perhaps related, one late weekend night, my sister and I were watching scary movies, and we heard the gravel popping on the driveway and saw a station wagon coming, turning off their lights, and pulling in and shutting off their engine. It was déjà vu all over again. What terrible things could be coming to us in the night? We didn't know the car, a station wagon no less, and they were hiding in the dark, waiting. I became afraid of the sounds of breaking gravel shells.

But on this night, when I turned on the outside porch light, there was my aunt and uncle from Indiana! We knew them from the time we drove there for the funeral of my granddaddy Charlie. They came for a visit?! No one came to visit us, and it was a shock! They were "passing through" on the way to

California for a long vacation. They were such sweet people. Sweet people were something we didn't have in our lives.

* * *

So, this is who we were. Living in the country, away from town, away from any police. Just having a sheriff somewhere in the county, if we needed them, was all we got and they were usually found around the ranches and bayou people to make sure we didn't have cattle rustlers about, checking on guns being fired at night by rabbit hunters out spotlighting or shooting wild pigs.

We had neighbors but they were not too neighborly. If you wanted friends, it was best to create them. We two kids lived in an emptiness in the country usually devoid of adults, which manifested in the aimless boredom of childhood.

And yet, here was Uncle Dale and Aunt Jenny coming to visit! But every time Kelly and I walked through the house, hoping to get to know them a bit, the talking would stop.

Right before they got into their station wagon to leave, a day or so later, my Aunt Jenny said to me, which I thought was so odd, "Jonny, if things get really bad for you and your sister, call. You and Kelly can come to visit us in Bloomington. We would love to have you, wouldn't we Dale?" For some reason, I don't know, it just stuck with me. How did they know about anything?

The family moved into town to be closer to the bar my dad bought, The Last Frontier, and my mom went back to work at the local newspaper as a proofreader, and us kids by that time were always wearing shoes. We were now close enough to walk to church at night, and school during the days for years afterwards.

Jon Bunn

Pennies in The Plate

I came upon Baby Jesus when I was very young,
I didn't have much schooling, we just fought for every crumb.
The days were hot and sweaty, we never thought
    there was relief,
We just played in the mud holes and ran around in bare feet.

The mighty and the brave were always somewhere uptown,
And we went to visit and laid our pennies down.
It was nice to see, where Jesus walked around.

The happy, the new, and the good, were just up the street.
They cut down our only shade tree where the sidewalk ends.
So, we walked to church at night, to ask for some relief,
And we put our pennies in the plate and gave away our grief.

   CHORUS

The temple and the tempest and all the lands in between,
It's where we built our house and raised the family.
We never had much money, if the truth would be told,
When you're covered in dust and down on your luck,
    all you pray for is rain.

   CHORUS

After dark clouds passed over, there was light for us to see.
The light at the end of the tunnel held promises, indeed.
We held on to life, alright, and kept the good memories.
It's the place where you put your pennies, and how you
    held your load.

   CHORUS AND END

The Toy

We were poor and only had one doll.
It was all we had. It was an old sock.
We choked a head onto it with a rubber
band. Then it was gone. The parent
took it and wore it till it got dirty and
the rubber band broke.

It Was The Machine

Perhaps when I was five or so, I found a hammer among some boards laying on the ground. Perhaps that's when I learned them to be two-by-fours. I found some nails and was going to learn myself how to drive them into the wood. The hammer was very big and heavy and after many taps and pecks, I was able to set the nail into the board without it falling out after I hit it and hurting my fingers.

Later, I learned that a smaller nail, smaller than a sixteen-penny nail, would go into the board without so much effort on my part and I would not hit my fingers with the hammer quite as many times. I felt I was learning something I shouldn't be learning. After all, many things I did in those days came with negative words and some kind of punishing event, to set the matter straight. Learning was a hard road to travel when I was five, perhaps different for you.

We lived by a railroad track. I would get to play outside sometimes, and I would watch the train go by. It was a big black steam train with a silver nose on it and you could see the man that was inside somewhere, pulling on the rope and ringing the bell as it slowly went by, shooting out big clouds of steam.

I can see it still, clearly, one day when the steam locomotive stopped on the tracks in front of my house, and another train was coming down the track the other way, and it came to a stop almost nose-to-nose with this one. One train was diesel, and one was coal. I don't remember ever seeing a steam train or smelling it again after that.

Learning to hammer nails into boards was an important thing to do. I don't remember any other toys I had or other things I had to play with, except balloons. I do remember one time around Halloween, one of the first I remember, when it was cold, and the day was gloomy, and it was late, almost dark. My sister and I were told to get into the house because of it, and we had to close the blinds to keep all the outside light from getting inside and we had to turn out all the lights inside the house and keep them from getting out of the house, too. We would sit in the dark and wait for "them" to go by outside.

We were told to be very quiet. That meant completely quiet. There was no "very" needed. We could hear them going up and down the street and sometimes they would knock on the door pretty hard, which was a scary thing. One time we were allowed to peer out through the venetian blinds and see them. Some looked like small people, and some were complete monsters.

We went through this every year. Halloween came and went. I asked why we didn't open the door, and the answer was that we didn't have money to spend on candy. If we let them in, they might get us and take all the candy. We just huddled in the dark. We kept the porch light OFF. The monsters would *steal* all our candy?

The one thing we did have for comfort was that there was a gas space heater to keep warm and we could look at the small blue flame and what light it gave off. Over the years that followed, we looked into those flames every Halloween and thought about lots of different things.

My hammering nails into boards was found out. Most comments were generally positive, although I did get some gruff for nailing into a board that wasn't used or cut yet. I didn't know when you could nail the board that would be okay. The nail was taken out and that was that. I wanted to nail one nail really close to another nail and have the heads of the nails form a little Lilypad path. What I learned was that I shouldn't nail a nail right close to another one because it made the wood underneath split. I had thought that wood just took all the nails you could put into it. I thought that was the reason it was wood. I learned differently.

Years later, I was told by a schoolteacher that a hammer was a machine. I didn't know that. I thought of the vacuum cleaner that was dragged around the carpet, making noise, and sucking up dirt—now that was a machine. How does a hammer turn into a machine? I was waiting for the magic of that one. How does that happen? You put a motor inside the hammer and that's a machine or a hammer inside a motor? I'd like to see that, too!

So much learning to do and not all of it went on in school. We boys gained all kinds of things away from school and we learned from each other and then passed it on when we got to the playground. Outside was where we learned the most. You didn't have to hold it when you were in the woods, you could stop right there and pee on anything you wanted to. Sometimes we tried to see who could pee the highest on the side of a tree or on the side of the barn if one was handy. No one got a prize or anything, we just found out who were the high shooters or not.

Writing with pee in the dirt—someone was always trying. Then distance shooting was a favorite, too. It was usually a big brother or an uncle who would win, especially when they were drinking beer. I liked the idea of hitting the water or trying to shoot out over a hill and see how far you could go. Next came writing your name on a big rock. My penmanship gradually improved.

Bicycles were the machines of youth. You fixed flats, did things with handlebars, and got your freedom. It was nothing to take off to someone's house or to go exploring. Then came lawnmower engines, scooters, and motorbikes. The heavy motorcycles came later, like with cars.

And then things begin to change. Telephones were on party lines to begin with, before they left the differing ring tones to alert different people the call was just for them. TVs—I don't think of them as machines. Things will change.

Typewriters are really machines. They soon will be electric; you could plug them in like the vacuum cleaner and they will just work all on their own. Maybe they won't need your fingers. I'd like to see that. Things will change, I'm sure.

Was He a Drunk or Was He Just Drunk?

I found myself in someone's yard, sitting in the grass and enjoying the afternoon with friends and family. They were sitting around in the grass, too, and on the porch, just talking and drinking beers and smoking cigarettes. They were all smoking cigarettes.

Funny, when I go back and think about it now. There had been a fire of some sort, and some cleanup had taken place, where several shovels of burnt stuff and charred matter were just thrown into the middle of the yard. What seemed disturbing was a large amount of the debris was made in large part by medicine bottles, mostly broken and spilling out the contents into the grass and on the charcoal. I was alarmed that no one seemed to pay any attention to the potential hazard. I sensed that something could get out of hand and threaten me somehow.

Part of the ugliness was in the color of the mostly broken bottles; they were ugly amber brown. Not something pretty. It reminded me of the color of a brown gallon Purex bottle my grandmother used from time to time. It had a bad smell that made me dislike that color.

Grownups were quite lazy after the big meal and just sat around smoking, but they watched me as I kinda poked around through all the little piles of colored pills. They were watching me to see if I was going to swallow one. The smell of the Purex made the impression that those pills probably tasted like the Purex smelled, even though you aren't supposed to taste pills when you just swallowed them. However, when one of them gets stuck in your throat, you wind up tasting it anyway.

A big man was close to me sitting in the grass with his shirt off. Old men did that to cool off when there wasn't a breeze. He sorta slipped over and fell and was then laying sideways in the grass. When I laid in the grass with my shirt off, I would get itchy, so I didn't do it much.

He would lean up and drink, no, gulp his beer, and lay back down in the itchy grass. He would try and talk to the other people around him, but slowly. His words would slur a bit, and his eyelids would open and close slowly, too. I didn't know if he was trying to go to sleep or trying to wake up. He seemed lost in the in-between.

He tried to keep talking somewhat. He began to make less and less sense. Some people were laughing at his antics. He became yard entertainment. His name was Charlie.

I was told to ask him a question and see what kind of an answer he would give back. He became funny. Then he was sad. I took a blade of grass and tickled his belly, and he would swat at it. That was funny. He could not keep his eyes open any longer. He drooled some.

I told him that he was going to be dropped into a burning fire, and he began yelling, "Noooo." He would not wake up, but he continued to talk his "drunk talk."

I remember it was on a Sunday afternoon and I was going to have to go to school the next day, so we left. We left the pills and the broken brown bottles, and the charred wood used to set the pill bottles on fire, which they didn't do.

I never figured out if he was a drunk or just drunk. Unknowingly, I began to learn about alcoholics and drunks. I was in first or second grade.

The Violin and The Ivy

I was little, like four to eight years range, when this all happened, and my skin still gets nervous just thinking about it.

It was one of the earliest times I can remember going to Dugger, Indiana, to see my grandparents who lived in a small crossroads coal mining town, along a coal seam that might take their house someday. I didn't know that part then.

We came from East Texas at the Sabine River. We lived in Little Cypress. We drove up there to see my Grandpa Charlie who was sick and in the hospital, somewhere, I think it was over in Bloomington. He had worked in the coal mines. Enough said. He was a great grandpa from what I remember.

Grandpa Charlie's house was at the intersection of two roads and the one that went beside the house went down to open strip mines that had not been worked for some time, and they were full of clear rainwater, and you could see deep into the pit. My fishing and swimming water was always a muddy chocolate back home.

When it was found out that I was still "learning" to swim, my Uncle Morris wanted me to come with him and go swimming in those strip pits, which was a dicey proposition for me. That water looked so deep, too deep. It's funny now to think that I was somehow more comfortable swimming in the chocolate bayous where you couldn't see the bottom than I was with the idea of swimming in the clear water of the seemingly bottomless strip pits.

My Uncle Slim was with us that day and he was the greatest of men in my young eyes, 'cause he knew how to fish! We stood on the bank and investigated the water, and he promised to jump in and save me if Uncle Morris let loose of me and I went down, down into the depths I could see into. All of us "men" had to surmise my survival chances and talk it up before the deed was undertaken.

To seal the deal and before the event was to commence, we all stood at the edge of the precipice and peed over the edge and into the quarry waters below. We men were a true band of brothers back then.

Uncle Slim finished his cigarette and flipped his butt into the still water below. Somewhere from the depths, a fish came out of nowhere and grabbed it and took it down.

My, I was startled!

The fish could EAT you and you couldn't do anything but get eaten and dragged down, and then you would look up and see all your uncles watch as you faded into the dark depths below.

The days there were always full of adventures.

After a time there, visiting, we had done enough and so we went back to the Texas bayous and the chocolate waters. We drove over to see Grampa Charlie and say goodbye before we left. He was in a hospital room that was in a tall building with lots and lots of windows. Both of us kids were too young and were not allowed to go into the hospital to hug him and say goodbye. A small speck in time that placed a moment of remembrance in a cache of regret.

Before leaving to go back down south, we stopped outside the wall of windows and were told to look up at the façade and say goodbye. We were given this and that directions to where Grampa would be in that wall of windows. Finally, when it was "close to the time," they said they would have Grandpa walk over to the window and look down on us, and then when he came to the window somewhere up there, we were given our cue to wave back, and he would see us, and we could have a real goodbye.

The Indiana coal fields were quite different to me than the tangle of cypress knees and Spanish moss of the bayou. Indiana had hills and I could ride a bike and really coast down a road, as opposed to pedaling all the time to get anywhere back in Little Cypress. It sure was great fun to go up and down those hills. We kids wanted to come back to Indiana and have some more fun.

It turned out that we got word. I cannot remember if it was by letter or by phone call, though we didn't have a phone for several years during that time. But we got word that Grandpa Charlie had died, and we were going back to Indiana to attend his funeral. I had never been to a funeral before, so I had lots of questions about it and what it was all about. What happened? I wanted to know.

We had a 1950 flathead V-8 Ford and it took what felt like days to get to Indiana from Texas. It was like a thousand miles! It was all two-lane roads and most likely we traveled about 45 or 50 miles an hour. We amused ourselves by playing a game called "Frog," which consisted of us playing with a rag and it was tied into knots that was supposed to look like a frog and we took turns hiding it around the car and then looking for it.

"Go find things to do and stay out of the house until we have to get ready for the funeral," was the order of the day, "and don't go far." The first thing I did was to go into the basement and smell it. I didn't have a basement at home or at the other grandparents' farm in Cushing, Texas. If anything, they had a root cellar with a door over it, to run into and hide if a cyclone was coming. It smelled like plain dirt, whereas Dugger's basement smelled really strange to me, and it was because we were smelling coal rock, something we had never seen or smelled. Grandpa Charlie and Uncle Slim had built a wooden trough that held water, and they kept minnows growing in it, in the basement, for fishing.

Even though Grandma was to be left alone, we were told, we did see her come outside to see us kids, and I saw her face was puffy. She called my sister and me to come inside with her and it was a solemn occasion we sensed.

Grandma Stella presented ten real silver dollars to each of us and said something to us about it, but I don't remember now what she said. At any rate, we went back outside to play in the apple orchard and hang upside down from the trees until it was time to come in and get ready for the funeral . That's when they gave us our first warning.

We went into a room that was really quiet, like right before a show was to start, and Grandpa was laying down in the coffin, and they played organ music for real.

When I asked someone about Grandpa and what happened, they said he has died and gone up to heaven to be with Jesus. The first thing I thought about, Grandpa sleeping in that room where they were playing him organ music, was my vision of him looking down on me through the windows of the window wall and now, I could see him behind the glass waving at me and I could look inside all those other windows into those rooms and seeing them full of talking and smiling people, all waving back at me. And that was what a funeral was.

I went to Sunday school and then to church at that time in my life and "sang" from the Methodist hymnal, so I was used to hearing "church music" played on an upright piano in a small church in Texas, where I got to put some pennies in the plate, as I was taught to do. I didn't mind hearing some organ music, but the "feel" of it didn't empty too many celestial pangings from the heart. I did get an occasional elemental vibe from the upright.

In a day or so after Grampa went up to heaven to be with Jesus and look down on us through those invisible windows and wave at us throughout eternity, someone asked where our big silver dollars were, the ones that Grandma gave us before the funeral. Suddenly, we came up short. We could not come up with them all. Some were missing from our pockets and so we went searching for them and found some of them on the ground, where they came out of our pockets when we were swinging upside down in the apple orchard.

We searched under the apple trees in the orchard and went into the barn where the tobacco hung and searched there, too, with no luck. With heads hung low, we came back from the barn a few dollars short.

It hurt Grandma and us that day. We thought long and hard about our mistake. After a spell, we meandered outside and started playing cowboys and Indians. I was the Indian, so I took off my shirt and only wore shorts, no shoes, either. We were barefooted for the summers anyway at home. The end of the day saw a bunch of tired renegades come inside.

We kids (me, my sister, and some cousins) got a dishrag, and took turns pumping well water into a milk pail and wiping off some of the sweat and dirt that we brought into the house. They didn't have a tub, just a milk pail and wash cloth to take turns with. If we were extra dirty, someone would put a washtub on the kitchen table and make you get in and stand there, while someone would wash you, head to toe. That's when they would wash off your dirt necklaces, too. I had to stand up naked.

I heard one of the grownups talk about driving to Indiana University that night to hear a violin symphony. I really put up a fuss to get to go but I didn't get to go.

"You're too young."

"It's too far to drive there and back at your age."

"You'll be too tired."

"You're too dirty. You are already itching too much and need to get clean."

I protested. I itched. I cried. I scratched. I started to break out.

"We'll put some lotion on the itches. You'uns go and have a good time."

They left me. They left me out of sorts, but they still left me. I couldn't stop itching and I scratched and scratched even more. Whatever was tried, it didn't work. Raising their voices didn't work. Telling me how to "rub instead of scratching" didn't work. The hours went by, the whelps grew bigger and were about to bleed. Some did. They brought in the last resort they had, an oscillating table fan. It only paused the agony.

It was on my chest, my arms, my neck, and the sides of my face. My legs, the tops of my feet, my ankles. I was burning alive. My crying was constant. The parents had gone to a violin concert, my concert.

It was poison ivy. I was covered from head to toe, literally. My sobs were increasing until I was gasping for air and exhaustion would stop me and I would sleep until I woke back up and the cycle began again.

Crying for my mom didn't work.

Dugger was a very small community, maybe a half mile, end to end. No phone. No car. Someone said to try ice. That was a problem.

The ice box was just that. It was a box that held a melting block of ice that would melt away and keep some foodstuffs from going bad and that was all there was until the ice man would bring another block of ice. One block would usually last about three or four days. Day three was tomorrow.

Electricity itself was barely an option. I remember a single light cord hanging down from the center of the kitchen ceiling, over the table and one more hanging in the front parlor. The one light bulb swinging from the center of the room cast weak light and strong shadows of black and white. It seemed to dance with pain as its partner throughout the night.

The raw red marks that were bloody scrapes quit bleeding and started to make yellow skin crusts.

In my delirium, my childhood brain rotated and melded my physical torments with the antecedents of my grandfather's death, losing solid silver dollar coins, a most precious gift, and contracting a severe allergic reaction to exposure to poison ivy that bastardized and corrupted my skin.

My situation left me in a dripping sweat and the salty water continued to torment me, lucid or not. My caretakers were present during the casual mention from someone about the violin symphony and then relief came. It wasn't instant, but the road of torment was turned.

A radio was put near my bed and its operator began searching for symphony music on late-night clear-channel stations.

Somewhere between WBZ Boston and WLAC in Nashville, violin music was found, staticky but discernable, and I remember being awakened to hear some, momentarily before falling away again. I stopped crying when I was awakened, and I smiled again. And my mind seemed to be able to begin sorting out the three plagues, as violin music played in the background.

My skin did develop impetigo but no one to my knowledge caught it. I have never developed a resistance to poison ivy.

The instruments I played for many years, some I still play, percussion, but no more. I did it as a rebellion against not getting violin lessons as a child. I began teaching myself guitar in the 1960s, starting with the 12-string, and I play still, and I am a songwriter.

However, nothing reached my emotions and soul, what little bit of that I had, like the sounds of the violin. I was awestruck when I heard it being played. I wanted to play one and learn how to do it. I thought that a violin playing at Grampa Charlie's funeral would have been better than that organ music. It was celestial. It was the instrument of my soul.

'Lil Johnson and The Sparklers

Growing up and becoming a man has to begin with lots of major events and in my young life and the first abrupt event on that road began with acquiring the stuff: raincoat and boots. The other name for it was goloshers or golossers or something like that. It sounded like a word we wouldn't use unless it came from an adult's mouth to another adult's ears, and that would preclude a child from thinking further about it, unless spoken to directly to by an adult.

It was a word that sounded vague, but maybe like a rare dish we might eat someday called goulash. It was something, at any rate, which would be fixed in the big heavy black iron skillet. It would be such a meal that a child would not be involved with it. The skillet would be too heavy for a small child to carry to the table and if it were hot, too, then way too dangerous. It would involve using a hot pad. Too much danger, right there. That was the line right there.

So, the raincoat and the boots—the galoshes—would only come in the color yellow, but since I had started the first grade a few weeks earlier, no one had to bring out the raingear quite yet.

I was lied to, though. I wanted some other color besides yellow. You just stuck out in yellow. "Everybody will be in yellow, don't worry." It wasn't so. There were different colors, but they were only worn by the girls. You'd be a sissy if you wore them.

Boots were another matter. I had to try on a few pair to get something that fit and that I could wear. They were cool but very stiff. I was told that I would be walking to school in the rain. After all, they had to walk in the rain and snow without rain boots and had wet feet all day at school. And if it still rained at the end of the day, they would have to avoid the big puddles, which was hard to do because it was always dark then.

It was arguable about the color choice of the raincoat and the only consolation was getting to choose what kind of snaps or zippers I wanted. If I picked the closures that were weak, if they broke, I still had to wear the broken-down raincoat until next year because they couldn't afford to buy another one.

I never had rain boots before, and so that was cool. I got them home and wore them around the house. There was no rain in the forecast, but I got to wear them for two full days. After the second day my feet hurt—a lot—and the tall sides of the boots rubbed sore spots on both my legs around my knees. No rain in the forecast and so I put them by my bed, kinda like the firemen did at the fire station. I soon forgot about them.

It was an eye-opener. We were shopping at Green's Department Store on Front Street. We hardly ever went inside to see what was in Green's, but since this was starting the first grade, the parents allowed us to go inside. The store had all these wires that crisscrossed the store up near the ceiling and they would attach sheets of paper on the clips, and they would shoot it across the store above everybody's heads to this platform, where a man stood and took off the paper and shot it back. The platform guy also had a big vacuum cleaner hose with pipes you could see into, and they would shoot those canisters around everywhere.

I got a pair of new blue jeans and a button-down, not a t-shirt, for school. The legs were too long, and I had to roll them up three or four inches to wear them.

"You'll grow into 'em."

They were stiff and had to be broken in, too.

My biggest worry was the length of the pants legs and them being way too long. What if they became undone, somehow? How would I get them back up my leg? When I got to school, I was shocked to see the cuff lengths on the other boys and was amazed that half of them would grow into GIANTS! I was going to be the runt of the class. Yee gads.

The "marching orders" finally came down from on high, and by the second or third day when the paper was handed out, we were told to give it to a parent to go buy this stuff and everyone on the following Monday was to bring that stuff to school.

The list was pretty cool. We were to buy *new* crayons—the boxes with eight or 16 crayons in them.

"Look into the box and see that they will have one or two rows of crayons. Bring nothing larger."

A jar of white paste, with the red top that was a brush, Vanilla paper, colored paper, watercolors in a tin with brush, a Red Chief notebook, two pencils with erasers on the other ends, and a one-foot ruler. Bring scissors, but only the ones with round tips and no sharp points.

The teachers, principal, office people, the cafeteria, and even the janitor all had the answers to just about everything. Lunches were 25 cents, and you got chocolate milk and a graham cracker every morning. Who in the world would ever want *white* milk? You got that at lunch, anyway, or at home.

It looked pretty good getting started at school. You had your own coat hook, cubby for art supplies, and real blackboards on two walls.

Getting into your classroom was pretty good, at first. "Sit anywhere." All the girls sat on one side of the room trying to insulate themselves from us boys, except for two girls that wore glasses. They got to sit in the front, so's they could see better. They already had glasses. Jeeze!

Some desks were singles and others were side-by-side tables. I got one of those side-by-sides all to myself. They were flat-topped and had little grooves cut into the wood that would hold your pencils, crayons, or marbles—IF you didn't knock one down to the floor and make noise as it rolled away and then you would get caught and you would lose your marbles. There were little cubbies under the desktop to put our things into.

It seemed to me to be that to get an education you have to lose your marbles at times. Boys tended to lose their marbles a lot, Girls didn't lose their marbles. Ha ha! They didn't have any! They all had to wear dresses!

There were five boys, but Mrs. Beverly said two more would come in later. Boys with boys, and girls with girls, unless something went wrong.

We had to learn things in school, that's how it was. We learned about stories and about sentences. If you knew anything else about sentences or words, you would have to have been taught at home because there was no schooling before the first grade to learn about stuff, except maybe at Sunday school. And all that was, was about people who lived in robes and tents. It was like a game where they showed you pictures of lots of people standing around and you always had to pick out the one that was Jesus.

Dick and Jane books seemed to be popular, but they didn't seem to do too much. They ran. They played. They had a ball. Boring stuff. We learned about words and sentences and then how to look at a word and divide it up. I fully remember most of it and can say that I have carried a bad episode with me throughout life as a result of one of those "learning times."

We moved through the literature of the Dick and Jane epics and the pictures in the book just about told you the story before you had a chance to learn the words. On such an occasion, I was called on and Mrs. Beverly took her yard stick and pointed out to me what I was going to try and read out loud.

"Please stand up and face the class."

It was to be a shining moment in my early career, so I stood up and read the passage that read, "Dick and Jane visited an is land," and I sat down, pridefully, knowing they were trying to trick me, but I caught the fact that two words were snuck into one. I divided it right there, in front of the class, showing my depth of English skills for all to see.

I was betrayed.

I was betrayed by Dick and Jane, sneaking in a trick word. It was a betrayal to all who read Dick and Jane, set up by the teacher, and ultimately delivered to me like a Queen taking a pawn. I was crushed. I remember those words to this day and will forever carry the scars. Her voice reverberated throughout all those four walls.

"Well, Jonny, that isn't right. Dick and Jane are showing you that the S in I-S-L-A-N-D is SILENT, and you do not say that letter! It is not IZ-LAND. It is an EYE-LAND."

That was the day I learned that words weren't always what you thought they were. Words could be very different than what they seemed to be.

How could I have known? I was standing there, in the middle of the room, pridefully demonstrating to the class my acumen and the word "NO" came from my teacher. All the other students stared at me in disbelief with their mouths hanging open.

My literary execution rang out through all the opened windows and throughout all the first floor of Anderson Elementary School, throughout the streets of the city, and as far away as the breath from a word could carry it.

✳ ✳ ✳

Walking in line was a remedy for something we didn't figure out. Boys tended to not keep their hands to themselves much, in line or in the classroom. We started out fairly well from the classroom door, where we always lined up, to go to the cafeteria, to an assembly, to the playground, or at the end of the day before the bell rang, to go home.

We would start out all right, but the line usually bulged a bit at the start, and then got wider and wider the further we had to go. Two lines going in different directions always get crossed up and sometimes we would lose one or two in the mingling and kids would be in the wrong line and so we would have to stop and reorganize ourselves before starting again. Finally, just to relieve ourselves of boredom, we would do it on purpose. Mrs. Beverly was a grandma's age, and she was victimized, would be the best way to put it.

The janitor would step in and help sometimes when he was in the halls sweeping. That seemed to me to be excessive. He had this stuff he threw on the marble floors and then he would sweep it up. It was like a mixture of coffee grounds and sawdust, and it was kind of oily and smelled like strong lemon and motor oil. It was supposed to pick up the dust on the wooden floors in the classroom and dry the rainwater in the doorway at the entrances. He had a room to keep his wheeled bucket and mops in, inside the boy's bathroom that was always locked.

Three of us boys got two more boys who were new; they had come the third week after school started. One of the new boys was assigned to share my desk. He was Cajun and his name was Evon (pronounced Yvonne) Gauthier, but he wanted to be called just "Evan." After two days, Evan was moved to another desk and shared it with the other new boy, Eugene Swiderski, who wanted to just be "Gene." He had a burr haircut and so had very little hair up there. They both came with brown grocery sacks and school supplies.

It didn't seem to be working out very well between Gene and Evan. So, Mrs. Beverly separated them. Gene's dad was in the Navy, and Gene, like his dad, wore real Navy shoes that came from the PX, the Navy store on base. He was sent to sit with me, and Evan got a desk all his own, like I had, until both of them showed up.

Gene's art supplies had to go into his desk, as the other storage boxes on the wall were already full. Just as well, we started art and got to cut strips of colored paper and then we glued them together to form paper chains that we could decorate the room with. We did that for a while and then had to put our stuff away.

Mrs. Beverly made a space among the wall boxes for Gene's stuff, and he put his stuff over there. And then, after a couple of weeks or so, Gene came to school with a new jar of paste. Mrs. Beverly asked him where the other jar was, and he said he had used it up. Mrs. Beverly frowned but said nothing more about it.

The next time we did art, we made more paper chains and Gene pulled an empty paste jar out of his desk to use what was left. As soon as Mrs. Beverly left the room, Gene took his tongue depressor paste stick, put a glob on it, and—I thought he was being "a funny butt"—he started eating his paste stick like it was melting ice cream. He was eating his jar of paste!

He admitted that he ate paste all the time! He had me try some, as I was his desk mate, and it was fairly okay. The taste was like mint or vanilla, I can't remember which.

Gene kept a jar of paste hidden in his desk for quite some time. And he ate quite a bit of it over that time. The teacher became suspicious. I could see her eyes pretty well. Her glasses magnified her eyes, and you could really see her eyes when she looked at you. Gene always wanted me to be his lookout.

Soon after that, before Mrs. Beverly announced art time, she stopped reading aloud to our class and looked at Gene and me with a squinty eye, and as I bumped his leg to warn him, she got up and came right over and put her arm in Gene's cubby and pulled out a spent jar of paste. Later, Gene said there was still some good lickings left.

"Gene," she said, holding the almost empty paste jar aloft for other kids to see. "Where did the paste in this jar go? Can you tell me and the class?" Her eyes looked like they were bulging. The class was frozen still.

"No, Mrs. Beverly."

"I see," she said. "So, I think I will have a new seating chart by the time the class comes in from recess. Would you like that, students?"

And almost everyone was excited to move to a new desk. I was just scared of what was going to happen to me. After all, I was guilty and was a paste eater, too. (Only one or two times, though.) I could wind up in paste-eating prison, too. This could be an organized paste-eating crime and we would be criminals.

Circumstances didn't look good. Now, all those girls in my class started to look at me, like they did at Gene. We were marked men from there on out.

The punishment phase began as soon as we returned from the playground. Mrs. Beverly began by having all the students stand up around the outside walls. She called each person and told them where their new desk was. Gene and I were the last two convicts standing.

"Jonny, I do not think you are involved in anything so you will remain in your current seat. However, Evan, you will move from the front row and sit with Jonny, and Gene, you will take his old seat up front by me."

My parole had come. I still had to share a double desk, but now it was with Evan. Few girls were affected, except for the girls with the glasses. They were separated because they were always talking to each other. Other than that, the reorg was over.

Gene was absent for two days following the classroom shakeup. On returning, Gene had a new desk that was a bigger one that had been used the year before by a big roly-poly boy. Consequently, Gene's legs didn't quite reach the floor, and they dangled, so, consequently he was always swinging his legs back and forth. His new desk had the cubby part, which was like a metal breadbox, was below the seat and when Gene was mad, he would strike the metal breadbox like he was hitting a drum. It was loud. Mrs. Beverly would do things with her eyebrows because of it.

I would just look over at the girls and roll my eyes and sometimes I would get enough of a laugh that it caused Mrs. Beverly to look at the girls and frown, which was the only kind of warning they would get.

❋　❋　❋

Mr. Janitor, or "Sir" as we called him, was all over the school doing work and he helped out the teachers all the time. If something was too heavy to move, or something broken, or a mess of some kind, like throw-up, the janitor was the man to do it. He had keys on a belt loop for everything, as his storeroom was inside the boy's bathroom, I would see him all the time. He worked very hard, and he would be sitting at times at an empty table in the cafeteria drinking coffee and talking to the cooks working in the kitchen. They were always wearing white, with white shoes, and hair nets that tightly went over their hair. They looked like nurses of a sort, like the ones that would be giving you your first polio shots a couple of years later on.

He was a man that always dressed in khaki shirt and pants. If Mrs. Beverly needed the janitor, she would always send a boy to find him, in case he was in his storeroom. I suppose he could help us guys with guy stuff, in an emergency or something.

Since Sir was around the kitchen, we learned to ask him to tell us what our dessert for the day was going to be. He also kept an eye on us boys when we were sent for our bathroom break, after chocolate milk and graham crackers. If we were acting up, he would relay that to Mrs. Beverly. If it were more serious, he would just say something to you directly, kind of like a big brother, uncle, coach, or a dad would do.

So, it was not unusual one day to see the janitor motioning to see Mrs. Beverly outside our door during class. Uh oh, could be he saw something, and it might involve our class, or probably us boys. They talked a bit. She didn't look at anybody when she reentered the classroom. Must have been a false alarm.

However, when we got our bathroom break the next day, Sir came in after a few of us were at the porcelain trough and starting to cut up. Mrs. Beverly could hear us in there with our loud voices and since she couldn't come in, she sent in the janitor, who caught several of us holding ourselves and pretending to shoot a stream at someone else. We were caught holding our— and silence fell instantly before Sir had a chance to say anything.

"You know, look at the messes you have left on the floor. It's ME that has to clean up after you. From what I see (looking at us red-handed, so to speak) you boys need to grow those things a bit more and learn to step closer to the lip. You can't get any in there?" He pointed to the inside of the urinal.

"Look over here. How could there be a puddle by the wall? If it ever hits that wall socket, it will cook you and your little Vienna sausage!"

We were mortified, embarrassed, humiliated, and shamed all at once. Some of the boys were telling the janitor how sorry they were, how they never would do it again, thinking about who peed by the light socket and could have died. How would something like that ever be explained?

When we got out of there and went back to class, the janitor stopped and whispered the story to Mrs. Beverly, so she knew it all. Boy, her eyeglasses REALLY made her eyes bug out at this one! There was head shaking, nodding, disbelief, smiles, followed by stern, controlled anger.

From that day forward the janitor was called to watch us boys. As there were only five of us boys, it wouldn't be worth the effort to divide us into two groups, so we continued to all go at once.

The slip-up happened when the janitor was on the third floor, tending to something, and the five of us went in to do our business. It was a bit off schedule, but Gene started swinging his legs to and fro and hit the metal desk box underneath his desk, banging it like a drum. Mrs. Beverly's brow didn't dissuade him from continuing.

"Why are you continuing to flail your legs? Look at the clock, the break is in a half an hour."

"I'm really needing to excuse myself."

All the girls stopped their schoolwork and began smirking among themselves. They knew about the sordid details. Trust me. Begging for the bathroom was so degrading on so many levels.

"Are the rest of you willing to wait or do any of you now need to go?"

Everyone grinned and grimaced fake cramps in unison, so she let us go early without the janitor standing guard. Big mistake.

Once we all got in, Gene declared, "I'm the one that peed by the electric socket, 'cause I got scared. It won't hurt ya, they were just trying to scare us."

"Do it, then!" And the others chimed in, "Do it! Do it! Do it!"

Gene grinned and instead of unzipping his zipper, he unbuck-led his whole pants, which fell to his knees, grabbed his 'lil

Johnson and peed a stream from six feet away, and painted the wall and all over the double wall socket, as we stood there in amazement!

Pee was coming down the wall like a miniature waterfall and the socket lit up and threw smoke and sparklers everywhere. Still cascading down, the pee drops would find the slots of the receptacle and added more flashes and smoke.

Burnt smoke and pee stunk up the small bathroom quickly. No one ever smelled burnt electric pee before. Gene gave it his all and the show just went on forever! No electricity jumped into his hand or what he was holding. The light never flickered.

We got scared and all zipped up, but the smell got all over us and our shoes and Mrs. Beverly, almost shouting, started in, "What on Earth is that awful smell? Come back out to my classroom immediately!" And she stomped her foot.

Things happened very quickly. Mrs. Oleatha Wignall, Principal, came into the Vice Principal's Office and Detention Room about a half hour later after meeting with parents, guardians, and a man dressed in a brown pin-striped suit, wearing cowboy boots and a Stetson hat, and a small gold badge with a silver star in the center. He had a string tie and a toothpick. When he shifted his weight to the other foot, his leather belt squeaked, letting everyone know there was probably a holster hidden behind his jacket.

Everyone talked in hushed tones, and no one knew anything. Parents were in the other room, separated from us. We were being taken out of the room one by one.

And so it began. The voice that called out the names came from the man with the badge. This would be the time you would get hugged by your mom and see the anger on your dad's face before taking *the long walk.*

We would soon learn to spell penitentshurray.

"Eugene Darius Swiderski." The door with the fuzzy glass window rattled open and then closed behind him. Two other doors closed and clicked shut, one after the other as they left, and all became silent again.

✳ ✳ ✳

My brush with the laws was all I needed to set me on a solid path. I made all six grade levels at Anderson and took all my opportunities. I took any job I could get, starting with chalkboard eraser cleaner, and graduated on up, starting music classes on drums. And before leaving, I made crossing guard, and got to wear a gold belt, with a festoon motif.

Grandma One

In most people's lives, at least the ones I know, there are those who hold positions of respect within and without the family. If you count all the different people in your family, you usually find someone, perhaps more than one, who fills that hallowed position and is revered and honored for their attributes, their struggles, their accomplishments, or their station in life. Age has a knack of validating one's seniority in that circle that is rarely disputable.

Grandmothers. They possess that *je ne sais quoi.*

Bina Electra Paine Bunn and John Marshall Bunn owned and worked a small farm in Cushing, Texas. Granddad also was a butcher on the side. They raised sweet corn, peanuts, watermelons, cantaloupe, peppers, crook neck squash, and lots of beans, like butter beans, lima beans, black-eyed peas, crowders, yellow wax, crème peas, and pole beans. String beans. Add eggplant, okra, cucuzza squash, luffa gourds, and dipper gourds. Pumpkins for a Fall harvest as time allowed. Carrots and potatoes.

Grandma canned, pickled, shucked, dried, and put up preserves: wild plums, figs, peaches, pears, strawberries, you name it. If you didn't grow it, you didn't eat. If you had extra, you swapped, bartered, or traded to get it. Bina milked cows, made her own butter, and cooked applesauce. She shelled pecans and walnuts for pies and cookies. She wrung chickens' necks, made soup, and took her turn at the plow.

By the time I grew from toddler to rug rat, the woodstove was replaced by a Chambers propane stove.

When they got their 12 acres along the road to Cushing, the Methodist Church found land close by and built the community a church.

Someone or somebody went to Bina and John's land and dug them a freshwater well, and they built a back porch that surrounded it, as well as the house in front of it. So, they had well water, right out the back door.

They had a helper who worked extremely hard for them. His name was Bob, and he was dearly loved by all the grandchildren. Bob was their plow horse that lived in the log cabin barn a hundred yards from the house. He pulled the buckboard wagon full of dried corn to the market and John Marshal rode him bareback to town every now and then to get mail.

John and Bina walked to the Methodist Church in their early days and went by buggy later in their years. It was in such times that I saw the glue that held it all together.

She would come to each of us grandkids that came to visit and, from her little black pinch purse, give us a few wheat pennies each, or a nickel at special times, for the offering plate before Sunday school and church after that. If we were good and didn't cause any commotion during church, we would get a reward of a little stick of Dentyne chewing gum. She carried that in her purse, along with the pennies and nickels.

Even back then I started to understand what meager meant. It was the love, labor, and sacrifice that surrounded each coin I came to know and found it such an honor to be given the tithe to offer.

Grandma exemplified the verse from the Bible: "But Jesus called them unto Him, and said, 'Suffer the little children to come unto me, and forbid them not, for of such is the kingdom of heaven'."

I could not fathom then what I learned many years later: what it was to face old age, that sweet grandparents would not remain frozen in time. I was never mature enough then to make a connection that they would slowly become infirm and unable to continue to be secure in raising their own food and would begin a long heartbreaking journey they could not stop.

✳ ✳ ✳

The three sons and three daughters all moved away, driven to seek their future away from the farm, and the sawmill railyard, and the impending start of World War Two.

And the Baby Boomers came into being and the grandmothers were waiting for them with open arms. They were excited to embrace, cherish the innocent ones, reweave, and strengthen the torn and frail fabric from that war, and beckon in a new age of post-war prosperity they never saw or participated in.

Xavier Cugat fired up the radio air with hot Latin music that followed G.I.s before and after World War II. He was the leader of the resident orchestra at the glamorous Waldorf-Astoria in NYC and carried his chihuahua, Pepito, on stage and in the movies. The dog was his shtick. They were famous.

We had to have one for our family, too. The confetti was flying in my parents' heads to get a dog like that. We named the dog Chi Chi.

✳ ✳ ✳

"Load up the kids and let's go visit Grandma and Grandpa in Cushing." Three hours away.

We two kids got gifts, besides getting a dog. My sister got a whatever and I got a tomahawk with a hard rubber top with feathers and a rubber ball-peen hammer. I thought it was not just a gift, but a "special" gift, perhaps the first gift that had hard rubber, like the wheels on my toy dump truck.

Of course, it was safe, I thought. It was rubber. That is all I needed to know. I had tried to drive nails in a board a few times and it was hard, and I had hurt my fingers with the steel hammerhead. Driving nails would not hurt, now, I supposed, because it was rubber.

My dad drove a 1950 Ford sedan through Nacogdoches County and north to Cushing. It was all two-lane roads, and we knew we were close because the state highway department

• 38 •

strung a flashing caution light across the road on top of the hill that marked the turnoff.

Chi Chi was a small little thing that snuggled next to Mom and shivered a lot. All the attention went to the dog. The big reveal of having a dog was about to happen. We pulled into the front yard and parked under the big sweetgum tree as my grandparents came out of the house and across the porch to the yard to greet us.

We barely got out of the car when we presented the "surprise dog."

"Oh, Clyde, what have you got, a baby dog?" Grandma asked my father as she held the shivering animal.

In an instant, we kids realized we were not the most important people to her anymore. It was that dog. We now came in a lowly second place. My sister got her hug next and then I got picked up and was going to be held for a hug. It was when I was small and pickup-able, and Grandma was still strong enough to do it.

"Look at what I got, Grandma," I said, so proud to have the attention. I held the hammer and the tomahawk with real feathers and instantly demonstrated how it worked by swinging it and smacking her on the side of the head with it.

I felt her snuggling grip on me instantly go limp as I dropped to the floor, and she yelled in pain and put her hands to her scalp. I looked up, saw her glasses were still on but askew.

Boy, did I ever mess up.

The sound came out somewhere between a hoot and a yell as she bent forward, and I was grabbed and wheeled around to really get it. Grandma raised her hand to stop Clyde from throttling me, stepping forward to shield me at the same time.

The story about me hitting Grandma was told over and over during the family reunions. Sometimes it was told that I hit her with the tomahawk and other stories claimed I used a ball-peen hammer. In any case, the story got new life when the relatives sat on the porches or in the yard, under the shade trees, after the big reunions. I had to stay away from the crowds, lest I trigger those memories, and someone would grab me and hold on to me during the telling. I guess I was Exhibit #1.

But now the folks have all died away, and there is no one to hear the story and no one to tell it to, and the farmhouse has been abandoned. But there is a thumbtack stuck to my memory's bulletin board on that one. It is still there.

And Then I'll Come Around

Well, I'm sittin' on a bucket in a rainstorm getting wet,
And I'm watching all my beans fall over
and the rain ain't got 'em yet.
And my task's not over, the rain's barely begun.
I'll weed and hoe in the sun, you know,
And then I'll come around.

I hear you fussin' in the kitchen.
You got your canning jars out.
Let me taste your little fuzzy peaches.
That will make me jump and shout.

Can you see the cornfield growing and the
    dew drops a-glistening?
Put your shoulder to the task before you, and
    the Lord will tell you when.
I'll see you in the morning and again in the afternoon.
You'll swing in the shade of the old sweetgum,
And then I'll come around.

BREAK AND CHORUS

Put your hands together at the table, where friends should be.
Count the blessings all laid before you and then pass the tea.
And my task's not over, I'll thank the moon and stars,
And you know since I love you so,
And then I'll come around.

BREAK AND END

Jon Bunn

Grandmother's Place

I headed back down that old dusty road,
In the shade of sweet gums, to the old family home.
The house on the hill is all trimmed in black,
It's the last trip I'll make and I'll never be back.

The road is dusty where the wheels press the sand.
There's nothing left of the orchard. The ivy claimed the land.
The old timber bridge has fallen in the creek.
No hands have touched it, and the wagon wheels are weak.

Looking back from the valley, up to the barn,
The whole thing is leaning and will soon fall down.
With its life almost gone and its people died away,
The good timbers are taken, and the rest will rot away.

The names of our children were carved on the tree,
With the mules and cows, we'll lose their memories.
The stories and the battles will all finally end,
And the whisper of possibilities will leave on the wind.

This old house is not lived in, no more children will it bear,
As it looks over its fallow fields where no one gives a care.
The hot sun and light breezes press the homestead down,
To the cool dust of slumber, where no one comes around.

Going Up The Country

I don't remember where the idea of moving came from. It was just the reality of it. We had lived in three or four other places and towns that were vague memories, but I just finished the 2nd grade and were headed to the country. Thinking about it wasn't something to do or to anticipate. We were awakened and told to pack clothes.

It was the visual picture of seeing the grown-up's mattress being dragged through the house and leaned up on its side in a horse trailer that was so odd. I never saw a mattress treated that way, and now that it was in the full sun, it had all these coffee stains imprinted on it all over. I could tell that some of the big blotches must have been sweat stains. I didn't know about the others. I deciphered that much, later in life.

But at that age, I only knew that I sweated, like any member of the family would. I had never thought it would go and do that to a mattress. I guessed that everybody in the whole world would have sweat stains. I thought it was probably coffee sweat stains. Tea was what it was at Grandma's. It was coffee sweat at our house. I was pretty sure of it.

I watched them lash the mattress to the sidewall and then talk about it. They stood there, looking at the layers of stains, and then unlashed it, and turned the mattress around and retied it. The other side was stained, too, but not as bad. And so, they left the second lashing alone and covered it up with a bureau and moved on.

We drove into the country and drove on a shell road to the house, the oyster shell popping as we drove in. We had a fence. We never were fenced in before. The big yard was used as a pasture. We were going to raise horses.

Little Jonny was going to get his own horse. And a horse was even better than a pony. They were sometimes mean. I could hardly imagine having a horse. Grandpa had one horse and that's the only horse I knew, and the only one I ever rode, until I got Strawberry. She was a Jenny mule and all white.

The road we drove on was an asphalt road that needed repairing. We learned from the neighbor kids, BB and Joanie, that we could walk in the fresh sprayed oil on the road after it cooled and walk in soft sand that coated our feet, and that could last several weeks or until we were caught. In front, next to the road, was a big, deep drainage ditch that was full of weeds, snakes, crawfish, turtles, cattails, egrets, and other stuff. This drainage ditch was one of the first things that needed exploring.

It was paradise. I was getting me a horse, and we could run around all day barefooted, catching turtles and big eating frogs, and picking blackberries almost every day.

I messed up quickly, though. I saw a little green grass snake gliding thorough the thorn bushes, and I caught it, and it bit me and wouldn't let go, like its teeth were stuck. It felt like the thorns on the blackberry bushes had me and so I ran into the house, and it was thrashing around trying to get off my arm, but it's teeth were stuck in my flesh. I had to yank it off, and the snake bite scratches started to bleed some. My sweaty arm and the blood mixed together, and so I rubbed the mess off on with my white t-shirt to show everyone it wasn't that bad.

They also didn't know the phone number of *The Orange Leader* newspaper, which is where he worked. They had to ask the operator to place the call for us. The neighbor got on the phone and talked to someone inside the phone about what had happened to me. She never dialed a telephone number. Just started talking into it to someone else; she was trying to get them to agree to stop talking so she could call the newspaper. The neighbors' phones were known as a party line; eight different people could get on their phones and hear everyone else talk. They were all talking at the same time as we were trying to leave, and someone was going around their house, trying to find the ignition key to start the car. It didn't have the usual three floor pedals and a shift arm like a regular car. It had buttons that stuck out of the speedometer on the dashboard, and you pressed the one that told the automobile what to do. But you still had to steer it, and you had to press the two pedals on the floorboard to get it to do something.

Maybe six or seven got into the car and everyone seemed to want to sit at a window seat, so everyone had to then roll down the windows to cool off the inside of the car. They even opened the two wing windows that helped direct additional wind inside the car.

Dr. Peters' expression relaxed when they told him it had been almost an hour since I had been injected with the snake's poison and as he took off the many wrappings that were bound and tied around the arm, he could find no puncture wounds and only some scratches. And since there was no pain or stinging or swelling and no blood loss, I was released to go home. I got to wear my bandaged wrist for two days to school, to show it off to illustrate how I survived.

The doctor and I talked about what I knew or didn't know about snakes, and he gave me *The Little Golden Book of Reptiles and Amphibians.* I read and learned about what lived in my ditch, my yard, the swamp, and the desert. Eventually, I learned all the poisonous snakes of the United States.

My first exciting find from reading *The Golden Book* was to discover and identify a Hellbender Salamander living in my ditch. Not bad for a 2nd grade graduate. A year or so later, by the 4th grade, I kept my first alligator. I caught and kept armadillos for short periods and had to turn them loose because I took too much time finding food. Then it was on to turtles, snakes, and racoons, followed by flying squirrels, hawks, owls, skunks, nutria, screech owls, and a monkey.

Well, it finally happened. We got our first telephone when I went into the 6th grade. This was neat. It was an authentic private line so nobody could pick up their phone and hear us talking on ours. We had to pay extra to get that part. In reality, there was not much to it. It sat on the kitchen table. We didn't know anybody so there was no one to call. It just sat there, we just looked at it and no one ever called.

~ PART TWO ~

The Little Cypress Sagas

Inscribed here are some memorable past events that may be called upon to perhaps guide a young lad or lass to build character and increase stamina in the years and decades ahead of them as they face the challenges of life. Although these stories and historical events occurred many years ago, these truisms from that bygone era will remain steadfast, and most of all, inspiring.

The Ranch

The ranch was located north and east of Adams Bayou on land used for grazing, and it abutted a stand of mixed hardwoods and mostly pine trees. Some small groups of houses were strung along a farm-to-market road headed into a crossroads at Mauriceville. Most people settled along FM1130 (farm to market), giving them access to the shipyards and Navy base in Orange, Texas and East Orange, Louisiana.

There was still one Native American family, the Tigers, living along the road next to the stand of tall pines.

Our spread never carried a name but was found in the lands in front of a large chicken egg-laying house, which was in the pasture behind us. Some of the pastures were low and they held water for a time after heavy rains and an occasional hurricane, which bred vast numbers of mosquitoes. I could walk into the back pasture, usually in rubber boots, and go to the bank of Adams Bayou, a short distance.

The blueprint for these sagas came from the television. We didn't have one when we first moved there from the city but got one in time. It helped me establish a legacy. When I got home by riding the school bus—it was the short bus, and we were teased about it—I would run into the house and turn on the TV and watch The Little Rascals show. It gave me ideas and set the mighty wheels of creative industry into motion.

My parents were newspaper folks and they both worked at *The Orange Leader*. He was a linotype operator and Mom was a proofreader. They didn't come home till after "dark-thirty," so I wasn't burdened or inconvenienced much by their presence.

There were many TV shows consulted for references, daily ones and then the hours of Saturday extravaganzas—Roy Rogers, Rex Allen, Gene Autry, The Lone Ranger, Sky King, Hopalong Cassidy, Lash LaRue, Gunsmoke, Paladin.

The Little Rascals were particularly inspiring. The shows were filmed in the 1930s or so and the Rascals seemed to live unique and adventuresome lives. The cowboy shows showed how to live in challenging times. That was true grit.

The Well Shed

We raised horses—Arabian, palomino, Shetland, donkey, mule, and cutting horses. We rode mostly bareback and rarely took the time to saddle up. More than half the time we wouldn't even use halters.

Our livestock had names, Shorty, Peanut, Speedy, Chief Yellow Hand, Bob, Fancy Pants, and so on. Strawberry was our white Jenny. She was solid white, except when she took dust baths and got her coat dirty. I could not read horse teeth and so I didn't know how old she really was, but the guess from those who looked at her mouth thought she might be a skosh over middle age.

Developing one's talents isn't always learned at school, or from one's parents, but through trial, error, and experimentation.

It was at just such a time when I was watching a shoot 'em up that I began to notice more closely the horsemanship of my hero cowboys. I saw that they were able to hide behind and on top of giant boulders and watch those cattle rustlers gather around the campfires, bragging about the big rustle they were getting away with by changing the brands on cattle and then trying to sell them or something. Usually, the good guy wound up slipping on a rock or something and the rustlers are alerted. And then a gun fight ensues.

The ringleader makes a break for it and tries to get away. The good guy, let's say Gene Autry, runs down the back of the boulder he has been hiding behind, and leaps several feet below, lands right in his saddle, and takes out after the rustlers.

I believed that maneuver took some skill to carry it off and it might be something I could do. After all, I rode bareback and all. I even was able to dip myself over the side of a galloping horse to keep myself from being hit by an Indian's arrows as I was being chased across the prairie or dodging bullets from a Winchester rifle. And to make it work, I always used a saddle to hang from the side.

Closely watching how Roy Rogers and Gene did it, I noticed they had their horses just standing behind big rocks and I didn't have any big rocks. There weren't rocks in the palmetto scrubs and rice fields to jump from. I would have to try something, but I didn't know what, just yet.

The well shed, as we called it, was really a windmill tower that had a large, galvanized water tank on top of that, where the windmill pumped water into it. The ladder going up to the storage tank was better than 30 feet up, but it was in poor shape, and a rung, here and there, was detached on one end or missing altogether. So, I decided to use the roof of the well house as my launch point, my big rock to jump from.

I led Strawberry around to the feed lot by the back of the well shed. She was just standing around and doing nothing when I left her there.

Action!

I had to imagine the climax of the action in my mind and shoot my way out of the ambush trap the rustlers devised. My ace up my sleeve was my hidden horse behind the saloon.

I faced my attackers head on and hastily retreated over the tin roof as they tried to corner me. I got one last shot at Bulldog and hit him squarely in the chest before I leaped—and then looked down. Strawberry had moved away and wasn't even close to where I left her.

I hit the ground hard and did a half roll. By me missing that mule, I could have broken a foot or been captured, tied to the mule, brought to the edge of town, and hung from a cottonwood, and The End.

My legs did hurt, but I had jumped off the side of my house many times without getting hurt, so I took that part in stride.

I had to replay the events in my head and refigure how to do my trick. Unfortunately, since Strawberry didn't have a saddle on, she didn't have a sense we were really doing anything together of any consequence, so she wandered away. Again, I hit the ground in a cloud of dust. Strawberry's eyes got big, her ears pinned back, and she looked at me in amazement and snorted.

My figuring produced this: If the trick could be done, I just need to set it up better. I went to the tack room and got some rolled oats and poured a hill of grain on the ground and put her in position. I could tell she was suspicious, but she ate the oats quietly.

I quickly ran to the ladder and climbed on the roof, checked to see if my animal was in place, re-ran the scene I wrote in my head, and then yelled,

Action!

It was superb acting, and the scene played to the end. Once again, Bulldog gets drilled in the chest. The sheriff yells, "Bang, you're dead," then "Bang, you too." He shouts out his commands, his boots are pounding and banging, as he stomps across the galvanized tin roof to his retreat and his get-away.

Strawberry wonders about the noise from the pounding tin and is now on full alert, she never sees the leap from the top of the barn and is not expecting anything as the sheriff sails through the air and lands on her back, pushing the air out of her lungs.

Did I mention that a Texas roping saddle is made to hold the rope that prevents the livestock from getting away once lassoed by the cowboy. That prominence at the top front of the saddle that was made to hold the lasso is called the saddle horn.

This young cowboy's "little horn" and the big saddle horn met each other soooo painfully. It was only for an instant. The gut-wrenching pain's talons gripped the rider's gut and anything else it could seize. Strawberry bucked straight up, gasping for the air that was knocked out of her lungs by the falling body that was to be sent aloft again.

Grasping hands clawed for something to hold on to—the horn. However, the saddle was only strapped loosely by one belly strap and not cinched up, and so saddle and rider slid towards the ground, while Strawberry rose further and further into the air. As her cargo pounded into the earth, she pivoted and dropped her head and front legs to the ground and exploded a mighty kick with her hind legs moving in unison, sending the saddle and temporary occupant backward and into the air once again, only to roll and tumble to a tangled halt, many yards away.

Sadly, no Hollywood film crew was there to capture the drama that day. But in my mind's eye, it was Oscar-worthy.

The Petrified House

I rode the short bus. That's how us kids got around in the country. There was not too much inclination on the part of the parents, despite our protestations and nagging, to haul us around. They used the car to go to work. An exception might be when we went to the drive-in on occasion.

My good friend Steve Phillips (Stevie is what his grandmother called him, to his embarrassment) lived at the other end of the school district's bus route. It was a ways away.

He lived out towards Mauriceville and his Grandpa Merriweather had a couple of horses and a few cows and a big barn to store hay in. Steve had a real hideout, and he said he even had candles to burn for lighting at night, which was exciting.

I would ride his bus to his house on Friday at the end of the week, after school, stay the weekend, ride into school on his bus on Monday, and then ride my little bus, Bus 13, after school to home. That meant three days of playing and no parents would be involved. I was told to try and keep my clothes clean. Steve and I got to work on the hideout, go to the woods and explore, and take our .22's and hunt.

Steve told me, before my first trip to his place, that he lived with his grandparents in a petrified house. "You couldn't miss it if you drove past it on 1132."

Sure enough, his house was petrified.

Mr. Merriweather knew about a reservoir that was being built, either the Sam Rayburn or Dam B, also known as B.A. Steinhagen. He also knew the people that worked there had located a petrified forest that would be flooded when the lake filled up, so he could have as much petrified wood as he could haul away. He took all the stones he could haul and built another room on the front of his ranch house and covered it in petrified wood.

Steve had a couple of horses we could ride, too. We played in the barn and roamed around. The plan was to sneak out of the house, once the grandparents went to bed, get some matches, and go and spend the night in the hideout. We burned candles and went into the woods several times that night and didn't return to the hideout until the next morning.

We watched a Tom Mix serial and cowboy shows and got a great idea. In one of the shows the cowboys had to go across a wide gorge in a cable car to discover the secret cave where the outlaws were laying low.

We wanted to ride a cable car over a gorge. So, we went into the barn and looked around. First, we needed a pully to make a cable car work and then some rope, the longer the better. Long ropes, wire, clothesline; everything was thought about.

As mentioned previously, we didn't have big rocks. The biggest and highest things around were the trees and then there was the barn and the hayloft. We could go as far away as our rope was long.

We didn't find any rope that was too long. If we tied pieces together to make it longer, the knots would jam up in the pully that was over the hayloft door, so we had to use what we had. We needed the cable car to hang under it and to be able to ride in it. All we could find was a peach crate, much too small for either of us.

Steve then said, "We'll get Dinky to do it!" Dinky was his little brother. "Let's go find him."

Both of us were tired from staying up all night but the new plan energized our enthusiasm. Dink might get talked into doing it. We never saw a problem with that. Little Dinky was small. I wondered if it was okay to involve him in this plan, but Steve told me, "Sure, it will be fun. I already put him inside Grandma's washing machine before and he rode around in it and saw that it was okay and thought it was fun."

So, this testimonial seemed fine to me and so we went looking for him. Whenever I saw Dinky (his Christian name was David Nickolas Merriweather) when visiting Steve, he always was dirty and rather unkept. And he always had cats around him. He would play with them, put doll clothes on them, put them in his wagon and pull them around, here and there. If he attracted a fly or two, you'd never know it.

"Look for cats."

We found Dinky almost instantly.

He was in the barn, below the hayloft, and he was riding his cats in a box, in his wagon. Steve took his box of cats up into the hayloft and he followed, he wanted his cats back.

Steve started telling him about this great ride he made and wanted Dinky to get into the peach crate and then he could be kicked out of the door for his ride down the rope in the nifty cable car.

Dinky was small. However, the crate was smaller. We managed to get him pushed into the crate, but when he got scared and didn't want to go, Steve came up with a bit of genius and told him, "It will be fun, and you can take some of your kittens with you and give them a ride. How 'bout that?"

The next thing was us, gathering up kittens to ride in the peach crate. The kittens kept jumping out, so we got some from his box to add a few more. Then Steve pushed him off and kicked him out of the hayloft – Dinky and the cats!

At first, it looked pretty good, like it was working. Dink and the cats were all headed down together, almost straight down.

One of Dink's feet and his leg came out the bottom of the peach crate and so did some of the cats. Dink was destined to hit the ground waaay early and wouldn't make the 20 feet.

And then the rest of the bottom of the crate gave way, but one of Dink's arms got stuck in the box and he was destined to continue down, hanging by an arm as the ground rushed to meet them. Cats were dispersed all along the way to the end. Dink glanced into the ground, one would say, and fortunately, being strung out with dangling legs broke the boy's fall but it did not break his legs.

When he got loose of all the lines and was about to wail, Steve got to him quickly and put two cats in his hands. "Check the cats," he told his brother, which got him redirected. I took the cue and raced around to gather up some of the kittens. I put them in the cardboard box next to Dink.

Steve said we better break down our cable car stuff and get rid of it before his grandpa saw it. Dinky went towards the garage with his cat box and Steve thought we should check on him.

He was in the shade in the garage with his box of cats. When the cats saw us enter the shade, they moved off and crawled under things and got out of the way. Two old cats were sleeping on the shaded steps into the house and didn't pay us hardly a mind.

Dinky told Steve he didn't like what happened and was threatening to tell Grandma when they got home from town. Steve told Dinky they could do something special if he kept quiet.

"You liked going back and forth in the washing machine, didn't you? Come and look at this," and he opened the door to the dryer next to the washing machine and turned it on so Dinky could see it run. He thought it could be fun and Steve egged him on to try it out. Dinky opened the door and crawled inside, then said, "Go." He went four loops before he yelled, "Uncle." He banged his head a time or two as he spun around, asshat to tea kettle.

"No lumps are going to come up," Steve said, after a cursory glance.

One of the pair of cats that had been sleeping looked up, rose, and walked over and rubbed past Dinky's legs. Dinky sat down to rub it and the other one continued to sleep.

Esprit De Corps, Alien Abduction, and Twirling Fire

That swelling of patriotism formed and grew in this young man, I suppose, from the large footprint and presence of the Navy base that was started in 1940, prior to the beginning of the Second World War, and built on the west bank of the Sabine River that emptied into the Gulf of Mexico at Orange, Texas.

It was a boomtown, both during the War and afterwards, when the troops came home. The Navy and allied shipyards employed hundreds of iron workers. The Navy built 24 landing craft and crafts that were destroyers, destroyer escorts, mine sweepers, and rescue boats. After the war, they built one of the Staten Island ferries for New York City.

Over 300 ships and other vessels created thousands of jobs, and the streets were filled with a mixture of civilian and uniformed Navy men and women. It was easy to guess what business, occupation, or concerns people were engaged in, by what they wore. That uniform said something and meant something. I spotted that right off.

The common denominator was khaki shirt and pants. Whether you were a shipyard worker or a Naval off-duty truck driver, you wore khakis. They were all over town all the time.

I could see many a time that a man in uniform was a point of pride. Sometimes when several of them walked up and met each other, they would always have one man that would be saluted to, more than the others. They just knew who that was, like everybody knew who it was in advance. On some occasions, there might be two of them in a crowd that got saluted to more than the others.

That's what I wanted. I wanted to get somewhere so's I'd be the one that would be saluted to, instead of the other way around. When I mentioned that to a sailor who was drinking beer inside my dad's bar one day, he told me he knew exactly how I felt, and he had felt that way before he joined the Navy, and he understood. I learned later he was a Chief Petty Officer.

"I've got just the thing for you," he said to me a few days later.

"This book I got for you will tell you everything you'll want to know. It is called the Blue Jackets Manual. It is the official book of the United States Navy."

Now, we were getting somewhere. My dream. No more being a nobody from nowhere. And I started to dream. I really wanted to learn something, as opposed to just going to school. This was going to be real learning; I was sure of it. The book had official pictures to help me go by.

I really started reading—goodbye to all that Dick and Jane stuff. This was *real* learning.

We started going to the library and I could check out two books at a time. I was ready to get a uniform. I could dream, right? My imagination fed on pictures of men in uniforms, and I could be a *bon vivant*, a person who enjoys a sociable and luxurious lifestyle. Looking up different uniform pictures just whet my appetite. The RCMP, the Royal Canadian Mounted Police rode horses. I rode horses. So, there you are!

"Epilates worn smartly, jodhpur pants starched crisp ... hushed tones and muffled voices ... crack a tray of ice cubes and serve ... the chest as a placard ... a swag of service emblems and campaign medals ... festooned the draped sash de guar ... a doughboy recruit."

I studied and studied the Blue Jackets Manual again and again to learn and remember everything I could. I learned the various rifle firing positions and practiced shooting in the back yard. I knew most of the positions; I got my first .22 bolt-action rifle and six boxes of .22 shorts for Christmas and was shooting a lot then. I shot lots of floating beer cans going down the Sabine River. (When the parents had people out to our river house on West Bluff they would throw the empties in the river.) Usually, I only got to shoot the single shot, so I would take my time aiming better and would make a better shot that way, before the river carried it away or it sunk.

Back at the ranch on 1132, I was blowing holes in the back fence when shooting a big Winchester '73. It was a .44/40, hexagon-barreled rifle that weighed a ton, at least several pounds heavy. I got to shoot it only sporadically because the ammo was expensive, and I had a time trying to hold it to my shoulder to shoot it. It was the gun I was given to use when we went deer hunting in Rusk County.

First Aid—bandaging the wounded, slings, compression … marching, saluting, swimming through the burning oil fires at sea when torpedoed. Lots to learn, so I studied hard. I just HAD to get a uniform.

Somehow, we could get on the Navy base as civilians and go to the PX and buy stuff. Some of my classmates wore Navy shoes and had Navy belts, too. All the shirts, pants, and things were too big and wouldn't fit me. Still, it was time I got me a real uniform.

We went to Levine's on Front Street and this time I didn't get a raincoat, and I did get a real uniform, but it wasn't Navy. It was the uniform of the United States Cub Scouts of America. What a feeling that was. It even had gold striping on the cap.

I started through the Cub Scouts first and displayed my bravery. The Cub Scouts had a manual. It wasn't like the Blue Jackets Manual, and it had lots of things to learn about and I could earn patches for my uniform, as I went through the ranks. I did get a bit of excitement to learn that we would go after the Big Three animals of North America: the Wolf, the Bear, and the Lion. I was to learn and earn the plaster casts of each trophy for my wall. When I finished the training, those mounts looked pretty fine on my wall. I hand-painted each one.

The time came when I accomplished all I could, and I was being promoted to a higher rank, which meant I was earning a new uniform. I was to give up the Blues and the next order of advancement—the Khakis! But, before I was advanced out, I had two duty calls to complete: the Cub Scout Jamboree (being held at the Navy base, how apropos) and move into my khakis. A man in uniform. Ah.

The Jamboree gave all the different troops a chance to show off some skill or craft. Ours must have been more general, as I don't remember it. I do remember cooking up a specialty culinary selection of bait shrimp and butter and (to their surprise) serving portions to the Scout Leader and Assistant Leader. They were quite surprised. If I could have cracked a tray of ice cubes and served, that would earn me one more badge.

The first assignment I took part in at the senior level was a Boy Scout program that was to raise money for our Boy Scout troop in the school cafeteria. The program included bringing firearms to the school cafeteria and displaying a variety of weapons we had from home and displaying them for a money-making event that sold beans and cornbread, a swell idea. The whole troop was to bring their guns.

People brought lots of guns: small semi-automatic pistols, lots of them with pearl handles, made for purses or small tackle boxes, revolvers (like cowboy six-shooters), Colts, Remingtons, Smith & Wessons (police revolvers), a couple of prized German Lugers, Colt M1911 .45's, M-1 Carbines with clips, shotguns (side by side, over and under, lever actions, pumps), high-powered deer rifles with scopes, and black powder arms, including a Hawking.

Someone even had a machine gun that was mounted on a tripod for shooting from a foxhole, and bayonets and other assorted knives, switchblades, and daggers. Of course, scattered throughout the displays and at the eating tables, we put out a dozen or so loose hand grenades, which you could get at the G.I. surplus store. Everybody knew about them. I was pretty sure that they were practice grenades, so we tried to put a couple of grenades on each of the dining tables before we served them.

My dad and I picked through our guns at home and brought in just a few: two Winchester '73's, a 38/40 and a 44/40; a black powder 12-gauge side by side; and a Civil War Springfield 45 caliber musket, a bolt-action .16 gauge with a clip. Dad said no one would be interested to see my bolt-action .22, so it stayed home.

Our troop studied the Eskimos, and I built a diorama with plaster of Paris that looked like real snow, and it had an igloo and a totem pole. We brought in a real walrus tusk that was carved into a cribbage board that Dad got during the Second World War while he was stationed in the Aleutian Islands.

It was a great bean and cornbread supper. At the end of the supper, I was surprised at who came over to the tables and picked up what rifle or firearms were there. Kids I knew. Kids I didn't even know. They owned those guns.

Since I was promoted out, got a new uniform, khakis and all, it meant that things would be a bit harder now. Going to the upper ranks, first off, meant that I would not be going to the weekly meetings by being dropped off on the bus ride home. And instead of cutting across the fields to reach our back pasture and walking, I would be going by bicycle down to the schoolhouse on 1132, a few miles away.

Going to the upper ranks meant I would meet new guys and have new friends. The first meeting was a get to know your troop, where hardly anybody knew anyone else. None of us knew what to expect. It was hushed tones and muffled voices. We got our patches and meeting locations assigned, gave dues, said the pledge of allegiance, and went home. I got a car ride from somebody that night but knew that it would, indeed, be a good pedal from there on out to attend the meetings.

And yes, as I suspected, I was assigned to the Little Cypress School. I looked forward to the next meeting and because the parents worked, I had to take my bike and ride down to the school and back at night. I certainly could not do that and be late. I didn't have a light on my bike, but I knew I could just take a flashlight with me. I'm a doughboy recruit. There wasn't much traffic on the farm road, so I wouldn't really see anyone else, back and forth.

The weather was still summer-like, being in the low 90's. It got dark late and so I left with plenty of light to get there and attend. On the way, I was thinking about what my uniform *could* look like when I got older and went to middle school and then high school.

Most of us cadets had our patches already and some guys wore their uniform shirts with their blue jeans. I only had some of my insignias sewn on, I didn't sew much, and Mom would do it on the Singer. Everyone promised to be in full uniform by the next meeting.

Everyone left the school by car to go home after the meeting. It would be just me on 1132. Someone offered to take me home and ride with them, but when they saw my bike, they said couldn't take me after all, and left.

In my excitement to attend the Boy Scout meeting, I forgot my flashlight. Well, it was waaaay dark and there was no moon. But it was just a two-lane farm road. But I didn't have a flashlight. I had to really pay attention to what I was doing to not get off the asphalt on to the gravel edge, slip, and go down. I could feel the road through my handlebars as I traveled along.

It was night, the *dead* of night was more like it. And suddenly, it was something I could not explain, but something that I felt. I veered off the new asphalt onto the gravel and my tires made a growling noise, I'm sure of it. The bike had just *pulled off the road, I could feel that as I held the handlebars.* Something was going on, I could feel I was getting disorientated, maybe because of the heavy smell of the new blacktopping I was traveling on. Even my tires sounded *wet!*

I tried to get my bearings and so I looked into the moonless sky, to where I could see the outline of the tops of pine trees that grew along one side of the road. I could go along for a bit if I kept my eyes looking straight up. I had the whole road to travel down, so I didn't have to choose one side or the other.

It worked, some, until both sides of the road were just flat pastures, and I struggled more. No more tree lines to see or to follow. To continue, I had to keep looking into the black sky.

Suddenly, my mind gave my heart a start, or a jolt, or whatever...

Within an instant, I remembered the conversation I had with Mom, telling me about the news of a man and a woman in their car, traveling a dark road and being overtaken and grabbed by a UFO! They were held as captives and the aliens performed *examinations and experiments on both of them before being released.* Barney and Betty Hill were dazed and lost five hours from their memories. They were captured from their car!

What chance did I have? What happens to me if I'm captured, with only my uniform left of me? My scalp and hair begin to tingle, as if I was being drawn into an invisible craft. How would *I* ever escape? They took Barney and Betty from the protection of their *car.*

The night had become pitch black, and I couldn't see my own hands before my face. What Mom said can't be true, I thought, as my heart pounded in my chest. Mom was a proofreader at the newspaper, and she read everything, so she couldn't be wrong. I was in the middle of nowhere, unable to see anything.

My favorite movie, *The Day the Earth Stood Still,* with Michael Renne, flashed into consciousness. I recalled the part where GORT, the robot, grabbed the Spaceman and took him to the rejuvenation machine as he struggled to get away. But it's now *ME* that is being taken away! I scrutinized the twinkling lights in the heavens and prayed they were not moving.

Where would this beastly machine from The Outer Limits land come from? Would I see them in time to make a get-away? Will they leave my bicycle behind for others to find, so they know I was taken? Maybe I should just sit here on the side of the road and wait for them. It was such a struggle to try and get home.

I looked down from the heavens and saw several kerosene lanterns at a highway barricade detour burning, their flickering flames placed along the road. I was momentarily blinded by the light as I looked upon them. An idea popped into my head—I could carry one of the bowling ball-sized lanterns with me to light the road as I went. The light blinded me, as I tried to carry one in my arm and steer my bike with the other one. I couldn't see beyond the dancing flame.

Stumbling along, kerosene sloshing from the blue ball lantern wets my pants and my new uniform shirt. Terrified, I continued on and hoped that my clothes wouldn't catch fire and burn me alive. I wondered, too, what kind of pain the Death Ray from the saucer would feel like before I succumbed. My balance wasn't working, and I couldn't balance the kerosene ball and peddle home. I'm soaked and would have to walk the gauntlet to the end.

✳ ✳ ✳

The incident on 1132 came to an end. It was behind me, and it was soon forgotten. No more thoughts about it. The summertime idles brought ample time for exploration, investigation, and experimentation around the ranch, in the woods, and beyond. My example is a parable.

It's like when the chickens are out and about. They laze about and look around for something to do or something to peck at. Kids living in the country are kind of like that, as well.

I was watching the usual shows, and a spark of interest flared when I watched people carrying torches and noticed a similarity in that the torches used by cowboys going into a hidden cave, or abandoned gold mine, were the same kind of torches they used in the darkest of Africa in the jungles. They were all burning the same kind of way. They looked the same, as far as I could tell.

I knew about fire and fires on camping trips, but our torches weren't as good, or as sturdy. They didn't burn as neat looking as on TV. Why? Maybe, just maybe, I could learn how to make a good one, to look like, and burn like the ones on TV. It was time to investigate.

I believed the best-looking torch handle would be a broomstick. The one that was in the garage looked worn out, so that one would do. No one would miss it; I was pretty sure.

The old broom straw on the end of a worn-out broom didn't burn well. The fire started slowly, made a messy flame, and soon went out. Besides that, the shape of it was all wrong. It needed to be round with fire, not a smoldering rag fire. When you swung it around, it would instantly go out. That was not going to work. So, I went to the tack room, got Dad's saw, and cut off the head of the broom. Mom found it the next day, when she was going to sweep in the house, and it was smoldering.

She was UNhappy.

I waited until after they left for work and resumed my experiments. I took rags and some wire and wrapped the broom handle in rags and tried it again. It smoldered worse and the rag ends wouldn't go out, they just smoked. And I had learned that I should hide the broomstick somewhere it wouldn't be found.

The mop! That would really work but I would really get it if the mop was found. First off, I cut the strings off the mop, so the fire would look good, which it did. I could already see it in my mind's eye, my great torch working.

My sister and her friends were taking baton classes and learning how to twirl. Drum and bugle corps were important things to get to do, marching in parades. I could twirl a little bit, myself. I could do horizontal twirling and vertical twirling with her baton. I thought if you could do it with fire ....! In an arena with the lights out!

I went to the edge of the property and retrieved the blue ball kerosene lantern I had taken from the detour barricade during the 1132 incident, unscrewed the wick top so I could get at the kerosine, and then soaked the trimmed cotton top of the mop in it. I lit it. It burned with a flame, a big flame. I started to twirl it horizontally. The mop handle was a bit too long.

After several spins and me waiting for the flame to go down a little, I switched to trying it vertical and was thinking I could attach another mop head to the other side and have two balls of fire. I lit the other one.

I dipped vertically and started to twirl. A combination of factors all came together at once. The mop handle hit the ground on the first spin. The burning ball of the other mop head stuck in my armpit, as my reflexes closed it shut. There was no hair under there to singe and burn away and there was plenty of skin to burn and loosen.

There was hardly a pause in the yelling and cursing with my juvenile vocabulary for some time after that. The damage could have been abated, somewhat, if I had worn a shirt, which I usually did not. The burnt area on both sides and into the pocket of the armpit held flecks of ashed cotton threading and smoking carbon remnants.

A merciful gift in the arm closing reflexively could have been that it snuffed out the fire's flames and the damage may have been lessened. NOT. It could have been iced down, but not something generally done or known about in those days.

On the stoves and kitchen tables, most southern families kept a can of bacon fat drippings that was the cure-all for lots of injuries. It would be put to use as soon as I could clean the burns up, after that I got it wrapped. Staying out of the sun was obvious. The sun's rays were exceedingly painful.

Running to the medicine cabinet to look for some medicine didn't produce much. A roll of gauze was all I had. I wrapped several layers of three-inch gauze around and around the arm and added bacon grease to the cloth. It was very odd to smell fresh fried bacon under my armpit. After a few days, the first- and second-degree burns were producing scabs that stopped the oozing, and the layered gauze absorbed a lot of it. I had to be careful the wound would not stick to my shirt. The smell of the bacon grease changed when I added mercurochrome (monkey blood) to the gauze.

Almost ten days later of tepid attention, the time had come to change the dressing. Since the gauze bandage didn't have any cotton or padding over the burn before it was wrapped, the scab simply formed, encompassing the gauze. How could it ever be changed? I didn't change it. It was about the size of a hamburger patty.

It was a very tender process to cut the bandage away from the area using a dull pair of scissors. I was slowly paying attention and had several wraps removed and thought I did it right. One wrap of gauze that was still attached and embedded, unbeknownst to me, I was sitting on. And when I stood up ... I relived the fire twirling all over again. The big scab tore right off my arm.

Ultimately, the parents never knew about the fire twirling mishap. Growing up seemed to be a process guided by other's directions and by personal discovery and happenstance, with a sprinkling of circumstances to flavor the stew.

The Bullet That Almost Got Me

I like to fish. I have liked it ever since I got to go fish on a riverbank and catch perch. I started out fishing in ponds and got to go to the beach down in Galveston and see all the dead fish that had washed up. It made me think about catching one, if I had the chance. The thing that got me is that I had to wade out in the water for a long way before I could hold a pole. I didn't have a fishing reel. It didn't make sense to me to stand in the water and hold my cane fishing pole and have the line go straight down into the water, only two feet away. The fish would get scared off.

Mom and Dad had these two friends, Pappy and Mary Wellington, from I don't know where, and they came and visited us at our house, and they pulled up in a new 1950 Chevrolet pickup truck. It was really neat. The starter pedal was on the floor.

They came to our house and took my sister and me to the beach, and they drove on the sand and away we went. There were lots of things that had washed up on the beach—fish, logs, orange and black tugboat lines, and we even saw our first sea turtle, though it was dead. We stood on top of the sea turtle's shell, and they took a picture. We got to go explore the beach and get shells. We found large conch shells and sand dollars. I always wanted to find a starfish. They were in every coloring book I had, but I never saw them on the beaches.

As time went by, and Pappy and Mary drove back to our house to see us again, Pappy had a big tarp over something in the pickup bed and he showed us a very large fish he caught. It was a red snapper or a bull drum, something big.

I got the first case of fishing pox, they said later. So, it was soon time to get stuff ready for a trip back to the beach. We didn't have any fishing poles. Nothing.

Dad came home one day from his job at the newspaper with a penny box of matches, not the book matches kind. The box had a paper clip sticking out one end and when I picked it up it was heavy. He said he had made the weight at work. He was a line-o-type operator, and his big typewriter-like machine had a big pot of molten lead on the end of it and he got the hot lead, poured it into the matchbox, and made it. It was what we were going to throw into the water, the next time we went to the beach. Then we wouldn't have to walk up to our necks in the waves just to get a line in the water.

I needed a fishing pole, and he was going to make me one to fish in saltwater. He came home one day with a big bamboo cane pole, but it was bigger than the ones we used on the bayou. He got a real fishing reel to go on it. It was a Penn 09 size, and it had Dacron braided line on it, a hundred-pound test, he said.

He took some clothes hangers and bent and cut pieces to wire the reel on to the pole and then he made eyes, for the line to go through and out the end of the pole. Those were secured using black electrical tape. I was then shown how to use my thumb to hold the line, with that big heavy weight on it and practiced how to cast it out. It was very hard on my thumb, but I learned.

I would cast it out and reel it back, time after time until I could get it out a ways. I did get it across the yard, but then, when I started hitting cars out in the street, he said I was ready to go out and try it for real.

Since we knew we'd lose weights and hooks, we knew we'd better get a few more weights made. And so, I went to where his linotype machine was and watched him ladle up hot lead into those match boxes. That hot lead was waaay cool, how it acted, and it would cool into any shape you wanted it to be in. It was like mercury, except that it got stiff and didn't change shape or drip away.

Pappy and Mary were going to go with us again to the beach and Pappy had this huge reel on his pole, and it was a real rod, too. His reel was a Penn 309, the biggest reel I had ever seen. It looked like he could put on a big bait and a mile of line. It had this chrome wheel that you could turn that made the fish have to fight more to keep from being caught. The reel handle looked like it was made of real ivory!

To get to the beach at High Island, we had to drive through a chemical plant. We would always roll our windows up. It stunk!

※ ※ ※

Then came the time that we were not going to the beach much anymore. I was standing in the tack room, scooping out buckets of horse feed and I glanced into a corner where stuff was piled out of the way, and I looked longingly at all those weights that we made and now weren't ever going to be used, or so I thought.

After feeding, I sat down with the latest edition of *The Shooter's Bible*. What a terrific book. It was filled with all these pictures of guns from everywhere. Since we had several, always all around our house, and I wanted to know about our guns, I was always reading. The sub-title was:

> *The most comprehensive and sought-after reference guide for new firearms and their specifications, as well as for 1000's of guns that have been in production and are currently on the market.*

Since our family owned a bar in Orange, The Last Frontier, lots of cowboys and ranch hands would bring in guns they wanted to sell, swap, or use to buy booze with. Guns would just show up and then disappear regularly at our house. I got to shoot some of them.

One of the draws of The Last Frontier was that it was a truly western-themed establishment. After working cattle, folks would show up and drink a few beers. When cattlemen and horsemen were either going or coming back from the auctions, they would come in. They came in from the Dorman Ranch, the Winfree Arena, Gus Harris's Farmers Mercantile, E.W. Brown's Ranch, the Stark's Ranch, and Pinehurst Ranch.

To recognize who was new in the area, Dad kept a blowtorch behind the bar and the ranchers were invited to bring in their branding irons, heat them up, and brand the wall. It was an attention-getter. When folks came in for a beer, they smelled fresh burnt wood, and knew someone new was around. Lots of beers were consumed when the walls smoked.

❋ ❋ ❋

I liked reading the gun books and seeing all the assorted sizes of the bullets that were shot out of them. I started making a comparison of what kind of shooting irons we had on our place, by caliber. I started with .22, .25, .30, .32, .38, .40, and so on, then switched to shotguns with gauges like 10 ga., 12 ga., 16 ga., 20 ga., and so on. I found this chart! It showed pictures of each of the bullets and their sizes as they went to bigger and bigger sizes. I remember it starting about .19, then .22, .25, on up and then up some more. The .50 caliber was a whopper. I wished I had one of those bullets.

Now, that's an idea—I'll make my own bullets!

Knowing what I knew at that point about bullets and lead, I figured it was just a matter of finding the right molds, melting the lead, and pouring them right up. How simple could that be?

The hunt was now on to find molds. I wasn't to the point of thinking about building any molds. I saw it as a matter of finding the molds that were already made.

I need to figure out how I'm going to melt the lead. Ah, the stove! It was electric, so I figured I could turn it up as high as needed. Now, where was I going to get lead?

Ah, the tack room! I remembered the lead that was just thrown in the corner and doing nothing. And since we weren't fishing anymore ... So, I went to the tackle box and loaded up on all the lead I could find. Now for the mold ...

For the few short years we lived in the country, our horses were part-time playthings to ride, do some rodeoing with, and to ride in parades. And they were for selling or swapping for something else. And there it was!

Sitting on the mantle, over the fireplace, was a trophy one of the horses had won. It was like brass or something, maybe copper because it was tarnished. Suddenly, it looked sooo neglected and unwanted. It wasn't shined or anything. The horse's name wasn't even on it.

Looking closely at it—if you ignored the silver handles on either side—it tapered down almost to a point before it flared to the foot it stood on.

A BULLET! Turn it upside down and there was my bullet!

I really thought about it for a good amount of time before I decided to do what I was thinking. Maybe three seconds or so. I leaped down the outside stairs to the tack room and started gathering all the lead I knew about in anticipation of creating a real bullet.

"Oh yes, Oh YES!"

I went to the stove and turned the front burner up to a rosy red. To melt everything down (still a bit unsure how much was really needed), I tested the lead sinkers in the largest cast iron skillet we had, probably the 12-inch one. The little split shot lead sinkers we used for perch fishing, those I dropped into the rosy skillet. They melted right away.

The trophy was only eight inches tall, and the base was less than two inches, so I figured six inches of molten lead would do the trick, maybe two cups would do it.

I started melting match box sized ingots and put in several, just to make sure. I was getting ready to pour. I placed the trophy at the edge of the stove, next to the burner. The weight of the cast iron skillet, plus all that lead, was very heavy. I used one hot pad and a small dish towel to protect my hands.

Upon picking it up, the molting lead moved around the skillet like water and shifted the balance and it was almost impossible to control it. I had to pour it quickly because the hot cast iron handle started to burn through the towel almost immediately.

I poured as best as I could, and the molten lead came out and spread very wide of the little pointy pour spout. It came out in a sheet, and I caught the middle part with the trophy, and it began to fill, so I kept pouring. The bullet almost got full, and the massive amount of hot lead instantly melted the small neck at the base of the trophy, it collapsed and poured two cups of molten lead into the burner and went through the stove. I dropped the skillet from the heat and more lead splashed across the porcelain top between front and back burners.

I was burned inside both of my hands. The lead was turning solid, and I had to get more towels and anything I could grab to get the skillet off the floor, where it was smoldering the lino-leum and making its mark prominent. I began throwing water on everything that was silvery and that was smoking. The room became steamy.

There was never a thought to wear gloves for any of this. It was July, for God's sakes. Screwdriver, butter knife, whatever I could find, I went at the task of removing as much of the spilled lead as I could, to cover up and hide the deed. Lead being pulled off porcelain leaves a trail of marks, like lead pencils do. It was a lot of scrubbing to get it off.

Below the front burner was the pots and pans storage area in the lower drawer. The drawer was leaded shut and it didn't want to open. I couldn't find a way to get fire down there to melt it, so I could move and unstick the pots that were fused together. I did manage to get a candle flame on the edge of a piece of a muffin tin and at that point, the jigsaw puzzle began to move somewhat and give me some hope. Some of the cooking pots I could move back and forth and so I had to sit there and work it until the lead would give up and separate.

※ ※ ※

I've thought about that little neglected trophy, and I began to think about the missing bits and pieces of how we got it in the first place. What could it have been for? We didn't race horses or anything like that. We just went to rodeos almost every week.

I wanted to be a calf roper, but I needed a healer to form a team—someone to throw the second rope to catch the steer's hind legs, after I strike the steer's head or horns. I was too young to drive to get to an arena. We had a great Arabian filly. She was fast and she was not that big. Fancy, we called her. She would be my horse. I could go out and jump on her back and ride her without a saddle or a bridle.

Our horse trailer was big enough to carry two horses at a time. We rode in rodeo parades in different East Texas towns and my dad was a sworn-in Deputy Sheriff. He would ride out on horseback and help people when we had bad storms or hurricanes, and the roads were cut off because of high waters. Many of the Deputies had horses and they put together a drill team to do synchronized riding as part of the rodeo programs at night. They would carry the flag around the arena slowly, and the people in the bleachers would take off their hats and recite to the flag.

Now, I got it. The trophy was awarded to my dad because he had the best horse and saddle in the rodeo. He was very proud of his handsome palomino stud, which he had named Chief Yellow Hand. Chief was too big for me—the saddle stirrup was too high for my leg to reach.

The parents went to Mexico on a trip, and they went to buy a saddle and harnesses for the Chief. They came back after several days loaded down with Mexican stuff they got over in Reynosa, Mexico.

The first thing we saw when they got out of the station wagon was a brand-new saddle and tack. Wow. The saddle was a chestnut fancy-tooled wide-horned Spanish roping saddle with covered tooled stirrups. They brought back a serape saddle blanket to go with the saddle, and two more serapes for us kids. Ponchos, too. Mexican pants and shirts. Belts, and other stuff. Dad showed me a new quirt, a new silver hackamore bit, and new Spanish large rowel spurs. I was going to get his old ones.

The major surprise for me was getting a new bullwhip, a ten-footer.

They really did it up. He wanted to look like a complete Mexican Caballero when we rode in the parades. That's why he got that trophy, it was for Chief Yellow Hand. We saw a western one time and one of the Indians painted a yellow hand on the rump of his pony. When we paraded, he would paint a yellow hand on our horse.

* * *

Oh, Lord, look at the mess. The trophy was destroyed, mostly melted away. I got the idea of hiding it, so I went to the attic closet door and threw it up there. With acres and acres surrounding the ranch, I could have just gone outside somewhere and buried it. Putting it in the attic was about as smart as the rest of it. I never thought of burying it. However, before we moved back to the city, I was curious and went to the attic to find it. And IT WASN'T THERE!

The Armadillo's
Seventh Drowning

After a brutally scorching summer and on to a still warmer than average October, Jonny rode the bus out and was back for another weekend of fun at Steve's petrified house. It was getting cool in the evenings, and they got ready to spend another night in the hideout together, and then they would run around in the woods and see what they could get into.

The cartoon shows were still on that afternoon when they stepped off the bus and went to watch some TV. They had no specific plans of what to do, other than doing something together. Sitting in front of the tube, they idlily watched what came on, until they got an idea for the next morning.

It was a matter of sneaking food stuffs out of the kitchen and stashing it in the secret hideout. With nothing on their minds, they proceeded to sneak it out in the woods and be ready to come back in time for breakfast the next morning. Afterwards, they just ambled out to the barnyard where Grampa Meriweather had been pulling a drag bar across a pasture that bumped up to the back of the barn, where they always loved to go and play. Soon, an idea came to Steve to get the horse, still in pulling harness, and hook it up to a pedal car that belonged to Dinky and figure a way to play at something. Unfortunately, the pedal car was a bit banged up.

"Dinky, I got a swell idea. We can make a carnival ride. We can get your great pedal car, and you can ride in it, and we will pull you across the pasture."

Dink had a brow of suspicion on his brother, and would need to be talked into it, whatever it was Steve had devised.

On concrete, or a board floor, the wagon could be peddled without any trouble. What Steve was thinking about, however, was to take his little brother across the field, pulled by the plow horse. Already it was making Dink nervous. Jonny could look out across the corduroy fallow field, which had once been cut into rows for corn that had already been harvested, and the stalks already removed and cut for sileage.

It was going to be a great ride! They could just tell. They loaded Dinky in the metal pedal car and Steve took the plowing reins and gave the horse the instruction to walk across the field, at a slow plowing pace. It was all so fine, Dinky was happy, going across the plowed rows at an angle, kinda up and down motion, like a carnival carousel would do.

But, the horse didn't like the constant jerking of the wagon up and down, instead of a steady pull. Jonny was walking way behind all of them, and the horse's ears began to tell a story of how it felt, which to anyone who could read horse's ears, it was clear he wasn't very happy, and he was getting more wound up the further they went.

The horse began to sully up. It wanted to stop and not go further. And then when he was commanded to go, he started pulling all jerky-like and the ride was getting to be not fun, in Dinky's looks, as well as the horse's. They reached the other end of the fallow field, and it was time to switch riders and go back the other way.

Steve and Jonny were deep in discussion about which of them should be the next to go and how much fun it was going to be. Both boys had watched the ears of the horse show hot and cold. Jonny was the guest, by rights, he should be the next one to enjoy the ride. But he explained that he was unfamiliar with the nuances of the conveyance and wanted Steve to go first. After Steve went, then he would go.

They were standing there for quite a long time, so long that Dinky got out of the pedal car and waited for the matter to be decided. A couple of cats came trotting out of the barn and joined Dink at his feet. Steve relented and agreed to be the next rider. But when he tried to get in, he was too big for the pedal car. It had been a long time since he'd even tried to ride in it, and his legs had grown so long that he couldn't even get his feet down into the cab. Ever resourceful, Steve soon found a scrap of a board and put it in the passenger hole and then sat down on top of that. He stuck his feet out in front and rested his legs on the hood of the toy car.

Next, it was discussed how the horse was going to participate in pulling the wagon. Steve could sit astride the car and then hold the reins on the horse and go along. They were tied together on the ends of the leather, and it made a convenient loop around Steve, so that he could steer with one hand.

Jonny didn't want to lead the horse. "You go ahead and go, Steve," he told his friend. "He looks a bit twitchy."

Two young barn cats were wrestling and rolling about on the ground, under the horse's feet and the cat ball rolled into a hind leg and grabbed the horse's ankle, unexpectedly. The horse's ears were pinned back on his head, and now they came up in alarm. That was the moment Dinky reached into a corn furrow, grabbed a big, dried, hard kernelled ear of corn, and chucked it into the horse's rump and yelled, "Gitty-up!"

Later, Jonny said when the horse bolted, he watched Steve's legs go straight up in the air and when they came back down, Steve had wrapped his legs around the front of the 1950 Ford sedan toy car and was holding on for dear life. He wasn't able to fall away and get away from it, as the plowing reins were tied around his back. He was going to be dragged for a spell—at least to the end of the pasture, where the horse would have to turn, and he would be thrown off. As he shot across the field like a missile, cutting off the tops of many corn rows, he bounced up and down, pounding on the board seat he had fashioned.

Dinky joined the ball of cats on the ground and rolled with laughter. Dry clouds of dirt kicked into the air, just like a dust devil! Jonny saw Steve, who had kicked free of the toy car, covered in dust and slightly bewildered.

It was the smallest rodeo they had ever participated in. When Steve got his wind and stood up and knocked off the dust with his hat, they sat back down in the corn rows to relive the challenge. Jonny started in, "Well, Steve, it looks like I'll have to give you an eight on that ride, pardner." And they started back in, laughing their asses off.

They looked at the crumpled-up Ford and could see it was a total wreck! The horse had shed the rest of the harness and was off in another field by then.

Steve said, "I'll never catch him this afternoon. I'll get a bucket of oats to rattle him back to the barn at feeding time."

❋ ❋ ❋

Johnny Weissmuller, Tarzan himself, was on the TV, and the boys started to watch it. Tarzan was always fighting wild animals, swinging through the trees on vines, and getting away from his enemies when they tried to put traps in the jungle to capture him. He knew all about snares and could always get away. He could talk to the animals in their language and his mother was a great ape. He also had a sheath knife, which he always carried on his side.

Steve asked, "Jonny, what kind of pet would you like to have and talk to? Do you think it would be a lot of trouble to have a chimpanzee for a pet?"

Jonny thought about it and then said, "When we moved from Orange to the country, I had a girlfriend, once, who had a monkey for a pet. She lived on Sixteenth Street and Park Avenue, across from the Piggly Wiggly, over by Shangri-la. When we used to go and buy groceries, you could see the monkey in this girl's back-yard and so, one day, we stopped to see the monkey. This lady came out with her daughter—that was my girlfriend—and we got to see it. They put it on a clothesline in the back yard and the monkey spent time behind the house, tethered to that clothesline, jumping around."

"Did you get to hold it? How did that feel, with his little hands on you and all?"

"He did jump up on me and I thought I was going to get bit. You ought to see those teeth."

"That girl pulled him away with the long chain she had on him, and it was all right, from then on. It was a spider monkey."

The girl was in the same grade as Jonny and Steve. She had this name he would never forget—Charlene Elsie Charlie McDonald. So, from then on, every time they drove by, they would look for the monkey. The boys started teasing Jonny, saying she was his girlfriend, and she had a monkey for her boyfriend. He invited her out to his family's ranch for his birthday one time, and they rode horses around the front yard of his house.

"We could make us a jungle hideout and build it in the trees, and we could cut some of those big wisteria vines to swing on!" Steve made the Tarzan yell —"Ah-iahhh"— and they both jumped up.

Then, Jonny yelled, "Bhawana, Bhawana timba!" like the jungle natives would say on the Tarzan show, and they ran off to the woods, stopping to get rope from the barn and the barn pully from the hayloft in case they needed it.

They were soon going into the darkest part of Africa, watching out for lions, tigers, and Cape buffaloes.

First off, after tying lots of sticks with vines and cutting poles with a hatchet that Steve had found in Grandpa Meriweather's workshop, they got the food from the other hideout to set up their new hide-away and started getting on guard, in case the enemy came down the trail.

They soon heard rustling in the forest and were ready to fight. They had found some rattan vines, growing straight, and made spears. Steve knew where some old bamboo cane poles were put away in the barn and they made them into spears, too. They gathered some kite string and went to the chicken yard and got fresh feathers to use.

Suddenly appearing in the clearing was the beast they had heard crashing around. It was one of Grampa's cows walking back to the barn to get to the feed trough for the evening feed.

It looked "vicious" to them, and it did have horns, although the points on the horns had long ago been sawn off. But it looked "dangerous," anyway.

They began to plot how they were going to capture this beast, even though the cow was walking at such a slow pace, it would be dark before she got to the barn. They had to think like Tarzan would. First, both had to make the Tarzan yell before swinging down from their hideout. They were going to track the beast and find a place to set up a snare, of some sort, if they could figure it out.

It was just a cow path in the pasture, but they could track the animal down. They didn't want to get too close, as it could turn and charge them at any moment. Luckily for them, it didn't challenge them, and they picked out a spot where they could rig up a snare. They didn't know how a snare would work, but they knew that there was always a big tree that was used and bent over to a trip wire that would send the animal skyward and be captured.

So, they had to stop and figure out how to do it. Other boys at school would set traps for flying squirrels and bring them to school in their pockets, after they were tamed, and sell them to the other kids. They could use the same trapping idea to a trip wire and catch their horned beast. It took a while to get it worked out so it would set and then spring.

Finally, both of them crawled out on the end of a sapling and bent it over. They used the pully from the hayloft to give them enough leverage to get the tree over and cocked. It was going to be a feat to capture the King of the Beasts. "Ah-iahhh!"

Once they headed down the trail and caught up with the "beast," upon closer inspection, the old Heffer failed to stir the blood of the two warrior Tarzans. She had been dry for a few years and was a bit skinny, with crooked horns and split hoofs. She was a Jersey crossed with another breed. Since the barn was just ahead and they had other things to do, they gave up the "chase of the Wildebeest" and walked past her on the trail, their mental energies for the safari having evaporated.

"Let's stop at the barn and get us those bamboo cane poles. They'll make great spears." Jonny followed Steve into the tack room and found a corner in the room that had lots of fishing gear that had not been used in years. It was all tangled and covered in dust.

Picking out some stout poles and continuing to rummage around, they located some boxes of old kitchen utensils and found a couple of steak knives with crumbling plastic handles, and they bound them to the canes. They now had deadly spears.

"What do you say, let's cross the road out front and go to the rice canal and do some spearing?" And so, they went across the road and along the canal bank, picking a few berries along the way.

"We have to learn to survive out here. What about the canal, how deep is it?" Jonny inquired. "Can we cross it?"

Steve was already taking his clothes off to go for a swim in the canal. "I've done it a million times. Come on in!"

The last thing they did was leave their undershorts hanging from the trestle timbers, so they would have some piece of clothes that would be dry after they finished. They got in and went to the other side of the canal and sat in the shade. Something was moving towards them in the tall grass, approaching them slowly. They realized their nifty spears were on the other side of the canal and they were now defenseless.

"Just stay still, Jonny, we might have a chance."

An armadillo poked his head out of the tall grass, sniffed the air, and finding nothing threatening, went back in the tall grass and poked along. It walked past Steve, who was frozen still, but then lunged at the armadillo and tackled him like a loose football. Then they both fell into the canal. Steve lost his grip on the armadillo and when he came up for air, he motioned to Jonny to show that he did not have the armadillo. They both froze and waited for the armadillo to come up and swim away.

Nothing happened.

No armadillo was to be found. Nothing was swimming in the canal. "Where did he go, Steve?" And then Jonny felt the scratchy fingernails of the armadillo on his foot and dived towards it.

"I got him, Steve!" He held the armored animal by his shell into the air. Suddenly struggling, the armadillo scratched Jonny's belly and Jonny dropped him, and the armadillo went back into the water and disappeared.

"We can't lose him! We'll eat him tonight in the jungle!" They stopped momentarily, looked at each other, realizing that this was real food.

"Bwana" one yelled. The other one, "Ah-iahhh!"

"How come this armadillo can't swim? I thought animals could swim."

"I've never seen one swim. Steve, have you ever?"

"No, me either. He's a submarine armadillo."

"For all we know he's down there, just walking along and getting away."

"Suppose so."

Since the two Tarzans had gone into the canal and had wet clothes, they agreed it would be nice to have something dry to put on.

Steve suggested, "We can take our wet clothes back across the road and put them in the clothes dryer and just wear our drawers home. Grandma won't say anything, she's seen me come home like this many a time."

"What about me?" Jonny protested "She'll see me."

"Probably not, she's on the back porch with pickings from the garden."

About the time they gathered their clothes up and started to climb up the trestle timbers to the road, they heard a car coming. Steve signaled that they should get under the trestle and hide till the car passed, but they were forced to get back into the water— in their drawers—in order to hide. The truck stopped momentarily on the bridge and then continued on. Now both were soaked, and their clothes were soaked, too.

Coming to the house, Grandma was sitting on the front steps of the petrified house, shelling beans. When the two boys came closer, she could see they had wet pants and teased them. "I suppose you two couldn't stop to pee on the side of the road? Looks like neither of you could hold it. Get dried off, your grandpa is out looking for that old Jersey cross and will be in by supper."

Oh, oh. That was the Wildebeest they were "tracking" earlier and the one they were going to trap! What should they do? They both had the same thoughts and needed to get away from Granny, so they could talk. Their minds raced.

Grandpa Meriweather's voice was heard outside. "You boys come outside here, for a minute," he says. They knew they were going to be caught at some time, and this was going to be it. It was a matter of which crime would be pinned on them, they thought.

Coming through the creaky screen door, they sat on the porch waiting for the worst. He had a cigarette in his mouth and flicked the butt to the ground, as he looked them over before he spoke. As an aside, he said to them, "Cigarettes are bad, don't smoke," before getting to the point. "I know you two are having a fun time and I want that to continue. I can see you are good friends. So, I want to say to you, who left the light burning in the barn tack room? It isn't a big deal, but we wouldn't want the barn to catch fire and burn down because we were careless."

Steve jumped right in and admitted that they were in there getting cane poles and apologized, and that was that. Dodged a bullet.

Their clothes were damp, either from the rice canal or being sweated under interrogation. Once they heard that Grandpa was looking for the old Jersey Heifer, they realized they had to do something and went to investigate their trap, in case they really had caught something.

As they started down the trail after supper, Grandma stopped them, asking them to take some sacks of black-eyed pea hulls out to the feed lot and suggested they may want to stick around. It was getting dark, and it was time to slow down and rest some.

Soon afterwards, Steve said, "Don't worry, they're old, and they'll be going to bed shortly. We can hide out at the hideout until it gets really dark and then we can hit the trail to the jungle."

In the hideout, Jonny said, "Let's sit here till the candle burns down and then we should go. Can't be too careful … if we get caught, we'll be in for it." So, they waited and both of them drifted off to sleep, until Jonny woke up with a start and got Steve up.

"What time is it? Did we sleep all night? We might get caught."

"I got it, I'll go in the house and get a flashlight, it won't take a minute, and we can go over to the rice canal and get our spears."

Waiting in the dark magnified any sound and Jonny heard plenty of them. He was worried that Steve would be found out, that they would have to leave the hideout and go back inside the house, and that whatever they trapped in the woods would be found out.

Steve had the flashlight and pushed the button to see if its batteries were good. Unfortunately, the wrong button was pressed, and the light locked in the ON position, and before he knew it, the light beam was painted all over the house. Shuffling footsteps were heard in the hallway, and he froze.

"What's going on in there, who's in here?" Grandpa said in a very gruff voice that scared the bejesus out of Steve.

In his quivering voice, he answered, "It's only me, Grandpa, I was just up to get some water."

"Well, what are you doing with that flashlight, going all around the house in the middle of the night? You've lived here all your life and don't need no light to walk through this house at night. Why you doing it?"

Thinking on his feet, Steve said, "It's just in case Jonny wants to use the bathroom. He's doesn't know our house, so it's just to make him feel at home, more comfortable."

"Oh. Then get your water and get back to bed now. And you two could sleep in. Tomorrow is Sunday, a day of rest …

for some," Grandpa added under his breath, as he turned and headed back in the direction of his bed. He stopped and turned around.

"And what are you doing with your clothes on? It's not near time to think about getting up?"

"Yes, Sir. I just fell asleep while we were talking, and never took them off yet."

"Good night, Stevie," he said back to him, making a point of using the word "Stevie" instead of Steve. The message was conveyed.

So, after returning, Steve had to tell Jonny every detail of the encounter. Then they took off for the rice canal and this time they had a flashlight to light their way. This was going to be a real hunt, and they had their spears with the steak knife tips.

What was out there were many dangers that could be found around the canal bank at night—starting with snakes. Copperheads, moccasins, rattlesnakes, and other non-poisonous water snakes could be in the grass banks. Larger animals could be the armadillo that got away, to start with, but then you could add the possums, racoons, nutrias, bullfrogs, turtles, bobcats, rabbits, wild pigs, skunks, and deer, all roaming around, hiding, or doing their nightly hunts and feeding, too!

By far, the most dangerous foe to encounter would not be slowed down by the tip of a rusted three-inch bladed steak knife on the end of a bamboo cane pole held by a trembling fifth grade boy. The American alligator lay submerged in water, showing only it's eyes and waited, sometimes for days, before moving from that spot. It could eat a pig or a deer or anything that may walk, swim, fly, or crawl down a canal bank. When spotlighted, because their eyes are above water, the reflection showed double sets of eyes. Jonny would learn that small bit of knowledge during the next few weeks.

A dead giveaway.

Leaving the canal bank and standing on the trestle looking back one last time, Jonny spotted a pair of double eyes in the water. "I suppose we can head on back and leave whatever that is for next time."

The two Tarzans had no idea what they might find. The only thing they were looking for was the reflection in the night of a pair of eyes, shining back at them. They looked for rabbit eyes.

Poking around in sometimes waist-high marsh grass gave cover to some things being pursued and the escape was aided being in cover.

"Big bullfrogs are croaking and that would be great to get us some frog legs, but I don't know how we can get them out of the water or get close enough to grab them by hand," Steve finally said to Jonny, after going down the bank for a while.

An explosion of commotion suddenly began at their feet, as the salt grass all around them turned into a maelstrom of thrashing grass and wings of calamity. They had stepped into a nesting flock of ducks, now rising into the air, going in all directions at once, honking, squawking, and sounding their alarms. The beating of duck's wings on each other and the grass made their escape fearful to the surprised boys, who also took flight and screamed their retreat into the night. The fear was intense but was gone in an instant. One of the boys picked up the flashlight and the other one stood up with the spears.

"Maybe we could just go back and look at our snare and see what goes."

With it being dark and in the middle of the night, it would have been unwise to give out a Tarzan yell, letting their enemies know where they were, and letting Grandpa know, too. They went to where the snare was set. Shining the flashlight ahead of them revealed that nothing was captured. However, the rope snare loop was missing and the tree sapling they had pulled over for the snare was snapped in two. Their eyes got bigger and bigger the more they investigated.

"We must have had a mighty beast in this thing. Look at how our trap was torn up! Where could it have gone?"

Jonny added, "Maybe it's wounded beast in this jungle, and we can't track it until daylight."

"It could be a BLOOD TRAIL we track. The beast could be cornered and DANGEROUS!"

Since their flashlight wasn't bright enough to track wounded beasts in the jungle, they returned to the hideout to plot their next move. They worked on the feathers that attached to their spears.

Steve stopped after a bit and looked outside, moving the burlap sack door aside to study the sky. "Jonny, it looks like the morning is going to break and we should get ourselves back into bed before Grandpa catches us."

"Did you notice that the cows are starting to moo a bit. It will increase until they wake him. You're right."

They had cereal that morning, as Grandma didn't want to cook bacon and eggs. Instead, they had Sugar Pops. Jonny told Steve's grandmother he liked the cereal and thanked her, then turned to Steve, picking back up on the story about the monkey.

"That Charlene catches her monkey when it gets out and runs through the house and this cereal is what she gets him with. She puts them in his cage when he gets out. Boy, you ought to see that monkey go to the cage."

Grandma Meriweather laughed. "Well, you two monkeys can help me this morning for a bit, before the sun gets up and gets hot. I need to pick strawberries and do some canning and you two can help me with the picking."

The two Tarzans looked at each other and smiled.

"I've got enough for you two to string some strawberries up and dry them. They keep better that a way, and you can use them for hide-away food."

The Tarzan show had an episode where an expedition was going down a river in the jungle and were attacked by a hippo who overturned their boat. The natives tried swimming to get away and one of the hippos got him.

Steve said, "I got an idea. If we had a boat, we could go float it in the rice canal and explore the 'Jungle'."

"Not before strawberries," the grandmother reminded them.
"Yes, Ma'am."

"Since all waters go down to the sea, I guess I'll know where to find your bodies after this adventure is over—just in case the wind dies in your sails, and you get stranded. Two of y'all get them milk pails and follow me."

After their servitudes were over, they went looking for some lumber to get started on their boat. How they built it depended on how much lumber they could find. They were perplexed with how to get it started and built. No matter how they tried, the wood wasn't right—too big, too wide, too heavy, too old, or Grandpa said, "No." And they had nothing for a sail, but Grandma solved that one. She gave them a whole bed sheet. But they had no mast unless they went to the woods and chopped one down.

"Don't use pine, boys, er 'Tarzans.' The sap will get all over you. Use some hardwoods, why don't you?" Grandpa encouraged us.

"Shipbuilding is hard to do, Grandpa," Steve said to him, as he walked by their stack of lumber to inspect what they had accomplished so far.

"Well, keep at it. I'll give you a hint?" The first lumber to use on your boat are pencils!" He laughed and walked away.

Tarzans looked at each other with puzzled expressions. They were both taking turns hacking at a victimized dead sapling they found and dragged to the cow path. Cut marks were evident on a select few areas and making a pole would be a day's worth or more for one piece of the boat. Grandpa was driving three calves and one cow by them, and he stopped to inspect their boat. He pulled up his horse and got off to look closer. He had gone into the farmhouse and gathered up a bunch of pencils, mostly stubs and used ones, some with points, and some that were broken in two, some with and some without erasers. A handful, you could say.

Without so much as a word, Grandpa made a "Humm" sound and laid down the pencils in a pile, saddled up, turned away, and walked the horse down the cow trail to another pasture.

By mid-afternoon, the mast pole was hacked on pretty much its entire length and the Tarzans were in the shade, finished with it, or at least finished with all they were going to do to it.

"Let's go swimming in the rice canal," Steve suggested, and away they went. They took off all their clothes and put them in the sun, where they would stay dry during all the splashing.

"Look what I got!" Steve emerged from the tea-colored canal water with three muddy Coke bottles, ones that had been there for some time.

"Look what I got!" Jonny held up the armadillo. "He was going down this same path. I saw him coming and just stuck out my hands from the tall grass and grabbed him. Let's see if we can make him swim."

It didn't work. Every time he was tossed in, he went to the bottom of the canal and walked out. They put him back on the bank and started to think about their boat. They dived around and looked for some more bottles and piled them up.

Going to the barn with several bottles, Steve stopped and looked at some yearlings sniffing the empty feed trough. It was like he was hit by lightning. Steve just dropped his bottles and started dancing around.

"You are not going to believe it. I got us our boat!"

"Whaaat?"

"Look right here!" And Steve had his hands on the trough and was patting it. Suddenly, Jonny caught on. They realized it was big and square and just the right size. But how were they going to get it off the side of the barn?

"I'll show you how we'll do it. Grandpa has some pipe in the shed. We can use it to get it off."

Like little busy beavers, they went at it and pried it off the barn. It was heavy, so they got the Red Flyer, loaded the trough on that and took it across the road to the bank. They were all excited until they realized they were up at the canal without a paddle. They went to the pile of wood they had gathered to build the boat in the first place and got planks to use as paddles.

They put their clothes on. Since they didn't know how far they would go, they needed to have their clothes on. If they went naked, they might be looked on as natives if they were captured. One of them got in and the other one handed him their paddles. Then the other one got in.

It sank instantly. It went to the bottom with them in it. Standing in nearly neck deep water, still in the boat, they were totally surprised.

"How could it sink?"

"It's a boat!"

The troubles began.

They got out of the feed trough. The feed trough didn't float. As they soon learned, the trough boards were soaked with something and trying to pull it up proved almost impossible. After several tries, it did move, but barely.

They went to the bank and sat down. "We've got to figure this out. We could go from here all the way down to the ocean. Remember, 'all water goes to the sea.' From here, it would go to the Sabine River, out Sabine Lake, to the Gulf of Mexico, we would be in the OCEAN!"

Steve was "figuring" things out about what to do.

"Maybe, let's take that piece of pipe we just used, and we could jigger it under the end I'm pulling on and see what we can get loose."

"Better still," Jonny added, "let's go get the mast pole we been cutting on, use two poles and see if that will break it off the bottom."

They went back across the road to the petrified house and dragged the mast to the water. Both made a valiant effort. It came up on one end and they grabbed it and pulled it to the bank. The water inside sloshed around and added to the weight they had to deal with, until they could get it to the bank and dump some water out.

Steve growled, "We better get this up the bank, at least, and get it back to the house. Listen, do you hear all of them cows mooing? They come in from the fields and are getting up and waiting for feeding before they're turned loose. Grandpa will hear them and go feed them and when he gets inside the barn, the trough will be missing and it's the end of the line for me. Our gooses will be cooked."

"So, what are we going to do?"

"I'll think of something."

"If we try and go across the road with the trough in that wagon, we'll be spotted right off and caught. Let's leave it in this tall grass for now and get to your barn, Steve."

As they got closer to the front of the barn, cows were every-where, and they were pushing to get in. Steve put out feed in sections, but there were so many cows standing around moo-ing, he had to open the other barn door and let more cows in, so they wouldn't start pushing on the door and break it in. It was near pandemonium in the feed lot. Steve saw his grandpa coming with his bull whip, cutting cows to change directions and splitting the herd in two.

Jonny saw his opportunity to make a difference, and he got a whip from the wall hook and waded into the herd to help Steve's grandpa move them out of the barn and into the arena. The cows were lively and moved away, especially with two whips working the herd. They got on the other side of the corral and settled down and fed on the grain Steve managed to dump ahead of his grandpa coming.

It opened a dilemma. If Grandpa got inside the barn, he would see the missing trough and know the real reason for the cows pushing in.

As Grandpa moved in towards the milking stalls, Steve saw what was about to happen and closed one side barn door back into place and pushed cows around to the inside. They jumped at the chance to get to the feed trough first and were milling around, looking for feed that wasn't there. Jonny grabbed a bucket of oats and spread it out and the cows started pushing and shoving around to get at the feed.

It covered the bare spot on the barn wall when Grandpa came, with a brow on, to locate Steve. "Who's not doing their chores?" He would find out. The cows had cleaned up the poured-out grain and were starting to leave and soon the bare wall would be exposed.

It was Jonny's turn. Thinking fast, he untied Grandpa's horse and sent him out of the barn with a swing of the coiled whip, which no horse wants a part of. Then, Jonny yelled, "Mr. Meriweather, Sir, your horse is getting away!"

The cutting horse was going away, running with the cows. He was in the middle of the herd, headed for the pasture all saddled up, and ready to go to work. For a cutting horse, running with cows is always fun. Grandpa would have to walk to the other end of the pasture to get his horse because he didn't have another horse to ride, unless he had another saddle. The other ride was not very broke in.

As soon as the two Tarzans got their wits about them, they make a mad dash to go across the road, load up the feed trough on the Red Flyer and get it back to the barn and attach it to the wall.

Not good. The kid's wagon had a bad wheel from the first trip across the cornfield and had decided to give up its usefulness by breaking. Three of the four wheels would not carry the thick and heavy wood board trough anywhere. Sitting on the bottom of the rice canal in the mud meant that it had ample time to drink up the water and waterlog. So, just like the American Indians, they rigged up a three-pole drag from the other side of the canal. They only needed two. The mast gave them the third pole.

But there was a problem. How are two, ah hem, boys going to drag that thing quickly across the road, get it to the barn and attach it to the wall before Grandpa got to his mount and galloped back to the barn and caught them red-handed? One possibility was to work all camouflaged up, so they wouldn't be seen from a distance.

The Farmall tractor in the shed, the one that Grandpa used to cut grass at Wilkerson's Cemetery on Highway 87, north of Orange, and others, was sitting there with gas in it and the ignition key in it. It could sit for months without being run and it would fire up. They gave their Tarzan yells and raced cross the road and fired up the tractor, took it across the road, drove it into the barn, unloaded the trough, and then it wouldn't start. It was close to the barn wall, and they were unable to re-attach the trough into the original drill holes.

Grandpa Meriweather was heard galloping close by and suddenly, he entered the barn, catching them red-handed.

"Boys, get that tractor fired up and come with me, I've found that Jersey cross cow, tangled in a rope/wire mess along the fence and she doesn't look good. She has been out there for a few days, and it looks like she has some cuts, and bleeding a little. I've got her sold and they're coming to get her tomorrow. I don't want her looking poorly. Hey, we can use that Indian drag you got hooked-up, so bring it."

Now, it is really the end of the line for the Tarzans. Once they moved the tractor, the busted trough would be discovered, and they would get it. But what happened next was a small reprieve. Instead of waiting on the boys to get on the tractor and go with him, he wheeled his cutting horse on a dime and bolted out the barn door. The tractor had blocked Grandpa's view of the trough. Once they got it started and moved, the jig was up. They were going to get caught, they knew it, and this was it. Once they helped Grandpa with the cow, they would have to tell them the truth, the whole truth.

The cortege appeared on the trail that led to the barn. In the lead was Steve driving the Farmall that was pulling the Indian drag that was stacked with barn tin and several hoops of barbed wire. Following, Jonny was walking along behind several cows with Grandpa on his flank, dragging their whips and keeping cows on task to get to the feed lot. In the middle of the herd, and not at all damaged and cut, was the Jersey cross. They drove the cows into the feed lot and secured the gate. Surprisingly, Grandpa went towards the house and not the barn.

Steve and Jonny immediately got the trough pulled over with the tractor and they got it re-attached to the wall, just as the gate swung open and Grandpa turned the cows into the feed lot.

Grampa saw that the trough was empty and looked at the two of them. "What have y'all been doing? Get some feed in here, chop, chop."

The two Tarzans looked at each other and smiled.

✳ ✳ ✳

The next morning, Grandpa Meriweather took the truck to the Farmer's Mercantile for feed and treats and took the boys to the Saturday picture show, which was actually two or three shows, cartoons, new reels, and such. They were early and the line had not started forming just yet.

Grandpa needed a new set of leather shoestrings for his boots and the shoe repair store was across the street. The window at the front had a display of something and getting closer to it revealed that someone had caught an alligator and put him in the window display. He was about three feet long.

"I want him, for a pet. What do you think? Will he be a good one? He isn't that big, and I could train him. Hey, mister, how did you get him?"

"Someone was hunting in the swamp at night and spotlighted it. They were looking for frogs and when they saw his double eyes reflecting in the water, they knew it was an alligator and they netted him."

They laughed it off and left.

Two weeks later, on a whim, Jonny's dad saw the alligator, still in the window, bought it, and brought it home as a surprise.

But that's a whole other story.

Three Swims to Glory

It's time to drop everything and go swimming. That's just how it is. Of course, it depends on an adult to get us in the station wagon and get us to the water. Let us find our swimming trunks or some cut-offs, tennis shoes for our feet and we are ready to go. It also depends on the driver's mood and how many beers they have recently consumed.

It took some planning, and we could not go swimming by just getting in the car and driving away. What normally happened was that we had to go for hot dogs, potato chips, Cokes, and beer for the grownups first. What our dad had going for him and several others, I came to find out much later, was that he would go to the 7-11 and buy big bags of ice from the icehouse that adjoined the store. He knew the owner, Mr. Peveto, very well, being a beer seller himself with our bar, The Last Frontier. Mr. Peveto would put a few six-packs in the big paper bag and cover it with ice to hide it from "the revenuers" also known as the ABC men, Alcoholic Beverage Commission, who might be hanging around on a Sunday to see if anyone is breaking the law. Mr. Peveto, to my knowledge, never did get caught.

Option #1. The standard places to head to were the beaches at Sabine Pass and McFadden and anywhere down the beach you wanted to drive until you found a great spot. Texas beaches were open beaches. You were free to drive all the way down to Rollover Pass, cross the bridge, get back on the beach and drive 20 miles more, till you got back on Highway 87 and caught a ferry to get to Galveston Island.

Oh, the beach combing we would do! The first thing to do was to go looking for shells and find all the dead fish that had washed ashore. It was unusual but we would find a few sand dollars and large conch shells. We would find dead turtles occasionally. Tugboats pushed barges up and down the shore and when one of their tow lines broke, they untied it and threw it in the water and the tides would bring these lines in. People who had beach houses would drape them across and around their places and drag bunches of driftwood up to decorate with. Feathers were popular, too. We made fires with the uninteresting pieces of driftwood, roasted marshmallows, and cooked hot dogs.

Saltwater fishing in the surf was a standard thing to do. Lots of people had large seines, sometimes a hundred feet long, that would take as many people as you had to get one in the water and drag the shallows for fish and crabs. You could rent them by the day if you didn't own one. On a good day, you could get fresh seafood by the wash tub full.

There were a few downsides. But as kids, we didn't worry about much and so just went about our business. Who would not want to go to the beach?

Suntan lotion didn't seem to work well. Probably because it washed off in the surf. Who would ever think to re-apply it?

Caution was always needed when running barefooted along the surf. Dead fish, particularly hard head catfish or gaff tops had very nasty spines with poison in them that would hurt like hell if you got one stuck in your hand or foot. The throbbing felt like being hit, again and again, with a hammer. It could bring you to your knees with pain.

Jellyfish. "Cabbage heads" is what we called them. We always knew that they would sting you and you weren't sup-posed to mess with them. They were to be left alone, which we did, mostly. They would wash in at high tide and they would be scattered around in the surf and beach.

Another one that would sting, they said, was the Portu-guese Man-O-War. I saw some friends of ours go to the surf and pick up a jellyfish and walk around with it and they showed us that it was just the tentacles on the bottom of them that would sting. But the Man-O-Wars were a different animal all together. Any part of their body anywhere stings you. Their tentacles could reach 30 feet!

We ran up to one that had washed up at the water's edge. Some Dilbert picked up an empty glass beer bottle and threw it on the blue blob and it splattered like jelly all over us. We started burning and ran to the surf to wash it off, which it did not. We got blistered skin from the contact.

Later, when I learned how to surf fish and stood in the surf, one of those things got on my fishing line and I reeled it in by accident and got it all over my hands. At other times, I would get it on my legs because the tentacles could be 30 feet or longer and strung out in the surf. We wouldn't see them and so we get stung. I started wearing pants into the surf, and shoes.

Poisonous fish weren't a bother to us. We never knew about them, especially coming into shallow water.

Oh, surprise! I stood in the surf, just fishing along, and wading barefooted. I moved down the beach, slowly wading and casting my cut shrimp. Everything in the water would eat a shrimp, so it was the go-to bait. As I stood there, I felt the sand move below my foot and something wiggled.

"Ha! I'll just catch it by hand. I'm already holding it down with my foot."

I reached down and poked my fingers into the mud and caught a small fish, less than a foot long, that was buried in the sand. From the instant I looked at its ugly fat face, I knew this wasn't good. The fish's face was situated on top of its head and pointing skyward, with *all* kinds of teeth. An UGLY S.O.B.!

Unable to let it go quickly enough, in the next instant I was ELECTROCUTED and felt it go through my legs, down to my toes, standing there in water. I was trying to describe to someone what had happened, and I remembered them laughing at me before I could tell the tale.

"You picked up a Stargazer—it's both poisonous *and* electrified. Bet you won't do that again, will you?"

Barracudas were supposed to have this poison called ciguatera. It only affected you if you ate a big barracuda, which we never saw. That was stuff you had to watch out for if you were in the Bahamas. Also, we didn't have Lionfish then, either.

"You're supposed to shuffle your feet in the surf when you fish in it."

"Why?"

"Because that's where the stingrays hang out and if you step on one, they will drive a spear into your leg."

Learned about that one, too. Some people would catch them in the surf, if you were there long enough, and they would either cut them up for shark bait, take them home and try and eat them, or the "good" fishermen would cut the barb off their tail, so no one else could get stung and turn them loose.

So, speaking of fish, the big downside would come if you got tangled up with a shark. When they occasionally came into shallow water in the surf, they could be bad news. I remember a few times over the years where someone at the beach got bitten by a shark, usually not bigger than four or five feet. They didn't just get you and drag you to a watery grave. They would take a chunk and leave. We weren't allowed to go down to the beach and see a real shark bite close up. That was called gawking.

Back in the day, no one knew about the baddest threat that's known. It is a flesh-eating bacterium that floats in the saltwater and shows up, up and down the coast, on rare occasions. I never heard of it until I was an adult. It enters the body through a scrape or a cut on your body. It can kill a healthy adult in three days. It is called necrotizing fasciitis. It eats your flesh so fast, you are already in DEEP trouble the moment you recognize you caught it. Survivors usually undergo amputations, where the limb or affected area must be removed within hours, just to survive.

Option #2. Big Cow Creek is for swimming. The next county north of Orange County is Newton County. It was a cool place to go swimming, so I was told. The first time I was there, I went with a bunch of men that worked at the newspaper and were drinking buddies of my dad. Some of them had hunting dogs and Newton County was the place we went.

"We're just here to run the dogs. So, don't get all excited about it."

It was cold winter days when they all got together with the tent, sleeping bags, cook stoves and skillets, a big bag of potatoes and an equally big bag of onions, a couple of gallons of cooking oil, coffee, and beer, as well as a fifth of whiskey. Oh yeah, several guns, three or four dogs, large bag of corn meal, eggs, and kitchen stuff.

We were going fox hunting. I thought it would be cool to get to tag along. I had never seen a wild fox before and I was told that I probably would not see one on this trip, which was odd, since we were there to hunt them with dogs. Were we going to be *that* bad at hunting foxes?

We sat around the campfire a lot.

"The dogs will do all the work," they said. It started to drizzle, so everyone got under the tent. I was in charge of keeping the campfire going and I enjoyed messing with the fire. Nothing else to do. Someone brought out a bottle of whiskey and they all started drinking.

"When do we start out to go hunting?" I asked.

"Not till after dark."

It finally came to "after dark" and one of the men took the dogs to a trail in the woods and turned them loose. They went down the trail till they were gone. He came back in 15 minutes, and they drank some more whiskey. Just then, everyone heard one of the dogs bark, and then another and another one chimed in. That is how they hunted foxes. The dogs chased them, and the men drank whiskey.

So, the men listened to the different dogs' barks, and they would name the dog that was barking. Some yelped, here and there, and some were mostly silent. As the hounds hunted and barked, we could follow the sounds of the pack through the forest as they changed locations.

"There's Joe ... he's tight to that fox. You can tell ... he doesn't bark much but when he yaps ... like that ... he's right on the heels of that fox. Listen for old Hank ... when you hear him, that means he's taken the lead on old Joe, and he gives a rest to his buddy."

"My redbone, Dolly Girl, is still with 'em. I can tell her bark. It is l.o.n.g."

"Skipper don't bark until after Dolly Girl sounds off. Listen..."

And we all stop talking to listen, and sure enough, Skipper follows his barks behind Dolly Girl.

When the dogs mostly stop barking and no one was "hot on the trail," Bob Hicks picked up his cow horn and blew a few notes. He let it rest for a few minutes, and then blew the same sounds again. It was the signal the dogs knew, and they knew it was time to quit the chase and come on back into camp.

"OK, Jonny, get us a good fire going. Them dogs will be hot and wet when they get here, but after they cool off, they will want to curl up and bed down. A good fire will help them get dry quicker and they won't shiver too much for the rest of the night. They'll be ready for some hoe cakes and water, I expect."

About an hour went by. The first dog, followed by another one, slowly walked into the camp. They stood by the fire, tongues hanging and panting. Once they got a hoe cake, just like he said, they came into the tent and settled right in.

Another hour went by, and Skipper finally showed up. By then it was getting lighter outside, and all the old drunken men start moving around. Someone got a pot of coffee started. The big skillet was slid back over last night's coals, and the grease was getting hot. Soon the onions and potatoes that were not eaten last night were reheated. Fresh eggs were cracked and added to the hot grease and "over easy" is made.

The day warmed up quickly and I explored Cow Creek. The water was crystal clear, and the stream was running right along. I could see what people said about swimming up here.

The creek got its water from a tributary off the Sabine River. The area was full of various kinds of pines. The lower section that flowed through the bottomlands was composed of beech and other hardwoods. The banks were rolling hills, and it was the best section of the 56-mile-long creek to swim in. You had white sand, a lot cleaner than at the beach, and no saltwater to deal with. Besides, this place had lots of shade trees to get under and we wouldn't get such bad sunburns. There were even rope swings there. Who wouldn't want to go to Cow Creek?

And so, during the summers, we would go to Cow Creek, too. The family would still get all the stuff together to go, like always—chairs and ice chests full of beer, hot dogs, chips, bottles of Cokes, the usual. Another trip to Peveto's Grocery before we pulled out to go.

Whether we thought about it or not, the hardwoods and bottomlands had cautions, just like at home. It wasn't swampy, but we did have a sense, perhaps an innate one, to not be surprised by our surroundings. We had snakes, like here at Cow Creek, but Cow Creek had some of the biggest Timber rattlesnakes around. Since they could swim easily and were not hesitant to cross bands of water, the rattlers usually gave a warning sign, their rattling, and so that was a good thing. But keep in mind that they grow to over seven feet or longer, and you better not fail to hear their buzzing if you got close.

The hospital would be an hour away, in the best of times, and if it happened on a weekend, traffic getting in and out of a two-lane highway, full of turns, might be a challenge. Just saying.

We brought along two distinct kinds of bar soap, LAVA for hard to get off stains, and Ivory Snow, which would float in the water if you happened to drop it. We would just leave it on some fallen log by the water's edge, just like it was our own wilderness bathroom sink. We would hang a towel and a couple of wash cloths.

Someone yelled up to the camp later in the day that they could not find any soap. It was all gone. Someone had to go to the creek and point out where it was sitting. That was me. It was gone.

Coming down the trail towards our camp was a herd of wild pigs and boars. We scrambled up the bank to get where they couldn't get to us and one wild boar got into the creek to cross to where we were, and he stopped and ran his snout into the branches and brushed by our soap log. Then he grunted and pulled out our bar of Ivory soap, and then just stood there and ate the entire bar of Ivory, mouth foaming up and grunting the entire time.

We carried no rifles to the creek when we went to wash up and we weren't going to get back down onto the ground until they vacated the area. The fox dogs in camp knew they were around and started barking. They were caged up and in the back of a pickup. If they hadn't been, it would have been a fight, and some dogs might have been fatally injured. We were lucky. It could have been us in that scrape.

Option #3. The Rice Canals and the Pumping Station. Without the pumping stations located throughout Orange County, water could not get into the rice fields in sufficient quantities to grow rice on a consistent basis, despite the lowlands and nearby swamps being full of water. Sugar cane needs water, as well.

It was just an option and laziness that got us to this option. People around home knew about a place to go swimming that was closer than Cow Creek or the beach, and this was it.

Rice canals were all over the county and that network provided water for the fields. Getting the water from here to there depended on large commercial water pumps to carry water from the Sabine River to various locations. It was chocolate, but cool and refreshing. Carloads of family and friends would show up on the banks by the station and jump in. It got to be a fun place. There were no boats and no skiers, just inner tubes and air mattresses, if you had one.

It could get a bit crowded, especially on weekends. The canal was built with clay soil, dredged from the adjoining ground.

You could go barefooted, most did. No broken shells, hardhead spines, or stinging things around, unless you wanted to count the blackberry bushes that grew on the other side of the fence. And with so many people swimming there, they would soon strip the bush of any ripe or near-ripe fruit. Just go elsewhere during berry-picking time, is all there is to say.

The Texas Southern Flannel Moth or ("puss caterpillar"!) was a cute, fuzzy little thing that would knock the fire out of you if you got stung by one. It stayed on tree limbs and could camouflage itself very well. The scorpion, with its two claws and long tail with a stinger curved over its body wasn't much of a contender. The moisture from sugarcane and rice fields was too wet an environment for them. Copperheads and water moccasins were shy around splashing water and stayed away. Usually, anyway. Same for alligators; they are shy.

The canal impoundment area adjoining the station building sat right over the canal. It was posted to Keep Out and to Stay Away, but then the people were good-hearted and plenty of people got into the habit of picking up their trash and taking it home with them, so as not to anger the station people.

The pumps themselves were surely covered with grating and other barriers to prevent something or someone from slipping below the chocolate water and getting sucked into the pumps and ground up like hamburger meat. No one to my memory ever got caught in a pump. It was absolutely unheard of. They thought of everything, we were sure. Safety first.

Who would not want to go swimming at the pumping station? Sometimes, we didn't want to be in a crowd, though you never knew how many people would be there until you were actually there and looking it over.

Driving down the beach was fun because you could see so many things that had washed up. Sometimes, though, access to good driftwood to use for building a wiener roasting / marshmallow fire was used up and you had to drive on. After all, the Texas coast is 451 miles long, so no crowding, right? Not always.

Someone else driving down the beach sees all your fishing rods staked out and thinks you're *really* catching them and pulls up next to you. Honest to GOD! So, the pumping station may have had a tinge of that, too.

And with that in mind, Dad comes up with this *great* idea to find our own, private, swimming hole. What? Okay, let's see this *great* idea. We could just go back to the pumping station and wait our turn. But *NO!*

First, he drives down the road that parallels the canal full of water and crosses Highway 87. On the shoulder, he parks the station wagon and gets out. Well, it *is* the same water, it's just further along the canal. This part of the canal was a bit lower than the discharge pumps at the pumping station. This part of the canal was about level with the pasture that surrounds us, for miles around.

"Right here," he says.

We are staring at the plainest rice canal in the county, we imagine. Except for scrub brush and saplings lining the banks, that's all it is. It's in the full sun. Since my sister and I are not great cross-English Channel swimmers, he goes to the back of the station wagon and gets a hatchet, goes to the bank, and starts cutting saplings, sharpening the fat ends to be driven in the mud to mark off a swimming area for us to swim in. The bank into the water is almost vertical but we can get in and frolic around. We could take inner tubes and air mattresses if we wanted to next time.

What we do is leave the saplings in the mud and maybe we can come back and swim there again. Now, with no one around, we go into the water and stand there. After a minute or two, we try to splash around a bit, to show how appreciative we are for the earnest effort. Wading to the middle of the canal and looking back, it was all cow pastures that surrounded us. With those saplings sticking out of the water, someone else was bound to see it. Then what?

That was pretty much it. Swimming in a cow pasture. The next thing we knew, we would be swimming in a cow pond, also called a stock pond. Actually, though, I never thought much, one way or the other, about going swimming in a rice canal. My good friend Steve Phillips, the one that lived in the petrified house, had one across the road from his house I would swim in, sometimes.

I slowly realized that having other people around did break the boredom of just standing in the water. Watching a crowd did have advantages. Having a few trees or having just one tree would make a difference, and we would have some shade to get under.

Idly wishing for a tree, I noticed that a gar or two came up to the surface and floated like sticks, motionless and waiting to grab a passing fish or small snake. The gar were two to three feet long. At least there was something living in this rice canal. Maybe a few catfish would be in it, too, I thought, and it might be worth putting out a line, away from our splashing, and maybe catching something.

❋ ❋ ❋

Coming home one day, I saw a copy of the newspaper on the table, and it was turned to a page, creased, and folded, so I was meant to see it. The article was under a big picture of a man standing next to an exceptionally large alligator that was hanging up, under a tree.

I read the story about a man out on horseback, checking on his cattle, and seeing this exceptionally large alligator sunning himself on a canal bank. For a bit of fun, he decided to try and catch this exceptionally large alligator and rode up on it and lassoed it with his rope. That was a mistake.

This exceptionally large alligator was having nothing to do with this cowboy and it swung its large tail around and did a death roll, like they normally do when they catch something to eat, to kill it, and drown it.

It knocked the rider *and* his horse to the ground! Rolling and rolling, the rope got shorter and shorter, and the monster got awfully close. The man had to shoot it. He then dragged it, using his horse, to a tree and strung it up. The newspaper sent out a photographer and reporter to get the story. It happened north of the Dorman Cemetery off Highway 87. I think the cowboy was from the Dorman Ranch.

The shocker of the story dawned on me, only after I read it a couple of times. The exceptionally large alligator that was captured was found sunning himself on the canal bank *exactly where we built the enclosure to go swimming in!*

Our splashing around would have drawn that damn thing over, and he could have *eaten us alive!*

You can look at life and wink as it goes by or jump in the water and swim with the alligators. Life is something to use so you don't lose your place.

Jon Bunn

Wader in The Ocean

I'm going down to see the ocean,
I'm going down to have a look around.
They say it's deep and it is wide,
I'm going down there, so I can decide.

I'll write a note when I get to the ocean,
I'll put it in a bottle for someone to find,
And when they find it and then they read it,
It says, "Throw it back in, sit down and watch it
    come back around!"

The great big ships and the little bitty boats,
I can't tell you why they float,
Up the Nile, with the crocodiles nibbling on their toes!

BREAK

I got new waders, to walk in the ocean.
I want to find some fish when I get there.
Those big old waves knocked me down and
    nearly drown me,
When I looked in my waders, the fish were in there
    swimming around!

I'll get a big pole, when I fish in the ocean.
I'll get a big bait and use a mile of line.
That big old shark took off for Cuba,
My line broke, thank God, save my soul,
    I'll catch you next time!

The Millicent Safari

It wasn't as if they had something to do. The April days were already hot. Sticky hot, to be exact. It was the usual situation—they had no money. So, now what to do?

Bird Legs was in his room, just piddling around and Jonny was at his house, just through the alley and he was doing the same. Nothing. So, they went to the "woods," the vacant lot between their two houses, to smoke cigarettes and think of something to do. They had no cigarette money, so they got on their bikes and checked out all the places they knew where they might find some empty Coke bottles. Without too much of an effort, they managed to get enough money to go back to the store they lived closest to and get their usual—a pack of Camel regulars, and a pack of chewing gum as insurance against some parent smelling their breath and getting in trouble for it.

They found an empty gallon milk jug worth a 30-cent deposit. They got the Camels for 26 cents, and the gum for 5 cents. Jonny had the extra wheat penny in his pocket, to make the amount come out right.

It didn't seem to be the greatest of times to go out and make money at anything these days. Jonny had a gasoline lawnmower and a gas can. Gas prices recently went from 14 cents a gallon to 19 cents, and if they could get a few yards to mow at 50 cents a yard, they would be flush. However, there was too much work involved, as it was just too hot, so they just went back to the woods and smoked another cigarette and made plans.

Their bicycles didn't need any work, and they could get around. Ideas were passed back and forth as to what they wanted to do. They went through a checklist of sorts to find something to do that both of them could agree on.

The idea that held mild promise was to ride their bikes out to Bluebirds Fish Camp, a few miles away, rent an aluminum boat, and go paddling around the edge of the local swamp. They could take a couple of .22's that Jonny had at his house. But the boat would cost them two dollars for the day. On top of that, they would have to ride their bikes out to Bluebirds with their guns laid across their handlebars and go along the edge of the Colored part of town. Someone would probably get nervous at two 14-year-olds with shotguns. That idea was scrubbed. They would be stuck having to go and mow yards for the money.

If they were lucky to shoot anything that was fit to bring home, they couldn't take it on their bikes back to town and carry their guns, too. Too burdensome.

And then—Jonny's got it!

He knew a place where they might go into the swamp to hunt, learned from when he rode the school bus at Little Cypress, where he used to live. It was a way away. The difficulty was that they would have to walk there. It might be a five- or six-mile hike. Jonny was used to getting up really early on Sunday mornings to throw a newspaper route and they decided to go then. It seemed to make sense to take off about 2 a.m. It was going to be a 20-block walk to get to the railroad tracks, but they could walk down the railroad tracks for another three miles or so and turn off into the final road that led to the last bus stop at the school bus turnaround, where they could enter the woods. Being up on the railroad tracks, they might shoot a rabbit or something on the way to the swamp.

Bird Legs got a single-shot bolt-action .22 to carry and use from Jonny, and Jonny got a Winchester .22 pump that was a better gun because it held more bullets. However, the single shot didn't weigh as much and was easier to carry over the shoulder.

They were excited to get out of the city and into the woods. Walking through streets and going along by houses caused sleeping dogs to bark as they passed. The honky-tonk bars had all closed at midnight and everybody would be in bed, in deep sleeps by then. Still, they decided not to talk too much as they passed by homes, so as to not wake so many dogs that the entire dog population would be barking and signaling other dogs down the line that some intruder or strangers were about. A car or two would pass by, but other than that, all the streets were deserted.

A police car was coming out of a neighborhood and stopped under a streetlight and paused. Even though Bird Legs and Jonny were a ways away, they were spotted by the police car, and the car turned their way. Since no one was doing anything, they weren't worried when the car stopped, and they were beckoned by the patrol officer.

It was a slow night for answering any calls he told them, and he wanted to know what they were up to. "You boys can go ahead and lay down your rifles in the grass and let's talk." He didn't make any move to get out of his patrol car and he sat there and talked on his radio.

They explained to the officer that they were going out to Little Cypress to hunt.

"Do your parents know that you are out here, in the middle of the night with your guns?"

"Yes, Sir," Jonny said. "My dad owns a bar at the end of Green Avenue, and he got home not too long ago, and I told him we're going out here to hunt. Yes, he knows. He wouldn't take us in his car, so that's why we are walking."

"I guess it would be okay to walk. No problem with that. It just seems a bit far to walk to hunt, I guess. So, I would guess that if I called him on the phone and asked him where you were, he would tell me the same thing?"

"Yes, Sir. He might need a minute or so to wake up a little."

"Officer Patillo here. I'm talking to your son and his friend who've walked almost out here to Echo with their guns, and they're telling me that you know they're going hunting. Is that true? Yes. They are. I thank you, and I'll send them on their way. Good night to you, Sir."

The officer then stepped out of the patrol car and went over to the grass and picked up the two rifles and examined them.

"It might be a problem if either of these guns are loaded. Are they?"

"No, Sir, we both know better than that. You do NOT carry a loaded firearm unless you are at the place where you are going to hunt."

"I'm glad you two boys are following the rules. I wouldn't want to get a call later this morning from someone over there at that housing addition that someone was shooting in the middle of the night."

"No, Sir," Bird Legs chimed in, now that the situation was over. "We aren't spotlighting rabbits up here. We don't even have lights."

The police car drove away down the road, headed to Echo Lane. They watched him disappear. A few minutes later as they walked further along, they spotted his car, lights off, half hidden off the edge of the road. They knew they were being watched.

"I can't believe we didn't get some kind of trouble, you and me. I never thought about us just walking around with rifles, right through the middle of the town. What are we going to do when it's time to come back this away? It'll be in the middle of the afternoon, I'm sure of it. Now, everybody will see you and me carrying guns."

They continued on their hike and were getting close where they would change roads to West Bluff and make it to the woods. However, they didn't have bug spray, like Six Twelve, in case they got into the mosquitoes. Even more important was the fact that they hadn't brought any water with them. They couldn't drink water from the bayou, as it was almost stagnant. Jonny knew this because the last time he had fished there, he caught a large Grinnell, and they stayed in blackish, almost stagnant water. So, that was going to be a no go.

It had been just cool enough that Sunday morning that the mosquitoes were not out. They started down to the edge of the water and looked around, being very quiet, for something to shoot. As it was already into the early part of Spring, the swamp rabbits would be getting the warbles and wouldn't be good to eat. It made no sense to shoot a rabbit and open it up and find it had warbles. By the time they walked back home, the meat wouldn't be any good, as it would not be cooled down. They let a couple of them go and never took a shot. It was hardly worth it.

Jonny was a few feet ahead of Bird Legs when he suddenly stopped and spotted a large turtle shell leaning up against a big pine tree that was growing on a spit of high ground by the water's edge of a slough. It was much, much bigger than a red-eared slider shell. It was the size of a large washtub, and it was just leaning up on the bank.

"Wow, would you look at that thing. I want that shell, Bird Legs! I had one just like it when I lived in Little Cypress, but it got run over by our horse trailer and I didn't get to make a bird bath out of it."

As they stood there looking at the shell, it moved! It turned out to be a very large Alligator Snapping Turtle, a loggerhead, attached to the shell. It was digging a hole in the dirt next to the pine tree and it was building a nest where it could lay eggs. As the boys walked up to it, she saw them coming towards her. She then started to move off the nest and go back into the swamp and get away. It had to be quick thinking, but Jonny saw a large tail and reached in and grabbed it. The turtle immediately swung its tail under the shell.

The loggerhead was extraordinarily strong and pinned Jonny's hand firmly under the shell. It then started to head to the water and swung about, opening its mouth wide and hissing, as it tried to back into the water and escape. Jonny was still attached. He managed to lift the turtle's hind feet off the ground, and that kept it from pulling him into the black ooze it came out of.

It took both boys to block the escape. If bitten, the bite of this large reptile would snap a leg or an arm bone in half without hesitating.

The shell that was given to Jonny had been given by a man he met when he was younger, who hunted these turtles in the swamps for their meat. The Cajuns and other folks prized their meat and would gladly pay good money to get one of this size. They were hard to get, and it took a special person to go into the swamps and look for them. They grew very slowly and one of them this size indicated it had lived many decades close to that pine tree.

When Jonny had gotten his first big shell, he had studied and read about them. He learned that they dug a large hole in the soft mud and stayed there for many years, waiting for something to step in the hole or swim by, which they then snapped and trapped. The man who had hunted them had a wooden leg because of injuries from fighting in the Second World War. He waded into the sloughs and bogs and felt for them with that leg. He was able to attach wire cables to them, somehow, and pull them out of their holes.

Now, Jonny and Bird Legs had found one of their own. They were stunned at what they caught. They sat there, realizing they were miles from home. They had *walked*, so now what? And they both had rifles to carry home as well! They didn't have a dime to even make a call home, to get someone to come out there and pick them up and bring this turtle home.

They looked at each other, "How in the world are we going to do this?"

"How much is this goddammed thing going to weigh?"

They sat on the bank and thought and thought. It was now hot, and the sun was out, not a cloud in the sky. They would decide to do something. They just didn't know yet what that would be.

And before they knew it, here came the mosquitoes. Most people described the bite as feeling HOT when they were bitten.

Bird Legs liked to watch The Little Rascals on TV, so his great idea was to use their belts and make a big sling between a big sturdy sapling pole and carry it out of the swamp that way—kinda like they did on Tarzan movies, where you slung up your dead lion or gazelle and walked around Africa with it. They didn't have a pocketknife between the two of them, and again, no water.

The guns were tied to the pole using vines they pulled off the trees and bushes. The turtle was attached to the pole, and they started walking out. They found a bridle path to walk out on and it was taking a bit of time to get adjusted to carrying the weight of that turtle and swatting mosquitoes. The turtle would open her mouth and hold it open for a bit, as if she were waiting for a chance to snap at Bird Legs, as he was in front. He kept wanting to switch sides and take the back end of the turtle.

With this being Sunday morning, not much would be going on and hardly a car would be out, except for the Pentecostals who went to the nearby church, and maybe someone mowing the yard or a pasture. When a car or truck passed them on the dirt road, they got some odd looks but that was about it. Interested but not interested.

After they took turns, a time or two, switching back and forth holding the front and back of the pole, they stopped under a shade tree and took a break. Jonny noticed just before they stopped under the tree an old rusted out '51 Chevy sedan slowed down and then turned round and came back down the road to investigate what they had seen—two White boys carrying a very large snapping turtle slung under a gin pole.

The driver was an old colored man who got out and came around to the side of his car. He walked into the grass slowly and took off his straw hat and looked at the big turtle with wide-open eyes. Jonny and Bird Legs were starting to beam with pride.

"Whoo ree, you boys sure got a big old turtle, yessir. How did you get him? Was he on a trot line or sumpin? That is a *fine* turtle. Which one of you caught him?"

"We both did," Bird Legs told him.

Jonny had to dramatize the story, just a little, and added, "We caught him with our *bare hands*." The old man stood there, waiting for more. "We seen her at about the same time, as she was headed to the water. She was on the bank, so, I rushed her and grabbed her by the tail, and she pinned my hands under her shell as she pulled up and took off for that slough."

"We had a tussle with her, there for a minute," Bird Legs added.

"You know what they'll do to you, if they get aholt to you? Them's the ones that won't let go till it thunders. That's what they say. Of course, it would just snap your han or laig right off. Them rifles would come into it too late to help out the victim by then. I suppose you all know about all that?"

The excitement of having the first conversation with someone over their capture of the swamp beast suited them to a tee. But in their minds, they didn't need to be reminded about how bad it would be to get grabbed by those jaws because whatever it grabbed, it would keep. Also, to figure into it, if it occurred on the highway, the one not bit would have to remain calm enough to get a bullet and then load it into the gun, before they could shoot it, and with their friend's screams and all that blood gushing all around. It wouldn't be like The Little Rascals, that's for sure.

The old colored man wanted to get that turtle for himself, and he was making it out to be very dangerous. He was old enough to have half of his black hair already turned white, so he had to have some kind of smarts about these matters. Seems like he knew about fishing. He opened the turtle's captors eyes a bit wider as they continued to talk about what was lying in the tall grass, mouth still set at full open.

"Me, I ain't never caught me one that big befo' and I have fished this swamp for going on many a year. What you going to do with it?"

"First off, we're going to try and get it home and then keep it. We saw it digging a hole to lay some eggs and maybe we can hatch them and get some babies. I got a bigger one than this, it's shell from a man, so I been reading up on it and want to see what happens."

"You don't say. Not saying you can't do it or not. Never heard of anyone trying do that. You got a ways to go yet to get 'em to town. Where 'bouts you going?"

"I live around 4th and Park. Bird Legs lives by me."

"How did y'all get here? Ya'll not big enough to drive out here ... I don't think."

The old colored man was still scheming a way to bring that turtle to his house, as he kept talking about all the fishing he'd done.

"I like turtle meat, and I could just as soon buy it off ya and y'all get some good dollars and we'll both be happy. I don't think that hatching idea will pan out. Never know, though."

"He raises and keeps pens full of snakes at his house, so he knows about how to do it. Ain't that right Jonny?"

The old man's eyes got really big, and he took a step back at the thought of having snakes around or even talking about them. He made one last pitch at getting the turtle for him.

"I will make you a better than good offer and I can buy 'em on the spot fo' $10."

They didn't blink, so he upped it to $15. And they were not going to budge. It was time for them to get going. They still had an afternoon to hike back to town.

"Boys, I'd tried my best to get me some of that turtle and you two have been fair all along. I can't leave you on the side of this road, so far from town and in the middle of the afternoon trying to make town. Can I do you all a good turn?"

The two of them look puzzled but said okay. The old man went over to his car and raised the trunk and offered them *and the turtle* a ride to town. It was a generous offer that was really needed, they admitted, and they accepted. They were grateful.

The old silver topped colored man driving into town with two young White boys was a sight to see, and them enjoying the time, windows rolled down and feeling the breeze. Occasionally, they would hear bumping and metal clanging, coming from the trunk. When they got home, the old man helped them get the turtle out. It had torn up the old floor matting rug that was in the trunk and pushed around the odds and ends of the stuff in there.

No one knew how to go about naming a turtle. No one professed any knowledge of such things. Many names were tried but they didn't seem to fit. Bird Legs finally came up with naming the turtle Millicent.

Several months later, the boys' turtle raising adventures ended. The loggerhead never did lay any eggs, but she did get one final victory—she took off half of the dog's ear when he got too close to the water's edge.

What Did I Think
About The Bar?

Oh, I went there sparingly during business hours. It may have been to go there to get a few dollars for something that was needed to be *bought*. (We never *purchased* things; we *bought* them.) It was the folding green kind. At any other time, it would be coins.

Sundays always. Late mornings—unless someone had a hangover, then it could be mid-afternoon.

We (my sister and I) would go to "rob" the jukebox and the cigarette machine of all the coins it held and dump them on the tabletop on one of the booths that were along the walls. We'd divide them, count them, stack them, and roll them in paper tubes to be counted and taken to the bank. It was easier for us to do the work, with our smaller hands. We were generally curious as to how big the pile of coins would be and how many tubes of money we would make. We never thought about taking even a nickel of any of it. It was just stuff on a table.

No pennies. Nothing works with pennies, no machines for pennies. Nickels for the gumball machine. They were generally used during the daytime by men who would come in during the middle of the workday to drink a quick beer or two and go back out to work for the rest of the workday.

The "fun in it" part was digging our hands into the piles to get the different sized coins for wrapping—nickels, dimes, quarters. Did we ever find 50 cent pieces? I don't remember, exactly. It was too long ago.

I remember when the cost of a bottle of beer went from 25 cents to 30 cents. It seemed the general discontentment about this could be registered by using pennies, instead of using a nickel with a quarter, when paying for a bottle or can of beer. It was noticeable. Some grumbling occurred. I saw it. Most pennies were wheat pennies back then.

Since we took the money from the jukebox and had to empty the box, my sister and I could use some of that money and play the jukebox all afternoon for free while we worked.

"Wake Up (Little Susie)" by the Everly Brothers played big on the jukebox during the week, as did "Blueberry Hill" by Fats Domino. We'd get a frown for playing any Negro music and it was soon removed from the box. We were a Cowboy beer joint, and the unwritten rule was that the music we played would be Country. Period.

At home, we had a hand-cranked Victrola that was inherited and only played 78s. We had the records at home, too. The Victrola was passed down to Dad because the Whitakers who farmed across the road from Grandpa Sugar and Grandma Bina lost their son in World War II and he and Dad were playmates when they were younger. The Whitakers' son was captured and died on the Bataan Death March.

My sister and I loved Marty Robbins and so did lots of barroom drinkers. "A White Sports Coat," "El Paso," and "Ghost Riders in the Sky," played a LOT.

"Hello Walls" by Faron Young, "Ghost Riders In The Sky" by Marty Robbins, and "Big John" by Tennessee Ernie Ford were three songs that captured my imagination because I began to think it was *me* they were singing about and later maybe I became haunted by them. I was "Big John in Chains" and died in the same coal mine as my Grampa Charlie in Dugger. Whipped in public with my whip set the die and I was tasked to endure a life of hardship, as it was played on the jukebox.

Kelly and I also had to reload the beer coolers and stack in the different beers, cans, and bottles for the coming week, and we had to clean, sweep, and mop the floors in the bathrooms and the barroom.

As a kid, I visited lots of bathrooms. The different bars I visited and was brought into were the scattered joints that lined the streets around the Navy base. The end of the street was the main gate to the base. The Last Frontier was the bar closest to that gate. Dad took me with him to just about all of those bars.

They had that *smell*. Warm, flat, stale beer, and hot piss ought to describe it pretty well, with perhaps a hint of bouquet of ammonia. I smelled it on Sundays and sometimes it was worse than at other times. And I had other places to compare it to.

For some reason that eluded me for a time, I noticed a five-fingered handprint was painted on the wall behind the commode, about six feet above the toilet tank. It was surrounded by eponymous contributions and snarky roughneck stabs. Infrequent urine trails altered and erased these witticisms as they dripped and drooled down to the concrete and linoleum floor below.

Only so many peanut-infused six-and-a-half-ounce bottles of Coke could be consumed, no matter who was buying.

The red handprint on the wall behind the stall in the bathroom in our bar perplexed me for some time until the "ah-ha" moment occurred when I saw a half-drunk cow hand attempt to "take a leak." He had one hand on the wall as he leaned forward to steady his aim as I left the bathroom. I don't know if the visual aid was helpful or not. *Not my business.*

✳ ✳ ✳

The end of the town went to the Sabine River, which was also the state line that separated Texas and Louisiana. The writings on the walls in Louisiana were all about the same as on the Texas side. The distinctions were small, except that on the Louisiana side, the drinking age was 18, whereas on the Texas side of the river the drinking age was different. You could be a man at 21 in Texas or go "across the river" and be a man at 18-ish.

I took a girl on a date to The Last Frontier. This was the first real date I had taken to the "bar." I met this girl at the city swimming pool and after seeing her there a few times, she invited me to come to her house for her birthday party. She looked okay. She didn't attend my school but went to another district. I didn't know if I would go because I had no transportation, other than my bicycle. She gave me directions for how to get to her house.

I went to the 7-11 and found a costume necklace for a gift. It was really *cheesy*, but it was all that I could afford.

I washed and ironed my clothes, as usual, and when I went to put on the best of my blue jeans, they had not been washed. They were not clean, and they had a tear in them. I had nothing else to wear. The only way for me to go was to wear a pair of my mother's jeans and they had *the zipper on the side*. I pedaled over to her house. The screen door to the porch had a big tear in it. She lived in the mosquitoes like the rest of us. Still, I didn't stay very long, my embarrassment at myself was too much. I got on my bike, and with every pedal, it was like I was being choked and crushed to death from my insides. I was sooo ashamed.

And then I met her at the movie theater. Her mother dropped her off there. We were to see the show at mid-day and then we were to walk to the bar and eat pizza. I kept my shirt *untucked* to cover what I was wearing, and the walk to the bar seemed *very far*, as far as I was concerned. My dad drove us back to her house, seemingly way across town. We didn't talk much by phone after that, and it ended. Her name was Judy.

The Old Last Frontier

Tell me about the old Last Frontier,
Where the shootings were few and the cold beers were many.
Let me drift on back to the day,
Where I could remember or throw them away.

Drift on back to the men that had guns,
They thought they were cowboys in the East Texas sun.
They'd come from the ranches and go to the town,
To drink up their beers and knock each other down.

How could you raise your children that way?
Beat up your women and fill your ashtrays.
Happy Birthday, instant replay,
For a swing and a sway and some more take-home pay.

Let the memories of "the good old days"
Find a place to rest in those sad old graves,
Bring them some flowers, now and then,
And recite to them all the poem, Gunga Din.

Bring them some flowers now and then,
And recite to them all the poem, Gunga Din.
Bring them some flowers now and then,
Recite to them all the poem, Gunga Din,
You're a better man than I am, Gunga Din.

Jon Bunn

Louisiana Roadhouse

He grew up in a backwater riverboat town,
Listening to honky-tonk and Creole sounds
Playing on the river and running all day
Scared to stand in line, as the doorman would say,

    "Got a card, boy? It's 18 to get in.
    Let me know, son, and tell me when.
    Pull your chère across the floor,
    You'll be a man when you cross that door."

Friday night I know you'll be at the V.F.W. Hall,
Like so many times before, I'll stand along the wall.
I couldn't ask you out, I was too poor to buy a car,
But I can get across the river to that Louisiana bar.

    "Got a card, boy? It's 18 to get in.
    Let me know, son, and tell me when.
    Pull your chère across the floor,
    You'll be a man when you cross that door."

    MUSICAL BREAK

I never worried about what you'd see in me,
'Cause I'll work hard for what I got, you'd see.
Got some wheels for the night, let's go dance and play,
C'est si bon, and les bon temps roule!

    "Got a card, boy? It's 18 to get in.
    Let me know, son, and tell me when.
    Pull your chère across the floor,
    You'll be a man when you cross that door."

The Black Cats
From Kentucky

Filled with excitement, the joy of the Fourth of July was one of the great times for kids. First off, it was in the middle of summer and so nothing else would be on the "social" calendar. Unfortunately, some kids were wrangled up by their parents and sent to Vacation Bible School (VBS), which broke into the happenings of summertime play time. But the rest of us prepared for the big event.

There were the inevitable rushes to go up to the roadways and hit the ditches in search of empty soda bottles to get money to buy firecrackers with. Once the money was secured, it was time to get on the bikes and head out to the firecracker stands to get as many packs of Black Cats as possible with your pocket change and to get bottle rockets for nighttime shooting.

Barring the occasional mishaps and a few burns, here and there, it could be viewed as a tradition. Oh, the days gone by!

And then, many years later, I was living a new life and future after leaving Texas six months or so prior. I had turned 16, was making new friends, and I was getting to know how to get around the city and discover where everything was. In the machine shop class I had taken the previous semester, there were guys who were beginning to drive, and some of them had cars, albeit old ones, that they drove around and used to get back and forth to the jobs that most of them had.

Some had jobs in grocery stores, stocking at night. Some had pizza parlor jobs, making pizzas, or making deliveries to college dorms, fraternities, or sororities. I got some tips about where to look for work and hitched rides to go interview for them. It all seemed to me to be like a club or something. They were great friends. We would get together to do things and go places.

I got a tip about a job opening at a restaurant, and interviewed and got it, all 75 cents worth an hour. Since business was slow during the summer, I spent time just kicking around when I was not waiting tables. Later, I found out that I could earn more money, up to $1.15, just washing dishes. I took it. That was quite a raise for me. I didn't make enough money to save any, but I was sure that things would work out. I was "living close," as some would say.

Every restaurant around had a "lost and found" bin or box where waiters would throw left behind items from tables they cleaned after the patrons left. I was able to pick through the assortment of scarves, leather gloves, and what-nots and got a few things I would use when I went back to high school for my senior year. Indiana was very cold to me, as I came from a warmer climate and wasn't used to needing heavy clothing.

But now it was the dog days of summer and David, a new friend (they were ALL new) dropped over to where I was living in a basement room I rented, and we took off to go his house to go swimming. I was amazed that he lived across the street from a stone quarry! I had never seen one up close, and that was where we were going to go swimming. He had been going across the road to swim for years.

The water was warm and clear—you could see to the bottom. It was like the water I swam in with my uncle when I came to Indiana for my grandpa's funeral many years ago, before first grade. I wanted to go and explore them and climb on the giant stones. We didn't have stones where I came from, where we lived close to the swamp.

We got flashlights and crawled inside openings between stones, like little moles. What a feeling that was, thinking about tons and tons of stone over our heads. I prayed we would not have a cave-in. It was the first time I had been under the ground.

Going back to his house to get cleaned up, David pulled out a grocery bag, reached in, and pulled out a big pack of Black Cats! I jumped at seeing them!

"Where did you get all of those?"

"They were left over from the Fourth."

"You have a bag FULL of them!"

"Yeah, these are the ones we didn't pop from last year. We can take them over to the quarry and shoot them if you want. I don't have any more cherry bombs. We shot them all up, but we can get more anytime. We just drive down across the river to Kentucky and buy them."

"Are you kidding? You can get them anytime?"

It was exciting to shoot firecrackers off into the quarry. It produced very loud echoes. After shooting a bunch, we returned to his house, went to the basement, and looked at his slot car set up, which was on a big plywood table. I never had such things as slot cars growing up. We didn't have money for anything like that. My money came from the bottles in the ditches or from mowing yards.

"We used to take firecrackers and tape two or three together and set them off to make a bigger bang," I told him.

David responded, "We can do that. We do the same. I've got lots of tape, that black stuff. And let's take them across the road and shoot them."

So, off we went into the quarry where the sound *really* echoed. I don't think I ever popped so many firecrackers in my life. My ears were ringing when we walked back to his house.

I returned to his house a few days later, went to the basement, and saw that David had his bag of fireworks poured out on the table. Since it was a drippy day and everything was overcast and wet outside, he decided to cut open some of the Black Cats and pinch out some of the powder and collect it onto a sheet of tinfoil he laid out. He must have been at it a while because he had close to a half cup of powder.

He gave me a pair of side-cut wire cutters to cut with, like he was doing. We could make twice the progress with the two of us working at it. Imagine how much powder we piled up in the center of the foil, probably enough to fill two hollowed out golf balls, maybe three or four or even more.

David stood up and took a step or two away from the table to get something, and then went back across the rug to the table and sat down to keep cutting firecrackers in two. He reached in front of him to pick up his side-cuts, and ... !

The concussive explosion lifted both of us from our chairs and we were thrown in opposite directions—I was thrown back into a concrete block wall, and David was lifted from his chair thrown to the concrete floor several feet behind him. The flash was blinding hot and robbed us momentarily of our sight and my ears felt like they were hit with sledgehammers, and I heard screaming sirens. I struggled to stand.

My chest, face, arms, and hands felt like I had hit the concrete floor face down, although I could see myself trying to get up and I knew it was my back that had hit the wall and not my face. But my hands, my hands—?

They were in front of me, nearly resting on the table when the powder ignited. The searing light moved over my hands and the flame was blocked by my fingers and the fire went above my eyes and burned the top of my forehead and hair as it expanded. My fingernails were intact. However, the flesh on the explosion side mimicked breaded chicken-fried steak. I could hardly close or open my fingers.

I tried to speak, and I felt my voice vibrating through the bones of my head as I called out. And then I saw David getting to his feet from the concrete floor and looking at his fried skin in disbelief, too.

The room was very foggy from the smoke of the ignited powder and as we looked at each other's hands, we heard a faint, muffled yelling from upstairs, and then his parents came running down the stairs. They gasped at the damaged hands we showed them. Everything they were saying to us was barely audible above the ringing in our ears. White smoke filled the room and things were blurry.

They checked the basement windows. Thank God some of them were open and so no windows blew out. We gave our explanations as to what we were doing and then we were escorted upstairs. They made a call to the family doctor to find out what to do with our burned hands. The remedy was to immerse them in iced water until the pain subsided and then come into his office immediately. The sirens in our ears screamed.

The tremendous pain from the flash burns came in waves that staggered us and each beat of the heart sent concussions of agony again and again. They filled the two sinks with water and placed our hands under the water and began adding ice. It was another excruciating ordeal we were not prepared for. It had to be done, the doctor insisted, to prevent further damage. Wrapping them to prevent any exposure to air was required. Any touch made our skin and bones ache with throbbing pain. Pouring water over our hands was the same as pouring molten lava over them.

The light in the kitchen allowed us to examine our hands close up, out of the smoke. This revealed to us the extent of the damage we had done to ourselves. Realizations soon set in.

"How will you get in and out of the house and though a door with those hands. You won't be able to open or close anything. How will you even eat? You can't even hold a spoon!" The parents just froze in disbelief.

David tried to make a light-hearted response that was not appreciated by his parents, who we had just scared half to death. They were out of ice and the icemaker couldn't keep up. It was time to go to the doctor's office and see what we were in for.

We were shuttled into his medical room and our hands were slowly unwrapped. The doctor was steel jawed when he unwrapped them and the questioning began.

"It will take some time to get over these burns and unfortunately, you may not like me the next few weeks. But whose fault is all this? You could have been permanently blinded or worse, you could have lost your fingers or your hands."

The parents assured him that he should get us wrapped up and bandaged.

"And there will be no pain medications from me today. You'll just have to bite the bullet and endure this."

David's parents seemed satisfied to just watch. They both had been beset with tremors, though their shaking had subsided some after arriving at the doctor's office.

✳ ✳ ✳

This can be the arbitrary point that roughly divides this saga into two or more situations we found ourselves in. The event itself on the one hand, and the effects of this tragic episode on the other. On the one hand, it was like walking on a sidewalk and stubbing your toe. And then on the other side, it was like tripping and falling down a flight of stairs. This will be the stairs part.

As delicate as the doctor could, he took his time and cleaned the flesh as best as he could, and where the skin was split or cracked, he applied ointment. It was a lot more involved than we expected. He worked on the backs of four hands and individually tended to 20 fingers. Each finger was individually wrapped and then an all-covering bandage was applied over the entire hand. From a casual observer's point of view, it looked like he was wrapping our hands in anticipation of us getting into the ring for a boxing match. It was going to be like a boxing match, all right. But the bell wouldn't ring on this one.

By now, the pain from the burns had subsided, somewhat. The ringing in the ears was still going on but the ears adjusted to the distraction within a few days.

How could we even get out of the doctor's office? We couldn't hold onto a doorknob. From here on out, everything became obstacles. Some things we thought about ahead of time, and some things we stumbled into and had to solve. Once we got to David's house, we couldn't get out of the car without help. "Oh God, what are we going to do about the BATHROOM?"

We were told that we should return in a week, and they would look at our hands and change the dressings. So, for the time being, we had to walk about with our hands up. The pressure of the beating heart when arms were pointed downward simply pounded our hands with pain, so we had to keep them elevated. To sleep, it brought increased blood pressure to our hands laying horizontally, which was painful in itself, but exhaustion would take over and we could sleep.

I spent the night at David's house. He had a sister about our age, and she was helpful in getting us settled in. We couldn't figure out how to take our clothes off. Thank God, I had slip on shoes.

Mrs. Jeffers started asking me, first off, the next morning who I had that was going to help me now that I am disabled. I just looked at her with a blank stare and told her, "No one. I don't have anyone around."

And here comes the problems. I wouldn't have a way to open and close the door to my room in the basement. I had a grandmotherly lady living upstairs. Actually, two grannies, so I couldn't expect any help there. Her grandson was in my machine shop class at school the previous semester and he was around, so he was a maybe.

Oh, God, my senior year will be starting in a few weeks. How's that going to work out?

And here was a real problem. I had a job as a dishwasher about 20 hours a week and I wouldn't be able to do it. I couldn't stick my hands in hot water and food waste from the restaurant for *weeks* to come. I only cleared $3 to $5 a week after paying rent. I would have no rent money and no food money. I had just lost my job.

I had been eating food on the sly at the restaurant and didn't make enough to get food any other way. I learned how to eat one meal a day. I'd run out of food.

It was time for David and me to go to the doctor's office and get the bandages changed.

"Which one of you wants to go first?"

"Makes me no difference. I'll do it and then, David, you can go."

The first layer, the outside wrap, came off first. The second layer seemed awfully wet. And when he got more of it unwrapped, my fingers looked like swollen sausages. Each finger was surrounded by a bag of skin, floating in water, twice their normal size.

"This is going to hurt a bit," the doctors, as he very gently covered the back of my hands with three or four layers of Kleenex tissues, each one soaking water from the sausage fingers. Not so bad, so far, I said to myself. And then—

Most of the flesh was dead and he grabbed a big handful and pulled it off. And grabbed it again and pulled more off, sending me into convulsions of pain. I shrieked. The nurse held onto me as he pinched and pulled everything that was loose off. It felt like he was peeling me alive.

He did it, again with the other hand …

I was re-wrapped in gauze like before and sent into the waiting room, where David was waiting to be next. He looked frightened. He had obviously heard me in the next room. I felt nauseous. I knew what he was going to have to endure.

❊ ❊ ❊

Here came another problem. The rent would be due, and I wouldn't be able to pay anything. I didn't have money for food, either. Working at the restaurant, I was able to grab something to eat regularly, but that food source was gone, too. Upstairs, Granny Strain had her house divided in two and her good friend Birdie lived on the other side. They had been friends since grade school and since their husbands had both passed away, they managed their situations by pooling what they got from Social Security. That kept the lights on and kept them in fuel oil for heating.

With me in the basement, I'm sure I put a strain on them by not providing my $18 a week rent. They were both in their

80's or older. They had told me a story about them driving their cows down the road to graze in a pasture that had eventually become part of Indiana University's famed Dunn Meadow.

Just about this time I saw a strange car pull into the gravel driveway and three people got out. In that same instant, I saw my sister, the one I'd left in Texas, coming to my door. What was she doing here in Indiana? How did she find me? How did she know where I was? I had had no communication with her, or anyone else, since I got on that Greyhound bus and left Texas behind. Seeing her was so abrupt and unexpected, it drove me to connect with all the things I had left behind. Anguish poured over me. I was almost to the point of heaving up.

I opened the door and stepped out and our eyes registered surprise. Kelly instantly saw that both of my hands were covered in bandages, and she was shocked.

She had found me by talking with my aunt. She and three friends had decided to go to California and drove from Texas on an adventure, ran out of money, and drove right into the Watts neighborhood of Los Angeles, in the middle of the Watts riots, oblivious to everything. The state troopers had the area barricaded off and the streets and buildings were on fire. These four White crackers from Texas were surrounded by the troopers and briskly redirected to leave the area. They decided to take the northerly drive home, via Bloomington.

It was a short, emotional visit. Kelly still lived at home and was still attending high school. My mother was still at home, and my dad was working offshore and gone for two or three weeks at a time. It was all pins and needles. As much as I worked to free myself and disconnect myself from Texas and everyone there, I still had those strings of attachments to my sister and my mother. I never expected to see either of them again when I left. The pain was too great, and I didn't have any solutions to anything, except to flee and forget. And now I had failed.

The progress I had made to get past the first six months I had lived in Indiana was torturous—from finding a place to live, to finding my next meal, to having warm clothes to wear, and to attending high school. With both hands wrapped, covering bad burns, I struggled to do simple things. Finding a job was quite a hurdle—how could I work at something without using my hands? Through circumstances, a reconnection had occurred with Texas that became worrisome.

Larry (we called him "Stork" in our machine shop class) was my go-between, between the grannies and me. I was able, with his help, to weather my hard times until I could get on my feet.

I had moved to Indiana with the help of my Aunt Jenny Sylvester, who had sent me money for a bus ticket and had given me a temporary cot at her house. When she found out I had burned my hands, she came over and washed clothes for me. Her sister, Aunt Mary Hardy, gave me a place to stay until I got back on my feet.

My senior year started, and we would be the first graduating class from the new high school. The old school had burned when a kid set the auditorium curtain on fire so that he would "discover it" and be the "hero" who put it out—except that it got out of hand. Go figure out the rest.

The first day of school was chaotic for me, for sure. I couldn't open or close a door. I couldn't turn pages in any book, and I couldn't write anything down or do any written homework. Someone naive might think that I had it made. "You can't make me do homework!" I would trade shoes with any one of my classmates. My hands were wrapped for another three weeks.

"Tex needs help, everyone." The word went out in our second-year vocational machine shop class. Stork let everyone know that I needed food and "the Boys" came through. Since most of them were from working class families and had part-time jobs, they were able to snag stuff from their jobs, food, so that I had something to eat.

I got a case of Chef Boyardee pizza mixes, cookies, Kraft Mac and Cheese, Kool-Aid packets, Thunderbird Wine, packs of sliced lunch meats, canned vegetables, and other surprise stuff. Suddenly, they began to realize that they could come by my basement room and "help" me with the Thunderbird, Mogan David, and Fall City Beer, and it was a safe place to stash it. Old Tex was getting to be a popular man on campus!

I soon got my bandages off and my hands into the air once again. They were sensitive and I couldn't expose them to the sun for any period of time.

I heard a car coming into the back alley and thought it would be one of my shop buddies, coming by to pick up a few beers or whatever and paid it no mind. Looking out the window, I saw a Yellow Cab idling and someone paying for their ride and then getting out. I had just turned back to the icebox to look to see if I had any beers or wine. The person knocked, which was a bit odd. My buddies usually just walked in.

I was truly shocked to look into her face. It was a face that was full of wrinkles and furrows, soft eyes full of tragedy and sorrow, lost in humility. Her smile had a hint of a long-ago time passed. She looked a bit frail as I opened the screen door, and we hugged. It was my mother from Texas, steadily walking in, holding onto my sister, Kelly. She held a Kleenex tissue in one hand and dried her eyes before anyone said a word.

The worry about reconnecting with my family from Texas had come to fruition. Memory brought back the yelling, the screaming, the crying, the sounds, the blood, the brutality, and all the ugliness that drove me away. Did the re-emergence of cowardice within me, once destroyed, now begin to grow again and drown me? Did the once-drawn sword do battle again as an eternal struggle to vanquish evil for the good for once and for all?

Who seeks water from a broken vessel? It cannot hold anything, once destroyed, so I wondered why I had these people at my door. I was back to learning the epilogue of my struggle for freedom and sanity, and they seemed like the next wave to bring chaos to my shore. I listened to the last travails.

Since the time that I was fortunate enough to grab that extended hand of friendship from my aunts and uncles, Dad had grabbed up a moving company truck, removed everything that was not his from the house and packed it up, along with Mom and Kelly as well, and sent them all away to live in Indiana. Wiped away the family till nothing was left. The final insult came from the movers, who rifled through our possessions and stole everything of value before they were delivered.

The remnants landed in someone's garage or basement, and Kelly and my mom needed someplace to live. It would have to be worked out. In the meantime, I got my bandages off and I was trying out my regrown skin. They were staying with me in the basement. I got the bed. Someone got the chair, and someone got the couch. It was too cramped. Upstairs, Granny didn't like it at all, particularly because I wasn't paying rent.

Kelly looked for work and found some at The Huddle restaurant, by coincidence the same place I had worked at earlier. Tips came in with the bill at the register, whereas wages were only paid out once a week. The tip money went away very fast.

Coming home after school one day, I noticed a strange car parked in the drive. Entering the basement apartment, I found Mom with a man, and they were having drinks. No job, no money for food, no money for rent …

I got him to leave.

"I can't have you here. I already did this before. You can't stay."

A putrid bile took the place of my own blood and pumped it throughout my body. She had to leave. She had go to one of my aunt's houses, or somewhere else. But she couldn't stay here. Kelly couldn't stay either. I didn't have food for them—I had people stealing food for me to eat, as it was.

Mom moved in with one of her sisters and got a job in housekeeping at one of the hotels. Going forward, I had very sporadic contact with her.

My sister went back to Texas, to a different town, and found work. She found a good man and they settled down, and they raised two boys.

✳ ✳ ✳

Here came a solution. Larry—Stork—came downstairs from his granny's and with the idea of the two of us going over to the RCA television factory and applying for jobs on the night shift. We would go to work at 5 p.m. and get off at 2 a.m. It would be full-time work, but it would bring us in *real* money! We wondered if we would be able to go to school full-time during the day and then go and work a 40-hour week at night. In my situation, I had no choice.

Here came another solution. Once we got oriented at work (we were both hired to work on the assembly lines), and got our first paycheck, we were on top of the world.

Larry spent increasingly more and more time upstairs because he was on the outs with his dad and needed to get away from him. So, his granny took him in. What started out as a refuge for Larry, soon became cramped because when the two upstairs grannies went to bed around 8:00 p.m., Larry came downstairs to hang out with me.

He let me know that Granny thought we were up to no good downstairs, with all the cars coming and going, late into the night. With us getting home about 2:30 a.m. it was getting to be too much for her. She was about to ask me to move out.

"There must be some kind of dope or something going on, Larry," his grandma said to him. "I can smell it."

We were burning incense, that was all, but she was not to be dissuaded. We were not smoking anything. We were against it, like most people. How she got that idea, we don't know. Larry did.

"Tex, what's going on is that all that smoke from our incense is getting into the duct work throughout the house and she's smelling it. Besides, she can *hear* us talking down here and knows about us having our stuff down here."

"Larry, let's move!"

We both had full-time jobs. I was out of my bandages. My rent was all caught up, and I was running on five hours of sleep a day.

I could make all my classes at school, but I was completely exhausted during my last period class. It was Government class. I had the class on Texas Government in Texas, before I came to Indiana, so I would already have a passing grade. I went to the back of the classroom and leaned against the wall and had to sleep. I talked with the teacher and told her I was working full-time and had no parents, and I was on my own. We agreed that I could participate better if I could answer some of the questions early during class to demonstrate I was participating, and she would let me be. So, I always had my hand in the air at the very beginning of class, answering a question or two, and then crashed until the bell. I had about an hour or so after school before my shift started at RCA.

I wired stereo speakers into console televisions on an assembly line, maybe 70 TV sets an hour. I wore these little rubber tips on my fingertips that saved my hands. I didn't know how things would work out, with me working full-time and going to school days. I didn't know how far I would be able to push myself before I had a total collapse. I just had to try it to see. My senior year would be ending soon, and I would be done with school.

I met a man at RCA who needed roommates to help him make a mortgage payment on some land in Greene County. He had just the basement built on the land so far, and so Stork and I moved to Greene County when school ended to help him out.

Looking back, I see myself picking up pop bottles from ditches one day, and then finding work building TV sets a few years later. It wasn't a matter of deciding which worked out the best. It was a matter of learning to put one foot in front of the other, and to keep moving.

Bird Shit and Fools

"Well, there's only two things that fall out of the sky and that's bird shit and fools."

I cannot remember when I heard someone say it the first time, so I don't know if I interpreted it as being dismissive or as an omen. Over the years, I have flipped that saying back and forth in my mind, trying to establish it in one camp or the other. I have put it aside mentally, but it creeps back occasionally since I myself have fallen out of the sky. A yin/yang thing.

The introductory event to me, back then, happened at the county airport. It was not near the grass airstrip I lived close to in my small town, but it was in the next county where we found ourselves standing on the side of the two-lane blacktop road that went by this airport. These runways were paved. I could not tell you who the "we" were. Too long ago, I suppose.

We were going to a show that was being put on for some reason with skydivers who jumped out of airplanes and fell for thousands and thousands of feet and then, right before they died, they had parachutes that would open and save them from certain death.

It was an *astounding* thing to think about, that someone would do that, in the first place, and in the second place, *invite* people to watch the skydivers plummet towards the ground and almost certain death!

So, we certainly watched what was going to happen from the road and, I am guessing, the reason we chose to keep from getting closer was our reluctance to get too close to the horrible deaths that might happen.

As the time for this event approached, we finally heard on a loudspeaker that the airplanes were now leaving, and they were flying *extremely high* to start off.

They looked like just regular airplanes to me, like the little ones you would see flying around that could seat four people. The little airplanes flew off into the distance once they left the airstrip, and then we could see them making slow banks and start around to come back over the top of us.

Then, the airplane's engine sort of sputtered and the planes slowed down, and this very long yellow streamer was thrown out and it slowly fluttered to the ground. I thought that a person was tied to one end of it but that was a marker of sorts they had to throw out of their plane to let the people know that the show would start soon.

Everyone was watching the big streamer and cranking their necks to see it go all the way to the ground. Everybody standing out on the road did not want to have their vision blocked by other people, watching a yellow streamer.

The big stadium speakers then began to talk about what we were going to see, and everyone was supposed to look up *way high*, find the airplanes, and keep our eyes on them because some people were going to jump out and we would see them fall.

They were such tiny specks, if you took your eyes away from them you could lose them in the blue sky. They were just tiny specks and very hard to see.

Suddenly, the falling people began appearing as they opened their parachutes, and gradually got closer and were easier to see. Now, we knew what to look for! And then they went back into their airplanes and flew up and off, until they turned around and were going to fall again.

This is what happened next. As we watched, it looked like the airplanes were on fire and you could see the smoke coming out of the back of the aircrafts.

Suddenly, the smoke left the tail of the airplane, and we could follow the huge arch of smoke coming down from the sky. It was the parachuters falling and carrying smoke grenades with them. They would fly away from each other and separate and then fly back together, and they held on to each other as they plummeted to the earth, their 'chutes opening at the last possible moment.

Never in my life had I ever seen such a death-defying display. My heart was in my throat, and I could not comprehend someone actually doing that. I was all agog to have witnessed it. The thought of it made me shudder.

✳ ✳ ✳

The first time, ever, that I was in or near an airplane was when I was carried into the cockpit, in my Uncle Marshall's arms, as he was a navigator for American Airlines at Love Field in Dallas. It was nighttime and I remember seeing the instruments: a wall full of them and they were all lit, like a Christmas display. It's a guess on my part, but I believe it was a DC-3.

Grass strips for landing were common in my childhood where most of the airplanes I saw were double-wing biplanes, like the Stearmans that were used as crop-dusters, to spray rice fields and such. Decades later, the airplanes were called Ag Cats. They were more powerful than the Stearmans and carried more gallons of spray before coming back to the airstrip to refuel.

I dreamed of having a biplane of my own sometimes, once I grew up and had a job, of course. I just knew I could build one if somebody would show me how.

✳ ✳ ✳

My first airplane ride happened when my Uncle Marshall and Aunt Evelyn sent me a ticket to fly home for Christmas—from Bloomington, Indiana to Dallas, Texas. I was in high school then. As an aside, Uncle Marshall and Aunt Evelyn never had any kids of their own, though they lived on Lovers Lane.

When I flew that day, I was the only passenger on a Boeing 727 jet, and the two stewardesses came and talked to me, once they learned this was my first time flying, and that I would soon be going to college at Indiana University.

I was going to I.U. because of the financial aid I was offered. I did not have any money myself. It was the tuition help and Pell

Grants that got me along. But not well. Not enough to survive and attend school.

I applied for work-study and got a job as a recording technician and recorded lots of music students who needed to meet graduation requirements. I did a portion of my work schedule on location. I was given a Willis Jeep to haul set-up gear from place to place.

It still was not enough to survive on. So, I got my first real job waiting tables at a restaurant named The Huddle. I earned 75 cents an hour, plus any tips I made. Twenty-five cent tips were earth-shaking for me. I had the weekend shift and worked from eight- and ten-hours days, always on my feet. I had terribly painful legs from working on concrete. College students were terribly cheap and bad tippers.

I had a room I rented in a basement, and after paying rent, I might show from four to six dollars cleared for the week. It was a tight "living close" situation day to day.

At the restaurant, the back kitchen prepared salads and cooked various foods that would be brought out and handed to the line cook to complete, plate, and have me serve.

In the back kitchen is where the walk-in cooler was. It had shelves full of strawberry pies, beef patties, fish filets, and other edible things. I was in and out of the walk-in constantly. The dishwashers worked back there, as well, running the automatic dishwashing machines.

I was able to grab a few bites here and there while I worked, and it allowed me to save an extra dollar or two. That meant I could buy a pair of shoes or a shirt, or a winter jacket, as I was not used to living in a place where it snowed. I only saw two snows in my life before then. Both of them were in the month of February.

College students who came to The Huddle to eat were always leaving something behind—a scarf, notebooks, an umbrella, and *gloves*! It was a lifesaver for me. Now things were looking up. I had steady food, a place to live, and some free clothes. Life was

Good. Later on, the G.I. Surplus Store completed my wardrobe, even with 13-button Navy bell-bottomed trousers.

I knew what a patty melt was, I could add a raw egg to my milkshake, and I could eat fish, now and again.

One day, at the start of work at 5p.m., when nobody would come into a restaurant because it was too early, these two men came into the empty restaurant and sat at the counter and ordered coffee. I was working behind the counter stacking clean dishes and getting ready for evening eaters, so I couldn't help but overhear these men talking about skydiving. So, I asked them about it, and it turned out they were both jumpers.

I mentioned to them about seeing skydiving back home years earlier in Texas. They both were from out of town. They said they were doing their jumping around Indianapolis, a world away from Bloomington.

Man, the memories of seeing people do that...

❊ ❊ ❊

And are we talking about *college*? On a wing and a prayer, I got admitted to Indiana University just by happenstance. I was riding my motorcycle along with two friends and we cruised through the campus to see the "attractions." One of my friends was scheduled to meet with his Admissions Advisor and we tagged along.

After meeting his advisor, the man turned to me and asked me if I wanted to go to college, too. I thought he was pulling my leg, but he again said, "Would you like to go to school?" I again laughed.

"I never had the idea I would be able to go. I don't have any money."

"Besides that, let's say you could get the money to go, would you?"

"It would be unbelievable to go. Nobody ever gave me a chance, so I just did not think I could. The counselors at school told me I should go and work with my hands and so they put me on the non-college plan and gave me business math instead of algebra. I have no foreign language. They gave me typing. But I have had woodworking, shop, sheet metal, machine shop, welding, and that kind of stuff."

"If you got the chance to go, what would you like to study?"

"I've always wanted to be a veterinarian," I said with pride.

His response back was, "That is the type of thing you would study at Purdue, which we don't have. Would you rather go here or there?"

"Right here, Sir. I graduated from Bloomington High School last year."

"Have you taken your SAT's yet? You need them to get in."

"Not that I know of. They told me there was no need in my case."

He forthrightly gave me financial aid paperwork to take and fill out. He explained how financial aid worked, with loans and matching grant money and set me a time to come back and take the SAT's.

I have never hyperventilated in my life that I know of, but I would bet you I must have been close that day.

The other people riding around with me already had their acceptance letters and both were well advantaged. One's dad was a well-known medical professional and the other one's dad was in the athletic department at Indiana University.

I was ignorant of the fact that people *prepared* to take the SAT's and had study workbooks and things to help boost their chances of getting the best scores they could. I mean, after all, *their futures* were on the line! I never had that kind of pressure in mine, to put a fine point on it.

My excitement came from them telling me to come to the exams with *six* sharpened pencils. On my best day, I never figured I had any more than about a third of one pencil and I was still seeing what I could get out of it, before using the extra ones I brought. I had to bring my letter back to the Admissions Office to get my SAT numbers explained to me.

So, the questioning continued between me and my counselor.

I left home at sixteen (15 ½) and any hope I thought I had for a future was to get a hardship deferment from a parent, where they would sign an affidavit allowing me to enlist into the Navy at 16, which they refused, so I dropped out of school and left home. I went to Indiana, "transferred" into my new high school and graduated.

It was a bit of creative explaining on my part, but the Financial Aid Office declared me an "Independent Person" and not a "Dependent Person." And then I got financial aid for college. However, I still needed to be accepted or declined for admittance, depending upon the final meeting I was going to have.

So, here we go. My name was called, and I entered his office and took my seat. He began looking at the different papers, arranging them just so, and finally putting them down. His review was completed, and he asked me for the letter I was carrying that had my SAT scores, but I had no idea what they meant.

"What did you think about the testing?"

"I'm sure I could do better; I didn't do any studying because I didn't know you were supposed to. I didn't know there were things you could get to help with."

"So, you took your *SAT's cold? Is that what you are saying?*"

"Yes, Sir."

Someone had told me if you didn't know the answer, to at least make a guess because you might get an extra one or two right and that would help you. At this point he just looked at me and then the paperwork with the score numbers on them and said to me,

"Do you know what these numbers mean? Do you have any idea?" And a big smile came across his face, and he almost made me a chuckle.

"No Sir, I don't."

"And with these numbers what they are ... and you still want to go to college?"

"I really do, I want to go."

"If that is what you want to do, I will give you permission and I will send you an official letter of acceptance within the next few days for you to go to college. Congratulations."

We both stood up and shook hands. *I am going to college!*

It was a challenging and exciting beginning, and I had several things I needed to put in place. Eventually, I needed to find another job. I was a machinist and welder at a Case Tractor Supply Repair Garage and working five and a half days a week and I needed a place to live closer to campus.

My grades the first year were average—B's and C's. I would work on undergraduate classes for two years before declaring a major.

I started college right at the beginning of the anti-Vietnam War movement, marching, speeches, cutting classes to attend rallies, having classes cancelled. Music. Marching. Counter-culture protests, organic food, communes, hippies. Woodstock. Monterey Pop Festival. Jimi Hendrix and Janis Joplin. July 20, 1969, the first man to set foot on the moon.

As if I needed a distraction. I was going from being a high school dropout to a college student. Since I was from a backwater southern town that began dying once the Navy base started leaving after the end of World War II and the Korean Conflict ended, I had no other experiences to measure anything by.

It seemed almost everything I did was new, novel, and fraught with possibility. Although I was the captain of my own ship, I was carried along with greater changes besetting the 1960's. It became an era known for radical changes. The '60's. Easy Rider. Life was divided between pushing boundaries on the one hand and establishing personal responsibility on the other hand.

A new full-length animated cartoon movie called *The Yellow Submarine,* featuring the music of The Beatles was the latest rage to see at the theater. It was a challenge to get tickets. Lines were very long, and each showing was sold out. The music was great, rave reviews. Record sales of the album lasted for weeks.

It was common practice when attending movies back then that the feature film would be followed or proceeded by a cartoon, or a news reel, or something added that was covered by the price of the ticket. The theater lights dimmed and went out and a dark screen emerged. A soundtrack started and loud crackling, popping, and snapping sounds filled the theater. The music soundtrack played the hit surfing instrumental, "Wipe Out!" It thundered throughout the theater.

Suddenly, what appeared on screen was filmed from inside a flying airplane with its side door removed, and then several people wearing goggles, helmets, and parachutes tumbled out of the door and fell into the sky. The camera continued to film them as they fell, and loud surfing music played. They were skydiving! And we were falling with them!

I jumped mentally and physically to see the rush of movement and sound, and music bombarding the big screen. What a rush! The crackling sound was the noise coming from the burning smoke grenade attached to a jumper's boot. I instantly recalled the skydiving show I saw as a kid. Now, here I was inside the airplane and hearing the sounds, too. Unbelievable!

It was as if I had been injected with adrenalin. I was hooked for life. I was willing to put it all on the line to make that first jump. Somehow and some way. I could not escape it. The rush of those old memories painted my conscious.

One of my friends who had attended *The Yellow Submarine* movie found a small skydiving ad a few days later in *The Daily Student*, the campus newspaper for Indiana University. The ad gave a time and location for a meeting and gave a price of $35 to take the instruction to learn how to skydive!

It was cold, mid 40's, dark and raining. I went, I was shaking. I remember seeing 40-plus people at the beginning, but attendance dropped steadily as the evening progressed. My friends told me, "Tex, you are *crazy!*" and "Hell, no." Not one friend of mine moved off that dime—i.e. none of them changed their minds about going sky diving. It was solo from then on out for me.

The skydivers had a place to teach the class. They had several parachutes and reserves (the back-up chutes in case the first one did not open). They had a few jumpsuits to wear that were bright orange, and a couple of helmets you could borrow when it was your turn to go. You were encouraged, if you stuck with it, to get your own jumpsuits and helmets.

They had the equipment, and I had the questions. I remembered asking a question after someone said to us, "that there are holes in the parachute."

I jumped. "Holes?"

"Yes, we'll show you a bit later, so let me show you this," and he took a toy parachute and a plastic soldier and tossed them into the air, and it rocked back and forth on the way to the ground.

"That's *not* what you want. You want this." And he tossed another one into the air and it came down without oscillating as it descended.

I was paying as much attention as I could during class, but I thought about me getting at least one jump before I "bought the farm."

It was amazing to learn how to fold and pack your own parachute. It worked on the simplest concept, and I could see how easy it was to work. However, that still didn't explain how they *would not* work at times, and you had to take other measures into account.

At first, obviously, I wanted someone who *really* knew how to do it and to pack mine. After starting to learn how to do it, someone half-heartedly asked me, "Now that you know how to do it yourself, who are you going to trust *now* to do it?"

"Hum," I said, "I never thought about that before." Another pause. "So, I guess I'll go ahead and do my own packing, from now on."

"Afterall," someone said, "You are already carrying another parachute anyway-in case that one malfunctions, you have a back-up!"

Now, I was feeling better about taking that last step out the door, which was coming soon. Some airplanes we were going to jump from had the right-side door removed all together and you could watch out the door as good terra firma faded away—it made my stomach squeeze tight. This was only my second time in an airplane!

The Jumpmaster looked at me sitting there, right by that huge opening where the door used to be and when a puff of wind made the plane jump, he must have seen my wide-open eyes and knew what I was thinking. The engine noise was loud, so he leaned over to get close to me and said, "Hey man, no reason to be scared. Hell, if you fell out, you have *two* parachutes, what are you worried about? Ha ha."

I never thought about the irony with what he said, still taking my first white-knuckled ride and jumping from a perfectly good airplane.

In the old black-and-white paratrooper movies, you see everybody standing up and hooking into a "clothesline" and then jumping out of the plane at the "right time." There was no need for a ripcord. Same thing for a beginner jumper.

The cord is tied to the back of the parachute with breakable string, which allows the person to fall away from the airplane 20' or so and the weight of the person breaks the string, and the parachute begins to open automatically. In learning how to skydive, the person gets to fall away with arms and legs spread-eagled with an arch to learn stability—so that you don't roll over and get wrapped into the parachute. They had you do it at least five times with a Jumpmaster watching, before being cleared to jump and start free-falling where you have your own ripcord to pull.

Some airplanes had a gull-winged door and when it was time to jump, opening the door let it fly open under the wing and out of the way. If the plane was flying, the door always stayed out of the way. It stayed closed during the ascent to jumping altitude and it was nice to have it closed when it was cold outside. We didn't practice getting in and out of the airplane when it was on the ground, so when the time came for me to jump, I was to put my feet out first (try this at a hundred miles per hour with the wind blowing on *your* legs,) reach outside and grab the strut with your hands (the brace that braces the wing from falling off,) and swing out and stand up on the plane's wheel, and wait for the Jumpmaster to line the airplane out correctly, and tell you when to jump.

(It was nice to find out later, that the pilot steps on the wheel's brake before you go out there and stand on the damn thing!)

It was nice to know that the pilot slowed the plane down right before you got out and stood up on the plane's wheel, with the wind being a "modest" 60 to 90 mph. If you waited too long on the outside, with the plane at idle speed, it would stop flying. So ... a parachute (two of them) was a wonderful thing to have.

I wore coveralls, boots, helmet, goggles, and main and reserve parachutes, and I stood on the wheel. The wind was like standing in a gale, the airplane and spinning propeller right there with you.

I was given the command to jump and arch my back, limbs spread. When you feel the parachute open, LOOK UP and see it is fully open and flying. That five- or six-second time lapse was an eternity, and the first glimpse of the parachute showed it was floating just fine.

Instantly, I noticed all the sounds were gone and a sublime quiet surrounded me. I checked my parachute again, just to make sure, and thought it should be the size of a circus tent. It was suddenly *very* small.

Looking down to steer towards the airport and a grassy place to land, I looked between my dangling legs, and I was not standing on anything anymore, a startling sight—my dangling legs!

Now that I had jumped out of a perfectly good airplane, I was ready to go again but we had a two-hour drive back to campus and other people were still lined up to take their first jump.

I was brimming with excitement when I gathered up my parachute and walked into the clubhouse. I met several people's eyes looking at me for any clue as to what happened and how it went. Some wanted to see me as an assurance that what they were about to do was all right and I met some smiles that relayed to me that we were part of the skydiving brotherhood, as they had already jumped.

Standing in the room, taking off my harness and reserve chute, someone said, "Well, how was it, Tex?"

I started singing a Ricky Nelson verse—

Fools rush in where wise men never go,
But wise men never fall in love, so how are they to know?
When we met, I felt my life begin.
So, open up your heart and let this fool rush in.

With that, I dropped my parachute and opened my arms wide, the singer ending the song. And, at the conclusion of that day, I recognized my Jumpmasters were the same two men that had coffee that day, four years earlier at The Huddle restaurant. They remembered that day, as well.

We formed a solid friendship and over the years we skydived together throughout Indiana, putting on skydiving shows in Fort Wayne, New Castle, Vincennes, Muncie, Anderson, and Richmond. We jumped for the 4th of July and other festivals, county fairs, and airshows. We put on a skydiving show for Little 500 weekend in Bloomington. I was the announcer for events when I did not jump.

Looking back, I logged jumps in California, Indiana, Kentucky, Michigan, Illinois, Ohio, Tennessee, and Texas. I recorded small accomplishments and major milestones that marked friendships along the way.

Over the years, I jumped out of a variety of planes. I fell out of six or seven models of Cessnas. The fastest plane to reach 12,500 feet to jump from was a Twin Otter. The smallest plane was a Tri-Pacer. The largest plane was Mr. Douglas (three jumps), a DC-3 airplane we jumped out of at the NCAA Collegiate Nationals in Carbondale, Illinois and we placed 8th Team for Indiana University. Again, to remember, the DC-3 was the very first airplane I was ever in.

A curious challenge came up one time to see how accurate a parachuter could be by flying with an open parachute over a long distance and reaching a target miles away. Three or four of us thought it would be a fun thing to try and several jumpers throughout the U.S. had fun with it.

Jumpers had to be at least 12,500 feet above ground level, have their parachutes opened by 12,000 feet, and float at least six miles away and try to land on a target disk of four inches, or as close to it as you could. I got within 20 meters of the disk with a round canopy, which was not a high-performance parachute.

The sport has certainly changed from the 60s and 70s. Parachute designs changed from rounds to triangles and to squares. Winged suits allow jumpers to soar like flying squirrels and cover great distances. Engines are being affixed to winged suits and may be used for military applications soon.

Falling out of airplanes was not enough to satisfy that daredevil adrenalin, so BASE jumping became a thing for some. B=Building, A=Aerial, S=Span, E=Earth.

With over 500 jumps I logged over a 15-year span, I've gone aloft in hundreds of airplanes and have landed in very, very few. I have used my reserve twice.

The first time was in a 12-man star formation at Spaceland, in Texas. One jumper overshot the formation and dived through the center. The vacuum created a vortex and sucked us all into the center at once. As the diver fell through the star, he kicked my reserve ripcord handle and it fired, leaving me alone in a cloud approximately 7,000 feet. from the ground. It was a long way down—a mile! I hitchhiked back to the airport.

The second time happened when I wanted to jump a friend's parachute, as mine was not very high performance.

It did not open at the end of the freefall and it just streamered. I used his reserve. I came down in an Indiana soybean field and walked back to the airport.

You may be able to guess what the skeptic in me said when I walked back in.

"There's only two things that fall out of the sky … "

Grandma Two

During the 8th grade, a few decades ago, all kids leaving and graduating and moving on to high school in the 9th grade had to meet with a career counselor and sit down and discuss in some detail their plans for what they wanted to do when they graduated high school and would then have a career or a future with some direction to it. God, how exciting that was! I certainly was taken aback by the idea that you could just sit down and pick your future. That was something I never knew—that you could just tell someone and go do it and live happily ever after. It seems that almost all my 8th grade friends didn't know about it, either.

Boy, did that get our intellectual juices flowing and salivating, rushing over everybody out of the blue, all at once. It was the pinnacle of life. It was still an adjustment for some boys to grapple with shaving one's face, using deodorant, and going home at night and having pimple wars in the mirror. But our entire futures were on the line before we could even choose one or a few.

What a caststrophe that was. Ninety-eight percent of America did not have color televisions, and we were off on the greatest frolic of our young lives. Our parents were shocked to hear about it, too. They had come out of World War Two, then the Korean War, and then the Cuban Missile Crisis. And their kids were *choosing* what they wanted, just like that?

I remember being told *how* to do it, when we finally got to sit and get started by the counselors. It was focused on one's interests, easy enough. I had many, so when I started choosing several, the person I talked to had this malleable face that slowly could make different expressions. The more I talked, the more expressions I saw and the less talking that person did, so I had to stop telling things and had to ask more and more questions to get anywhere.

They had these *files* stacked everywhere and they had one with my name on it. They hem-hawed while looking at the file and then looking at me. John Glenn hadn't flown in space, yet.

"For the next four years, you have got to concentrate on what you want to do, to have a chance at being successful," they said. "Your grades just look average, Jon."

"Well, nobody told me I had to have great grades. And for what? Most of the people I know here at Lutcher Stark Middle School did not have those kinds of things, either. So, now what am I supposed to do?"

"You can follow your passion and hope it turns out. Where is your interest presently?"

"I like hunting and catching snakes. Is that good? I know a lot about them. I got bit one time and had to go to the doctor really quick."

"Snakes? I don't know if you would have a *career* doing that, and so with your *grades*, you need to be very practical. We have two career paths. One is college bound and the other is vocational, and *your* background shows you will be better suited to a vocational tract, using your hands more than your mind. You won't need the SATs. I'll fix you right up! Now, it seems that catching snakes is largely using your hands. The practical skills will be a great path for you, and I'll put a four-year curriculum together for you, I hope you will like and do well."

Dismissed.

❄ ❄ ❄

I was loaded down with vocational classes at a young age; Leathercraft, Wood Working, Sheet Metal, Welding, and Machine Shop, and I was admitted to college. Twenty years later, I used those vocational skills to make a living while working on a degree.

Between times, I worked for a lumber company, as a carpenter for Wegmiller-Bender. I did remodels of houses and apartments. Some jobs were short duration, and some involved building houses from scratch, from basements to roofs. During the better weather periods in mid-state Indiana, roofing was the busy work, and it ranged from deck and patio covers, to complete tear-offs, and re-decking and shingling roofs.

An unusual job came in from Princeton, Indiana, where a tornado had come through and destroyed and damaged houses, barns, and other structures. We were sent to work 12-hour days to help as much as we could, meaning we would not be traveling back to Bloomington on a regular basis, so we gathered sleeping bags and tents and slept in the front yard. Apparently, the tornado picked up the house just a few inches and set it back down, an inch or two off. When we got there, only a windowpane or two were broken. The homeowners cooked our meals, did our laundry, and we could use their shower.

✳ ✳ ✳

Returning to Bloomington after three weeks in Princeton, we had a tear-off and re-decking job in Ellettsville. It was an old, but well-kept house at the edge of town. It was quaint, had a nice garden, a fenced-in chicken house and yard, and a garage that was stuffed with an accumulation of old, once useful things, stacked to the ceiling. Iletta and Herbert Wiley were in their "late" years: late eighties, but still getting around. She called him "Burt" and he called her "Ida."

We were expected to start and finish in approximately four and a half to five days, including cleanup. Our stacks of shingles were already on the job site. First thing first was to tear off the old shingles. We did it using flat blade shovels and then before we started to re-shingle, an old brick chimney that had been sealed up since they switched to gas heat from coal many years ago had to be taken down, at least to below the roof line, and the new roof would be sealed over it with plywood. The chimney was in bad shape. Several bricks were missing, due to the freezing and thawing of loose bricks that eventually worked themselves out and fell, hit the roof, and slid to the ground. The whole thing was tottering on collapse.

Sitting in the shade and having lunch with the crew, Bert came over to "shoot the breeze" and we got to talking about the house and its age. He wanted to take me to his garage and show me his fancy coal stove. They had to move it to the garage to get it out of the way when they converted to gas, and he wanted to give it to me.

It was a grand old stove, in great shape and had chromed footrests all around it to rest one's cold wet feet on and dry off while getting warm from the cold and snows of winter. It did look like it should be converted to a liquor cabinet, although it would weigh hundreds of pounds and was hardly movable.

"Well, it's too bad you can't take it. It's been here in the garage for a while. We had wanted to give this stuff to our daughter. Now, she's raising our only granddaughter and doesn't have room for anything we put back for her. They moved to Kokomo and left it all here and that's that."

"That old chimney is about to fall into the living room," he added, "and I'm glad it's coming down. Ida keeps finding bricks in the yard that have fallen off that thing and I keep telling her to stay away from where you all are working, or someone is going to get hurt."

"Well, Sir," I told him, "we will be very careful when we start taking the chimney down. It's very crumbly, and it moves when we even walk close by it."

"She's using them bricks out in the chicken yard to build a pathway—been at it for years. You'll just have to watch out for that old woman. She won't listen to me anymore."

"We'll be extra careful," I said. "I'll make sure that we don't throw any bricks away and she can have all of them."

Back on the roof, the whole roof needed decking with plywood, then covered with tarpaper, and then shingled. It had two shingled roofs on it already. The best approach was to deck the roof frame from the bottom, adding plywood, nailing it down and continuing going up till we get to the edge of the chimney, and then pull off a few bricks by hand and slide them to the ground on the new plywood decking. Care had to be taken not to just try and push the whole thing over and have the whole chimney come down at once inside their house.

I kept a watch for Bert's wife coming too close to where we were working, and sure enough, she left the chicken yard, pushing a small wheelbarrow, and started picking up a few bricks to take away. She got too close and so I went down the ladder to see her and to assure her that she would get all the bricks, and I would tell her when it would be safe to get them.

She decided to go into the house and let us continue to work.

We turned our attention to getting the bricks off the chimney, to slide them to the ground, and then to cover the hole that was left, and deck it over to the gable before laying down tarpaper, in preparation for nailing on a new asphalt shingled roof.

One of the other carpenters said, as he reached for the top bricks to remove them, "Look at how these things come off. That mortar is just a pile of sand, and..."

At that moment, the brick slipped out of his hand and dropped down through the exposed attic and through the living room ceiling to where Iletta was. Everyone gasped and started yelling to make sure she was okay, but there was no answer. And then we saw her across the backyard, coming back with her wheelbarrow to get bricks.

"Good Lord, folks, let's get this chimney down now that we know where she is, and get this thing decked."

The loose bricks, sand, and grit tumbled and slid down the new plywood sheeting and dropped into the yard and it was done. The bricks were down.

Iletta came around the house, once again, and resumed picking up her bricks. She was right below us, but all the bricks were down, so she moved closer to get some that fell into the flower beds, next to the house.

Someone went down the ladder to get a roll of tarpaper and came back up. I went to get one end of the roll and pull it across the deck, now that the bricks were down.

As I walked into the loose sand grit left by the crumbled brick chimney, I slipped down in the grit, and I threw my tomahawk roofing hatchet straight into the air, as I flailed for balance. I watched the hatchet hit the roof and slide, as if it were on ice, down the roof and toward the ground.

Iletta was stooped over picking up bricks. She had a few in her wheelbarrow. Her hose were rolled up just above her knees and she was facing the other way as I yelled, "Watch out," and I calculated within that instant that it was already too late. She was rising up and turning around when the hatchet struck her behind and above her temple and drove her to the ground. We heard her mighty grunt.

I slid down with nothing to slow my fall and was able to push off the roof with my boots, sailing into the yard with an impact, and rolled, tumbling to the ground, missing the brick pile on the ground.

She was on her all fours, grunting and grasping for breath as I got to her.

"I'm so terribly sorry, are you all right? I'll get your husband, just hang on!"

I could not find any blood, just a bruise and an egg-shaped swelling on her scalp. The others got there, and I ran to get Bert. I saw him coming out of the garden, carrying a hoe he was about to hang up and I was yelling to him, "Please come quickly, there has been an accident. I HAVE HIT YOUR WIFE IN THE HEAD WITH MY HATCHET. I'm sooo sorry, I didn't mean to do it!"

That was about the same time as he asked me, "How did it happen?" I told him, "It was about the bricks in the yard, and I lost my balance and dropped my hatchet, and it slid down the roof and hit her. Please come, hurry."

Bert didn't show any excited emotions and turned back to the wall and hung up the hoe. He then took his handkerchief from his pocket and wiped his sweaty face and then the back of his neck, replaced it back into his back pocket and we walked at a leisurely pace to where Iletta was sitting in the grass, where she was being attended to by the other men.

As we walked over, he said to me, "Well she is a stubborn person, and I told her not to get around all of them bricks. It just about serves her right. We'll get her inside the house, and I'll tend to her, she'll be alright."

"Do you think we need to call an ambulance or something? We don't have cars here to take her anywhere, at least until our boss comes by this afternoon to check on us. Can we use your phone to call our boss and find out what we should do? Is that all right?"

One of the hands contacted the lumber company and called for David Bender, but he was out on a call and would not be coming back to the office today. Bert didn't have a car that ran, so there was no way to get her to medical aid.

Bert sat her in a chair in the shade and she did look marginally better. It must have been a glancing blow. She was holding a wad of panty hose that she was using to dabble liquid Campho-Phenique from a bottle onto her head. It was running down her face, wetting her hair, and wetting her blouse. The smell of the remedy was thick in the air.

Her speech was less slurred, and Bert got her a glass of lemonade and sat with her. He finally talked us into returning to the roof to keep up the good work and we climbed the ladders once again and returned to pounding nails in near silence. The hatchets hitting the roof sounded like a flock of woodpeckers.

The Boss drove up. Completely without a clue as to what had happened, we got to the ground and cut off his path to the front porch while I told him that we had had an accident.

"I slipped on the fallen chimney grit and fell into the yard. I didn't mean to, but I HIT ILETTA IN THE HEAD WITH MY HATCHET. I DIDN'T MEAN TO!"

He looked at me and the other stunned men and staggered to the front porch, where Iletta was sipping lemonade, dabbing herself with Campho-Phenique, using an old wad of panty hose, and Bert came out to the porch.

There were all kinds of "We are SOO sorry. Can we do anything? Has she seen a doctor, what can we do?"

The thought of a lawsuit was eminent in David's mind, but Bert calmed him down. As an act of contrition, David went into their house and used the phone, to call in to the office to report the accident. He then took off his suit jacket and tie, went to his truck, got a hammer, and crawled up on the roof and helped us finish the job.

As he was standing on the roof, tying on his nail bag, he looked down at where the accident happened, he said his heart raced, just to think about what could have happened, how it could have gone very wrong. His hand went into his nail bag to get his first handful of nails, and one nail dropped from his hand, hit the roof decking, and slid towards the ground.

Just underneath the eve of the house, Iletta came from under the eve, pushing her little wheelbarrow that had a few bricks she picked up from the ground and loaded in. She looked up at the men peering over the edge and staring down at her. She smiled, gave half of a wave, as if to say, "It's okay now. I got the last of the bricks." Just then, the nail David dropped had now slid down the roof and fell behind her head to the ground. The only ones who did *not* see that nail fall were Iletta and Bert.

David and the crew were working at a fast pace, with the clear intention of finishing this job and getting off the property as soon as possible. It was later, a week or so, that one of the other carpenters told him about dropping the brick through the ceiling and into the living room. David about had a hissy over that.

I Woke Up This Morning and Found a Dead Cat in My Yard. What Do I Do Next?

My neighbor just asked me this question. He is standing in his yard wearing a wrinkled, half-buttoned dress shirt and pajama bottoms. So, I asked him these questions:

"First off, is it really dead?"

"How do you know it's dead?"

"Did it move any?"

"Have you touched it?"

"Can you poke it with a stick to make sure it's dead?"

"If it isn't dead, then what?"

"Do you hit it to make sure it dies?"

"Wouldn't that be humane?"

"Aren't you supposed to put it out of its misery, so it
   doesn't suffer anymore?"

"Do you need a bigger stick?"

"What if it meows?"

"Will you still be alright after hearing all that?"

"What do you do if it isn't hurt that badly?"

"Do you know how to see what kinds of hurts
   it may have?"

"Do you know how to diagnose?"

"To diagnose cats?"

"What do you know about cats?"

"Can you tell me anything about cats, to me, so I will
   feel better about you going to fiddle around with it?"

"What if it bites you?"

"Can you tell when a cat gets mad?"

"What if it has rabies?"

"Do you even like cats?"

"Do you have gloves to protect yourself if it's alive?"

"Will you try and put it in a sack or try and hold it?"

"Can you describe the cat?"

"Is it big?"

"The grass was kind of tall—you couldn't see it well?"

"Is it a short or long-haired cat?"

"Have you seen it before?"

"Does the cat belong to someone around here?"

"Do you know?"

"They prowl around a lot, and it might not be from
     around here?"

"Do you know?"

"Do you think it might have gotten out and escaped?"

"Have you seen any lost cat posters tacked
     to telephone poles?"

"Is it young, medium aged, or old?"

"You can look at a horse's teeth and tell how old they
     are. Do you think that would work for a cat?"

"Did the cat have a collar?"

"Did you poke it a little or really poke it repeatedly to see?"

"Is your stick flimsy or is it a stick, stick?"

"Did you see it in your yard yesterday?"

"How about before that?"

"It could have been there for more than a day or two,
     or longer?"

"What do you think?"

"Is it stiff now, you think, after you poked it?"

"How about before?"

"Are there any flies on it yet?"

"Is there any smell to it yet?"

"Is your stick strong enough to flip it over to look
    at the undersides?"
"What do you think the undersides looks like?"
"Is your stick long enough so you can flip it over
    without you having to smell it?"
"Is it wet, and did you get any juice on you?"
"Can you see any maggots squiggling around?"
"Can you do that by yourself?"
"Do you need help?"
"Is this the first dead animal you have beaten with a stick?"
"Have you seen feeding maggots before?"
"That doesn't bother you?"
"In some crime shows on TV the detectives put Vicks
    VapoRub in their noses before seeing stinking dead
    bodies, but would you do it with Vicks in your nose?"
"Do you have any?
"Maybe you should just bury it, you think?"
"Some owners will be greatly upset, can you imagine?"
"Not knowing?"
"You still think it's the right thing to do?"
"What color is the collar?"
"If you put a poster together and describe the
    color of the collar, maybe that might help?"
"You could remove the collar and wash the blood off it,
    that will help identify the collar's color, couldn't you?"
"It might be a good deed to go around the neighborhood,
    knocking on doors, and showing off the collar to
    them when they come to the door, wouldn't it?"
"Could you find a cigar box to put it in, maybe decorate
    the insides like a miniature coffin like a cheapskate
    or I mean to say, like a *keepsake* for them, that would
    make them feel better once they hear your story?
"Minus beating a dead cat to see if it were alive?"

"Since you don't have a place to bury the cat, it
would not be nice to tell them you threw
away their little Kittie in your garbage can?"
"You can't flush it down the toilet, huh?"
"If they saw your poster nailed to the telephone pole and
came over, wanting their little fluffy and it was still
in your garbage can before the trash truck came and
they had to dig it out, you think that would be bad?"
"Maybe, don't nail your poster to the telephone pole
until after the garbage truck comes by, but what
are you going to say you did with it, anyway?"
"I sure hope you won't have kids with them when they
come by. What are you going to say to them, anyway?"

Whistling Dixie

There are many events, circumstances, opportunities, and happen stances that mix throughout the lives of college students, before, during, and after the college years. The memories for most will culminate in successes of varying degrees, mixed with regrets, disappointments, and the pressures of life, family, and career.

So, in *medias res*, Vincent Price, a very notable actor from stage, television, and radio, and a movie icon in horror movies went to Indiana University and gave a lecture about his career on stage and screen.

He was a delightful raconteur that evening, and the program concluded with a post-production Q and A. Indiana University's Theater Department was situated behind the auditorium, and to a great many theater majors, this was a must-attend event.

As a kid growing up, I watched every horror movie that was broadcast on our three-channel, black-and-white television, and went to every big screen picture show I could. It was that love of those old films that drove me to declare a Speech and Theater major many years later, when I entered college.

I was fascinated with "monster make-up."

That night, I was able to converse with the Master of Horror and ask him "Who were some of your favorite fellow actors?" He dipped his head towards me and leaned in for added effect when he answered.

"There were many, and Peter Lorre was one of them," Mr. Vincent Price said. "What a great man. I realized early on that I would not be satisfied to just try to always be the leading male in a production. They are sooo boring. You already know they'll get the leading lady in the end. The leading man is always boxed in, and everybody knows that he will win. But—"

And here, he took a long pause and looked away from me to the other people attending his lecture, and then back at me. "The villain—now *that* is what you want to be. He's the one who can try anything and barely loses in the end. Now, that is a great role to have, the villain."

"As far as other actors, again, Peter Lorre. But my favorite—" and here, he paused and looked about, and we were all mesmerized— "is Boris."

He then shifted his mood to emote more lightheartedness, taking a few more questions, before saying, "Goodbye, my dear friends." And then he left.

It was exhilarating to see him, listen to him, and talk with him, if only briefly.

From that meeting, I began to develop myself as a character actor and studied Konstantin Stanislavski. *I will be that great method actor. Who could argue against Vincent Price?*

A couple of "character" roles sometimes went a little wide of field such as in the play, *Automobile Graveyard*, by Fernando Arrabel. It was an absurdist play that is a parody of the Christ story. The characters in the play are frequently childlike but seldom innocent. They are prostitutes, murderers, and torturers. The set was assembled from several actual wrecked junkyard cars stacked on stage in the background.

One of the torturers was my friend Deborah May, Miss Indiana of 1970. I taught her how to crack the bullwhip she was going to use on stage, so that she could do it without taking off her ear. I played Automobile #2, the persona of the populace.

Johnny Johnson was an anti-war play where I had a firearm (shotgun) loaded with ammo blanks, with a shotgun sound that activated a mechanism that blew out the guts of the actor on stage. It was quite graphic for a stage play and it was presented during the Vietnam War. It was a provocative show.

Another character role I was cast in was in a public television drama pilot that was shot with a V.H.S. camera—at the time the latest technology jump from previously having to shoot with 16mm film. I was the lead male who would be chased from a bar, pursued down an alley, and shot in the back and killed. The cinematography plan was to do a close-in shot of me getting the bullet in my back.

I wore a 10" aluminum plate taped to my back, inside my shirt, and a plastic baggy filled with Hershey's chocolate syrup, with a detonation charge inside the syrup. I had the detonator button in my hand. We were shooting in black and white so there was no reason for using red-colored blood. The "blood" showed better in chocolate.

During the filming I was running towards the camera and then past it, and that loosened the tape holding the bag, and the charge pulled away from the 10" plate. It was at the base of my neck when I pushed the button.

I hit the ground, thrashing to get my shirt off, and crawled and rolled over, and then dragged myself into a puddle of alley water. My skin was burning with scalding hot chocolate splatters. My collar smoked some.

"Great job of getting shot and dying, but it was too long, and you didn't die soon enough. Why don't we re-shoot that last scene?"

As the director talked, I felt the scalding hot chocolate go down my back and drip inside my pants and down my leg. That part didn't make the cut, either.

Play On The Local Radio

He came into the station one day,
With his guitar in his hand.
He wanted to talk to the station manager,
Wanted to talk directly to the man.

He had an old guitar, you know,
And a girl in his band.
He had a lot to say, he said,
And wanted to play on the local radio.

    BREAK

He got up to the microphone, and
Loved it like his son.
He gathered all of his courage up, and said,
"I'd like to play another one."

His words weren't that powerful,
And his rhymes were off to the side,
I felt bad for his girly-girl, because
He wanted to play on the local radio.

    BREAK

He danced and he wiggled from side to side,
He forgot he wasn't on TV,
His girly-girl left when he hit the microphone,
He wanted to play on the local radio.

He was kiss-your-ass happy when he got paid.
On his bumper and guitar case
Were two radio station call letter stickers,
'Cause he played it on the local radio.
'Cause he played it on the local radio.

PART THREE

Grandma Three

My first wedding day came during a week of heavy rains in New York City. I was hoping for clear weather, like the weather Elizabeth and I were having in Houston, which was our hometown. The clouds did abate on and off. We had gone to a Justice of the Peace for the license a few days before, and the rehearsal dinner was at the posh Tavern on the Green in Central Park. It was a wonderful luncheon.

The rain was gone as we pulled into the basement of the World Trade Center on the wedding day to park. We both remembered and remarked about the attempted bombing in that basement by Islamic terrorists a couple of months before. But we saw no damage or construction where we parked. Perhaps it was in the basement of the other Twin Tower.

We were married at Windows on The World at the Twin Towers and had the reception there, looking out over Manhattan, and down on the Empire State Building, and out to the Statue of Liberty. It was the top of the world that day for us.

We were new homeowners and moved to Jersey Village, Texas. She was employed by Conoco, and I was employed by Continental Airlines as a company recruiter. Continental's owner, Texas Air Corporation, led by Frank Lorenzo, was on an overly aggressive takeover agenda and was buying other airlines, in order to dominate the airline industry in the U.S. or gut them and sell off the pieces.

Eastern Airlines, under Frank Borman, was bankrupted in fighting the takeover in 1991. The business term became known as arbitrage.

I could fly wherever I wanted to in the continental U.S. for $20, Hawaii for $30, and to Australia for $40. Life was pretty good.

Children came along and I needed to be home. I found opportunities to make a difference by recruiting high school students to attend school after their graduations to get a *career* with an associate degree, and not just a "steady job."

After a few years, I was promoted into management as Admissions Director at ITT, training new employees, evaluating staff progress, traveling to different high schools, and attending career fairs. It was a ten-hour-plus day, oftentimes six days a week. Added to that were company business travels, nationwide.

Over the years, I thought about the "swell times" I lived during junior high school as an average student and how the "career" people did my choosing for me. What direction and outcome did they foresee for me? I was just an occupant of someone else's bus into the future. Without giving me any input and *asking* me, I was pigeon-holed and dropped-kicked to Jesus.

In those times and places, my future was driven by people who were products of their environment as well. The hometown had a Navy base and lots of shipyards which employed welders, pipe fitters, machinists, hard hat divers, painters, roustabouts, drillers, truck drivers, electricians, carpenters, boilermakers, millwrights, and cowboys.

Throughout high school, I was not propelled or encouraged to have a great desire to attend college. My future was decided by my 8th grade counselors. I was dismissed by others from attempting any "pre-college" classes such as algebra, upper science, a foreign language, chemistry, and so on. How could I have realized that this course was putting me at a great disadvantage if I were to want to gain entrance to college at some time in my future? Financial aid was never spoken about or mentioned. If you had money, you had advantages. Yes, things can always change, and doors do open, but—

Kids need to know that they don't have to settle for second class status and that education is the ticket to a future with success in it. Unlike the fortunate ones who somehow had the money to pay for college, many students just give up before graduation and drop out. I talked to many who were in that situation. Hand-to-mouth, or hit the streets and be a rap artist and make a million dollars overnight.

Getting to students before they gave up was the challenge, regardless of present circumstances. It was heartbreaking to talk to so many kids who only needed to be encouraged. I had a staff that worked on housing and transportation, ride sharing, and part-time work while they were attending school. It was a reward for me to see them graduate and become successful, in spite of themselves.

The streets can be a destroyer of young souls. I became involved with many students who were in gangs, slinging drugs, or worse. I had students who slept in their bathtubs at night as protection from stray bullets. Some were down-and-out homeless.

I would periodically see and meet their parents or guardians who were frequently second- and third-generation gang bangers themselves.

Going to school was an either/or proposition. It was the first stop on the way out of jail or the last stop before going to jail.

I had to train a staff that was prepared to deal with all of it. Part of that learning curve came from home visits, where a parent or guardian would need to be involved, need to care enough, and try hard enough to support their kid by just showing up and being an active part of their child's life, for however much longer they had.

At the dawn of the coming of the computer age, traveling around Houston at night, we relied on a directory book of maps that my admissions people carried with them. When we did house interviews, we relied on those maps and a flashlight, so we could see at night. Most of the visits did not occur on well-lit streets. Some neighborhoods were just 'hoods. So, having me along was a great assurance. I should mention also that reading maps at night started to become a challenge. My vision needed to be improved, and I got my first pair of glasses. In the nick of time, I think.

One cold and windy night, we tried several times to find the house and had to drive away and go to a 7-11 to get more accurate directions. We didn't have cell phones; they hadn't been invented yet. The latest gadget was a pager.

Not a judgement, just observations, the house we found was at the end of a cul-de-sac. A car or two were parked in the yard and side yard and the steps to the house were just wooden steps to the door. As the door opened, a dog under that porch barked a few times and gave up and went back out of the wind to a warm place.

All the windows were covered with plastic film and stapled around the window frames and the inside was dark, as in a shadeless table lamp with one lightbulb burning. It was cold inside the living room. I don't know if we took out all the heat from the room when we opened the door, but I did notice a natural gas space heater in the middle of the floor burning brightly. We could see our breaths.

These types of heaters had ceramic waffle inserts that glowed when the gas flame blew against them, and the ceramics would help the combustion of the flame and throw radiant heat outward. This was the type of heater I grew up with, but in a five-room house. The smell of the burning heater in this small room made our eyes water.

I knew there was a round tin cover that could be adjusted to let in more air during the flame's drawing of fuel into the heater, so that it would cut the noxious fumes down considerably. The air in the room was *very* smoky and would not be good for anyone to breathe for any period of time.

The room was almost empty of furniture: a table for the lamp, a broken couch with no cushions, just some scattered blankets, and no tv and no rugs, just wooden floors.

Before anything else, the kid whose family we were visiting, Darrel, said to us, "Just a minute, I'll get another chair for you to sit in. I need to tell you, 'cause you said it would be important to have a parent here, but she's got called into work and had to leave. I didn't have a way to call you to let you know."

My partner responded, "We got turned around, Darrel, and we went to the 7-11 to call you to get better directions. I was trying to call you on the phone, but I got no answer. The clerk told me how to get here."

"Well, Sir, we don't have a phone. We just use the neighbors, and they're not home, " he said, and sat the chair down and sat in it himself. I was standing by the heater next to him.

I offered to reset an interview time, as he invited me to sit down on the couch, which was closer to the space heater. I was going to sit down on the old blankets on the couch that I assumed were the dog's. It was lumpy, and when I instinctively went to move the blanket away from me, to even out the seat, the couch moved! I heard a noise from the couch blanket and was startled to see an incredibly old Black lady with white hair. She stuck her head up, out from between the covers, and was obviously as startled as we were. Everyone was transfixed. In that instant, time stood still.

Darrel was mortified and talked to his grandmother about what was going on and let her know it was all right for us to be there. She had awakened to find two White men, wearing suits, in her house. From that point she seemed confused but then laid back down in the pile of covers.

"I *swear* to God I didn't know she was in here. My momma usually has her in the other room when it's this late."

Grandmother stirred again, raised her head once more, looked around, and went back down into the covers.

We were standing from the surprise, still, and so decided it was the perfect moment for us to say goodbye and let Darrel take over caring for his senile grandmother. We rescheduled.

My partner drove us away and looked at me with a wry smile. "I can't even believe it. You sat down on his grandmother!"

Tavern on The Green

She walks around in Central Park,
In the rain, before dawn,
Crown in hand, bag of clothes,
Sometimes fed, always cold.

She stood at her cake, with a smiling crowd,
He never showed, she looked around.

Kids jump around at a birthday party,
Streamers wave, it's just another day.
Cap and gown, graduation day,
Pictures taken; she moves away.

She stood at their cake, with a smiling crowd,
She was never there, they looked around.

　BREAK

The children play and sail their boats,
Feed the pigeons and then go away,
Without any food and a place to stay,
Her hunger grows, what a shame.

The wet, grey sun has gone away.
That emerald ring doesn't shine today.

Like an old re-run that's been around,
You know the ending, it draws no crowd,
You take a glance but not a stare,
You walk on by as if there's no one living,
At the Tavern on the Green, at the Tavern on the Green.

Jon Bunn

Lovely Enchanting Venice

Ah, pictures of single-oared gondolas floating by on the canals, weaving between the brightly colored red-and-white barber polls, ribbon-sashed boatmen pointing out the marvelous architecture of the old stone buildings which descended directly into the gentle waters, the quaffing of delectable smells of freshly baked breads and piping hot Italian pizzas. All of this draws the tourists to partake in culinary delights at the chefs and shopkeepers beckoning to serve their guests once they step onto the docks and streets of a city that grew from the influences of the Roman Empire.

NO. NO. NO. WRONG. This Venice is NOT that one! This Venice is located at the absolute very bottom of the 2,320-mile-long Mississippi River of the United States. It is the terminus, the end, the last vestige of soil being deposited by the outflow of the Mississippi River into the Gulf of Mexico. This place is inhabited by people who wear denim blue jeans and khaki work clothes every day, have dirt on their hands and clothes, and wear the stains and scars of a life of toils in and around the oil business and the service industry for the mega-sized oil giants and a few independent drillers and exploration companies who hustle for a piece of the black gold laying offshore. This is the gateway to the waters that are full of drilling rigs and platforms that become the chess pieces where drilling, pumping, and exploration companies leave from to place their pieces throughout the Gulf of Mexico. This is the very last point of dirt before open Gulf waters begin.

The docks are full of supply boats taking on food, supplies, and equipment. Deck hands, roustabouts, mechanics, welders, cooks, engineers—all are present. They are in the process of going offshore or coming back from living and working 12-hour shifts, or on service calls. It is a place that is busy 24-7.

No place for slackers, malingerers, or pretenders. Being here means money. You earn it and go home. Some lucky workers get their rides to and from the job sites by helicopter, some by crew boats.

The work shifts vary between what skills are needed, when, where, and how much. It is a scarce commodity to find someone working 8 to 5. Some assignments were scheduled for 7 days working in a row and 7 days off. Some went for 10 days on and 5 off, 20 and 10, 30 and 30, 3 months on and 1 month off, and any combination thereof. The activity surrounding the need to locate, find, drill, and capture oil, transport it, refine it, and sell it to America or anyone wanting to buy it was like drops of water dancing on the surface of a hot skillet. It never stopped that level of intensity unless a hurricane was in your lap.

This story of Oldster and Young'un illustrates what it was like to get employment in those times, the early 1960s. That same scene does not exist anymore, as technology changed the game.

Oldster was injured. He was shot in a fight with a Navy sailor and his recovery to using one of his arms again was lengthy. Once the arm was well enough to use, he needed to make a lot more money than selling beers at 30 cents a bottle in the bar he owned and operated. He got a lead on a job from one of his regulars and pretty soon he went offshore to work as a cook on a seismic survey ship. The money would be the solution for his medical bills. Insurance in those days did not cover much, so a better job solved it.

It was not hand-to-mouth times, but it was close. The press of hard times was upon them. He thought about having the Young'un go to work with him, as it was during the summer. But one issue remained the obstacle. The boy, just leaving pre-pubescence and getting dark hairs growing under his nose could not work in the Gulf of Mexico without being at least 18, and he was just 14. What a shame, or so he thought.

Oldster's lawyer, who was working to get a medical settlement from the Navy over the shooting, told him that it would be highly unusual for someone to work offshore even at 16 because of liabilities in the oilfield. Certainly 14 would be a *real* stretch. They would need to go before a judge to get certification that the Young'un was "of age responsible" to go offshore. They tried it, all three went before the judge, and it was granted.

When the next round of shifts took place in Louisiana, they drove from Texas to "the end of the Earth" to work offshore. And it was the end of the Earth, too. It was on the complete other end of the state and then a long drive down to the bottom of the Mississippi Delta, to Venice, Louisiana. The judge issued what was known as a hardship deferment.

Oldster was the cook on the ship, and the Young'un was assistant cook/pantryman. The job was to assist the cook in making three meals a day, serving, cleaning dishes, pots, and pans, cleaning the galley after every meal, cleaning the mess hall, sweeping and mopping the floors, taking out the trash (throwing overboard), cleaning the bathrooms and the shower, making the beds, washing all the linens, and making coffee every day.

The shift began at 4 a.m. and didn't end until 4 p.m., 7 days a week for 10 days on and 4 days off. Then repeat and repeat.

The vessel was approximately 150 feet long and it was a seismic survey ship. It had two very large steel drum reels that were wrapped with a large cable, and on deck, next to the reels were rows and rows of floating buoys that attached periodically to the cable and let out into the Gulf and trailed behind.

A second boat, a chase boat, followed this boat at some distance behind and it was carrying a hold full of explosives in fifty-pound canisters. It was a repurposed shrimp boat that carried depth charges that would be set off with an electric signal once the dynamite was thrown overboard and reached the specified depth. The electric impulse was registered along the large cable. It picked up and read the lines and they were printed on a seismic printer, then given to the oil company to read and locate oil deposits in the floor of the Gulf or sold to any other company interested in purchasing them.

The depth charges were just like the depth charges seen in World War II war movies, bombing submarines. They made loud noises through the hull of the ship, hour after hour.

The two ships used for the seismic work were either owned or leased to Global Marine. The company was owned by Howard Hughes and was also famous years later for building two Exploration vessels, the Glomar Challenger, built in Orange, Texas in August 1968 as a research vessel, and later still, the Glomar Explorer in July 1974, which was a vessel that was built to raise a secret Soviet Nuclear Submarine that blew up from the detonation of a nuclear weapon it carried and sunk in 17,000-foot waters.

The Young'un thought the trip took forever and was anxious and apprehensive when they pulled into the parking lot to store their car and unload their personal baggage, and then walk across the street and board the seismic ship, which was tied against the dock.

It began in earnest. "Put your stuff down here, go there, move that over here, give me a hand. NOW. Leave that."

It looked like a grocery store was being loaded with shelves full of stores, and boxes and boxes of the same thing. Where do you put it all, where does it go? A few men were on the deck, adding floating buoys, and carrying some of the boxes through the hatch and then down the steps into the aft hold, which was in front and to the starboard and port sides of two very large twin diesel engines in the storerooms.

"Get them boxes down into the hold and put them somewhere. We'll rearrange them later, after we're under way," Oldster barked.

The first item the Young'un picked up to carry was a 25-pound bag of sugar . He then descended through the hold and down a steep and narrow set of steel steps to one of the food lockers. It was a challenge to move up and down the steps with awkward things. "One hand for you and two for the groceries. Don't drop anything, just keep moving."

It went on for hours and finally they took a short break to go move their stuff into their bunks and get settled in. The bow is where all the workers' bunks were located. Oldster already had his bunk looking like he was all moved in when they got below. Made sense, as that is where he he'd been for several months. The Young'un was bunked above him. Not a large bed, as space was at a premium. Most bunks are oriented bow to stern to make it easier to sleep during the ups and down of the waves, once underway.

The Young'un's bunk was set on the bulkhead, port to starboard—sideways, left to right. The bulkhead behind his and Oldster's was the freshwater tank for the ship. The gangway ladder dropped right at the feet of Oldster's bunk. He needed access to the kitchen, and it was a priority location.

"There's your sheets and pillowcase. Get it made, get a blanket, maybe two, and meet me in the galley."

When he got to the galley, they had frozen meats and veggies to put into the freezers that were on the wall and lashed closed with ropes and hooks. It began to dawn on the Young'un that the boat, er ship, might move up and down enough to open the freezer door and so, it is needed to keep the groceries where they need to be. Looking about the galley, he noticed that most things had straps and hooks on them. Hmmm?

"Let's go topside, I need you to climb that ladder and I'm a-gonna start throwing food up there for you to store." He climbed to the roof and was walking between two diesel exhaust stacks. Looking down, he saw Oldster and another man catching produce and stacking it on the deck.

"Behind you is a large plywood box. I'm gonna throw you all these produces and you stack them up and put them in the box. We don't have room to carry fresh produce very long. Don't have enough refrigeration. They'll have to go up there until they're no good and then they go overboard."

The first thing Oldster tossed up was the cantaloupes. Some hit hard and split in two and some were just cracked. Young'un looked down with a question on his face and was told they weren't going to last, so throw 'em away now or throw 'em away later, was the response from Oldster. But Young'un just could not do that. He loved cantaloupes and so he set one or two aside in the veggie bin for later. After all, they were going to be thrown away anyway, might as well take a bite or two, here and there. And Lord, they were good! He was up there by himself and all, so no harm, he supposed.

Coming back down the ladder, most everything was close to being stored and out of the way. He said to Oldster, "Where is that nigger man? Is he going to throw any more stuff up to me or what? Him and that Mexican about covered me up. They busted four or five of them cantaloupes. They work on this boat?"

"They don't work on this boat. They work for the grocery wholesaler. And you might not want to call him a 'nigger' and you be careful how you talk around them people."

Young'un started down the ladder, thinking, *What is he so uppity about? He uses that "nigger" word all the time. Never said anything to me about it, and now he's got twisted over it?* He paused. *Never told me NOT to say it, that I can remember.*

They went to the galley. "You and I will start off here, every morning. We'll be getting up at 4 a.m. and getting breakfast ready.

"This," he said, pointing at the coffee urn strapped to the shelf on the wall, "is the first thing to make when we get up here. See all these dishes piled up? That's because no one has been here to wash 'em. They won't do it, and now with you here, you'll be in charge of keeping this sink free of dishes. Might as well get a pot of coffee ready for the morning. Usually, the captain or first mate will be in the pilothouse round the clock on different shifts and so they'll come down here and get coffee, pretty much all night long. Those three steps up? That's the bridge. You'll meet them tomorrow. They will not be on board till later and you will know it when they are. They'll start the engines and do checks before we pull out later tonight."

So, with the preps done and foodstuff up, Oldster said they could turn in and sleep till 4 a.m.

Men start showing up and coming down and getting into their bunks. They eyed the "new meat" but didn't say much. Just as the engines started was when Young'un had dozed off. He woke back up and lay in his bunk. They were soon underway, and the engines ran smooth and steady. He noticed immediately that the water behind the bulkhead, which was next to his bunk, occasionally sloshed. Not too bad, he thought. Nice smooth ride. He thought he'd sleep like a baby.

The lights in the bunkroom were turned out. It was DARK. Young'un realized that there were no windows. It was pitch black. Someone went up the ladder and propped open the door for light.

The boat reached the end of the breakers and went out of the channel and into open waters. The engines added many more rpms, and the sounds became a LOT louder. Things started moving around. In the dark, Young'un couldn't tell what was what. It was disorienting. In and out of dozing, he never got any real sleep and then Oldster's alarm clock went off.

"Let's get up, give you 10 minutes."

Woozy or wheezy, one of the two, Young'un felt maybe a lack of sleep, or maybe not, but he knew it was time to move. The coffee pot was on, and the coffee smelled half-burnt. It had been on all night, and half of it was gone. "Pour it out and make new coffee. The men will be getting up in 20 minutes. They'll eat and need to be on deck at 6 a.m."

All the haggard and sleepy men emerged, took turns in the head, got coffee, and made small talk till breakfast was served. The more things that Young'un did, the more he wanted to get back to bed and lay his head down for a few minutes. He looked out the porthole and the ship was slowly rocking from side to side, sometimes jerking front to back. Now, it made sense to be leaning a bit against something to steady oneself. His head and his body began pulling itself in different directions, first one way and then the other, then both parts were pulling and moving in opposite directions at the same time.

"Eat something, it might make you feel a bit better."

It did not. What came next was that his cantaloupe feast of last night seemed a bit high in his throat. He thought he did not eat that much. A few minutes later, it was higher than that. It was creeping upwards, and he thought he could stop it by swallowing it back down. It persisted. Then it got worse. And then it became worser than that. The ship seemed to be fighting him, and it was trying to keep him off balance. It was succeeding.

Even the food smells were now tainted and raunchy. He went to the head and leaned down. Puffs and smells of blowing urine odors constricted his throat and he spewed orange salvoes of flotsam into and about the split top toilet seat and adjoining floor. He was heaving in spasms, and muscle fatigue talons held him from moving away from the porcelain altar. Oldster managed to gather enough of him and his clothes to put him on the rail and he hung on until someone provided a chair to collapse on.

Everything was spent, everything was gone, yet his spasms were persistent and holding on mercilessly. The ship soon settled into a slow rolling cadence. He would try a couple of saltine crackers as the ship wallowed in the troughs and as the deck changed directions and began rising again, his discharge would blow out and a new cycle began. He thought his underwear would come up through his mouth.

It lasted for two days non-stop, mostly with intermittent gaps. Oldster carried the load of cooking, cleaning, pot scrubbing, cleanup, and orderly duties. On the third day, the ordeal was over.

Upon completing his baptism, Young'un learned his routine, gazed out the back of the ship, and enjoyed riding on the stern when the day's work was over. Occasionally, the captain would let him ride in the second mate's chair from the helm and he could see into the water from a good vantage point to see vertically. Many a time, he would see large schools of fish dash away from under the boat when their schools were crossed in the Gulf. The large fish gave him fishing fever.

He was able to fish sometimes during the evenings if the ship was at anchor. He caught dozens of fish one afternoon and several of the deck hands came to watch him land them. "Oh boy, look at the fish dinner we'll get from this!" As soon as they left, he kicked them off the deck and back into the water. He realized that they were wanting him to clean, cook, and serve them dinner. No, not on his watch.

The purpose of the work in the Gulf was to map and shoot grid lines and create seismic charts to be analyzed, used, or sold to Big Oil. The cables that were put out were a thousand feet long or longer. The ship would go in a straight line for over a mile or so before turning 180 degrees and shooting a line in the opposite direction. On some of the shoots, the dynamite charges were close enough to explode close to reefs that held lots of species of game fish—snappers, groupers, tilefish, sharks, tuna, mahi mahi, tarpon, swords, tripletail, amberjacks, wahoo, hogfish—and the list was almost endless.

After a day of dynamiting and running the ship in the opposite direction, large, gorgeous fish could be gathered and pulled from the water, just floating by. They kept a gaff and pole handy just above the wheelhouse, in the event anyone wanted to try and gaff one. The ship was too big to maneuver around, so they just took their chances and hoped one would be close enough to gaff. Young'un was not very lucky, though he saw thousands and thousands of fish float by.

In some respects, Young'un was a bit luckier that he realized. Having his bunk sideways seemed to be a bit more comforting than sleeping headed bow to stern. Well, it did seem that way.

His big duty, which came somewhat regularly, was his laundry duty. The men that worked in and around the ship had their duties and they did get dirty and went to bed that way, causing Young'un to have to change their bed sheets before the 10-day work cycle ended, and they went home. Young'un found two types of dirty. There was the top sheet above the mattress dirty and the below the sheet under the mattress dirty. Quite the discovery, he felt.

When he was changing the sheets on all the workers' beds, he discovered a vast array of reading material hidden under the mattresses, certainly of an "adult" nature. Well, well, what the hell. How does one know what the stories are about if you don't "read" them?

They were picture books and showed physical skills that probably wouldn't be learned in gym class. It was an amazing library. It wasn't the *Playboy* magazine snaps, with hints of blushing, and cleavage suggestions. This was full-frontal-to-back, 360-degree literature. One of the men passed by a bunk when Young'un was changing sheets and he mentioned he did not want his magazines moved around. Enough of a scare to warrant judicious non-involvement in library science.

The captain was a short man and spoke with a heavy Cajun accent, but Young'un would take his time and, by listening carefully, get what the man was saying. The 10-day seismic boat trip would be over in a couple more days and the way out of the Gulf and headed back to Venice was fair sailing. It was right after lunch and Oldster and Young'un were standing at the sinks and talking about nothing in particular when Young'un commented, "I think I like the captain but he sure is hard to understand with that coonass accent. He must have been around a while..."

Oldster jumped back a step and got a brow on. "You need to watch how you say things on this boat. People don't need to take your sassy mouth and you being 14 or not, they may blouse it for you. Get yourself on better behavior."

Young'un thought about what was just said to him and shot back, "I've heard you use 'coonass' about a hundred times in the bar, just like you say 'nigger,' like it was nothin'. That's how you talk at home and that's how I learned to talk like you."

At that moment, the captain opened the wheelhouse door back and hooked it open on the bulkhead. The door was opened, and he heard the conversation going on and heard himself being called a coonass. He looked at both of them.

"Not to get into yo' bidness, sha, but I been called a coonass a lot. Where I comes from on tha' Bayou Teche, we just Creoles, us. My kins was all French when my peoples were put here. We don't use tha name much 'cept in close friends."

He gave both of them a look and turned and climbed the three stairs back to the helm. The vessel this whole time was running on its own and no one was at the controls or checking the horizon.

Both the cook and the pantryman were zipped up tight, solidly embarrassed, and were not going to say another word.

Young'un thought, *It doesn't put me in a good light. Could've told me that was how to say it right.*

✳ ✳ ✳

The issue about why we couldn't use pejoratives was one of the strains and divisions that grew between them that never seemed to get fixed. The rude habits of the parent were taught and passed down to the children, but then became a cause of disagreement that widened between them for many decades.

Martin Luther King's assassination became a humorous event for one and a tragedy for the other.

The ship went back to the dock in Venice and the end of a work cycle was concluded.

The captain said to Young'un, "It's good to have you aboard. I hope you'll make another turn around, sha?"

In another three weeks they were back, standing at the docks in Venice, looking for another hitch. Here came the groceries and they started loading in. Same bunks, same duties.

While the stores were being loaded, Oldster noticed the stores brought to the dock had increased and he had a sense the boat might be loading extra provisions because they were planning to be out more days than what was scheduled.

Four men, dressed in slacks and long-sleeved white business shirts came aboard and settled into the main salon and spread out the contents of their briefcases around them. They were clearly not the type of men who would be getting their hands dirty.

These were home office types and everyone on board tiptoed around them and gave them a wide berth. Oldster was told these men would be "riding with us" for a few days and then we were going to take them back to shore and drop them off at the docks in Morgan City.

Young'un made the beds for the four men in the center section in the bow of the sleeping quarters. The four bunks that had been taken over meant the four usual deck hands who slept there had their work schedules cancelled for this trip. He was told that they had free run of the vessel and that they were in charge, and he was to do what they said while they were aboard. Young'un had an immediate dilemma—what to do about the "library." He decided to leave it alone. Maybe someone else might be interested in the acquisition of skills or mental attitudes.

The corporate men did not get up with everyone for breakfast at 5 a.m. They waited and wandered in after 8 a.m., when they brought out their briefcases and took over the space. When choppy seas were either predicted or present, the salon's tables were tableclothed with cotton fabric and whetted with water to prevent the plates, cups, pitchers, and serving bowls from sliding around during rough seas. It took some getting used to, sticking your arms onto wet tablecloths for every meal. It was just unappetizing, that's all.

Here was another peculiar happening. One of the men had a cordless Remington shaver he brought to the table and after he ate and Young'un cleared his dishes away, he would sit there and *shave at the table! He put his whiskers all over everywhere.* That was really pushing it.

This was a rough trip into the Gulf, and they were being tossed about. The sinks in the galley were deep, like two feet deep. Washing dishes was a chore, Young'un had to reach down into it to scrub. It was hard on the back. All the burners on the stove had rails around the burners to keep the pots full of hot food from sliding off and scalding someone. A few times during the week, over-easy eggs would creep up the side of the skillet and sometimes they would escape. Cooking could be an adventure at times. The ship being 150 feet long didn't make any difference, it could have been 300 feet, and it would toss them around. It was tiring to be in high seas and fight to hold on while trying to work.

"Rescue at Sea!" is what the Cajun captain called it. A call came in from the converted shrimp trawler carrying a couple of tons of explosives that was following the seismic ship that a mishap in the galley had occurred, and they could use a hand. They needed some supplies and needed to come along and transfer foodstuffs. They would be going into Morgan City for repairs and needed things like macaroni and cheese, coffee, and loaves of bread. The seas had calmed down and the water was flat.

They came along side and Young'un met the pantryman from the trawler. His name was Jesuee du Monde. He was 17. His name meant, "the high ground" or "the high place." His ancestors came from the mountains in France.

Jesuee said to just call him Jesse, as it was easier. Cajuns eat rice and lots of it, with every meal, it seemed. Jesse was going to make a big pot of rice to go with the beans and he spilled the bag of rice into the sink. He decided to just wash the rice down the sink, and he made another try at the rice. After dinner, the sink clogged up and they let it go till the next morning. Jesse poured a large pot of hot water down the sink to wash it away.

The next morning, they heard a muffled bang and went to the galley to look. Afterall, they carried hundreds of 50 lb. canisters of dynamite on board in the hold. But it wasn't the dynamite. The bag of rice that clogged the pipes swelled up when the hot water treatment occurred, and it exploded and burst the pipes, sending cooked rice all under the sink into the black water holding tanks and they overflowed, as well. They had no plumbing. They had to go in.

With the seas being rough and rougher, they could not steady the seismic cable enough to get good readings and handling canisters of explosives was a dicey proposition. They could get repairs and back out, but they would lose a day of shooting. It was decided that both vessels would head to Morgan City.

Clean sheets were in short supply, so the plan was to drop off Young'un at a commercial laundry to get the sheets, pillowcases, and other linens washed, while the corporate folks went to the bar for some R&R.

The kid got covered up, no pun intended, and the linens were ready in four hours or so. The corporate folks had a roaring good time using a corporate credit card was what they had for "emergency use only."

It was mid-afternoon when they headed back to the docks and loaded the linens and started back out. The shrimp boat would follow; repairs would be finished late. And so, the seismic boat was to head out, ride the anchor for the night and be joined by the other boat and start shooting the next day. Three of the corporates headed back to New Orleans, and one stayed to oversee the shooting for the next few days before he left.

It was late that night when the seismic boat arrived at the anchor spot. Some wind and blowing rain hampered a quiet night in the bunks. The boat kept moving around but the weather was expected to be calm by mid-morning. It lingered.

By the next morning, after breakfast was over, the shrimp boat was still in port completing repairs and was expected to get under power shortly. Without the dynamite, shooting seismic lines simply had to wait.

The weather downgraded more. The seas increased and went to five- to seven-foot waves—too high to try to handle a 50-pound canister of dynamite while trying to detonate it. Waves became higher, still.

The captain said they should go in. Corporate said to ride it out, as it was expected to fall off. It did not. The shooter boat decided not to head out and stayed in port, refusing to leave the docks, and radioed the captain. Both captains thought the margins of safety weren't there. They discussed what to do.

One year before that, on September 3rd, Hurricane Carla had formed and within a few days the winds had gone up to 145 mph, then to a higher wind speed of 170 mph that devastated Galveston, Texas, and the Louisiana coast, damaging or destroying 50,000 homes. None of the deck hands wanted to be caught at sea with a monster storm like Carla forming. Everyone was getting extremely nervous.

Oldster and Young'un heard the name Carla spoken. They had experienced it firsthand in Orange, Texas, on the Louisiana state line in 1961. They were not happy with the idea of having such a storm upon them. Carla was Young'un's first hurricane.

The equipment operating costs for this two-boat exploration was at five figures every day. The disagreements were turning into shouting matches. The captain was the one responsible for everyone and everything, and his word was absolute. The corporate man standing there arguing with him had the purse strings. He could hire and fire at will.

There was no second mate on board, and no one had the ability to operate the ship. No one else had the skills. Now the weather downgraded even more, and the seismic ship was dragging its anchor. It could not go on. If the anchor fouled and couldn't be pulled up, they would sit there and watch the waves come over the ship's gunnels until something else broke, they took on water and went down or declared an emergency and waited for the Coast Guard to arrive, weather permitting.

The captain refused to stay on station and left the wheelhouse to go check the engines and the pumps. The seismic engineers aboard tried to intervene and mediate a solution. Those above deck tried to reach a consensus.

The auxiliary power was running, the pumps seemed to be in order. The Cajun captain stayed in the wheelhouse and talked to the shrimp boat captain in Creole French, so the corporate man was in the dark. The anchor needed to be reset for safety. They were riding the anchor to disaster and the captain told the corporate man his last straw was to contact the Coast Guard and give them their location, in the event they got snagged on the bottom and couldn't free themselves. He knew they might need to abandon ship.

The captain talked in Creole French to the other captain and to Jesuee. When the captains went off to talk, Young'un began his education in what the "rescue at sea" meant.

The captain began to prod and goad the corporate man into calling the Coast Guard. Corporate now refused to comply. The deckhands were alarmed at what was happening. Someone came in from the deck. They had been checking life rafts and life jackets.

That set off a round of increasingly angry shouting. The vessel lurched in the wind and the boat felt like it had slipped its mooring. The bow swung around and was stern to the wind. Something below caught, the ship lurched, and then swung back around, bow to the wind. A couple of men standing at the aft hatch slipped on the wet floor, while the others grabbed something to hang onto. Some pots from the galley came out of their bins, rattled around the galley, and fell to the floor with a clanging sound. They were re-secured.

There seemed to be a lull, after the pots and pans went crashing around and then the ship was secured. After a minute or two went by and things had calmed down, the captain said to no one in particular that the anchor needed to be reposi-tioned. That didn't seem to raise any objections from anyone, so he stepped to the dashboard and fired up one engine and moved the bow forward and the anchor raised and pulled free. He maneuvered forward about 100 yards and redropped the anchor. Letting the engine go to neutral, the ship backed down and the anchor gently set again.

The portside engine was spinning but it wouldn't start. The men in the salon blankly stared at the captain as he tried to start it again. It failed. They were all watching him, and it would not start. He looked at all the faces of the men and then to Mr. Corporate, locked a gaze on him, and without a blink, he spun the engine, and it was clearly dead.

The captain just sat and didn't move, letting others commit to some action or comment. A long pause ensued.

The wind was heard outside, and it was still battering the portholes of the superstructure. A voice was heard to say, "Now what?" And then, more silence.

The little captain said, "Da vessel is goin' to the dock. Nobody in tha' right mine can stop it, sha. We lose tha' other one, we done los' this vessel. Strap yo'selves in, we headed back."

The corporate man sat there, dumbfounded. Some people got up and some went below, and some stayed in the salon. Oldster said to Young'un, "Make a half big pot of coffee."

It took quite a bit of work to get the anchor freed from the bottom, but it was finally winched in, and the vessel turned to its heading and limped towards safer waters and the dock. In the back of their minds, the crew kept an ear out, listening to the last engine they had on the way to the docks. Many ships were headed to the docks at Venice, or were already in. It was picking and choosing when the harbormaster would clear them for arrival.

After a bit of coffee was passed around and the deckhands wedged themselves into places where they could snuggle in and ride out the rough trip, they seemed relieved to be headed back, and relieved they would get an extra day's pay.

Mr. Corporate was grousing in another corner about not getting another day of shooting and felt it was a little suspicious that the port engine failed, just at such a convenient time as to put everyone on the docks. Oldster heard the man's words and suspicions. He was somewhat skeptical himself. "We'll see."

When the ship was close to land and headed into the channel, Young'un was at his bunk, packing his clothes in his duffel, when he noticed that Oldster had already packed up. He also noticed that the things he always left behind and left for the next trip were not there. His calendar wasn't there. His alarm clock was missing, along with his night reading lamp.

Both of them were in the galley drinking coffee and Oldster pulled the plug on the coffeepot. "This is not to be spoken about, you hear?"

"Okay."

"Go down the ladder like you're going to one of the storerooms and go to the right of the starboard engine and look down on the top of the valve cover and the fuel lines. Don't let anybody see you and come back here and tell me what you see."

Young'un went off for a few minutes into the hold and came back with a big grin on his face.

"Well, what did you see? I can tell you missed something, come on."

Down in the hold, along the valve cover he pointed out to Young'un, "See? Those are hammer or wrench marks where the fuel lines have been smashed flat. He done it."

Young'un looked down at the hammer strikes, "Well, that little coonass ..." then he looked up at his dad before saying another word.

Young'un walked into Green's Department store, once home, all on his own, and bought himself the first suit he had ever owned. He had nowhere to wear it to, yet, but he had his first suit.

Adverse Possession

"First, let me apologize to you. I should not have said to you or implied that your feelings are not important. But, let's face it, we seem to be going around in circles these last few meetings and I think it will be time, very soon, that you hit a breakthrough in your behavior before we must end your sessions with me, and you then can seek guidance with someone more suited to your 'special needs.' My schedule will change at the end of this school year, and I will be leaving the university. It is not cold outside, and yet you are here all bundled up, once again. Earnest, it's going to be in the mid 80's and yet you stay bundled up to your neck, and you are always fidgeting and moving around. What seems to be going on with you?"

Keeping his head tucked halfway into his raincoat and without saying a word, he stood to go and as he rose from his chair, his unbuckled pants slipped down and fell to his ankles.

The psychology intern jumped back and shouted, "Earnest, what are you doing inside your raincoat?" and then hurried out of the room through the door where the double-glass one-way mirrored room had two staff psychologists observing her interviewing skills and manners with patients having problems that she thought were real patients. They were there to evaluate her crisis management skills.

As she entered the lab room, the two psychologists had large grins on their faces, and she knew in an instant that she had been set up. Then the "Earnest" she had spent time with on a few occasions entered through another door, hesitantly, not wanting to be swatted by the intern. He finally showed a slight grin as the tension eased.

"Your name is Tex, is that right? I never met you in person but your friend, Kip, told me you were an actor and finishing your degree in the theater department. I'm Dr. David Lambert. Nice to meet you. I was going to speak to you at our cocktail party but missed you. Thanks for being one of our 'patients'."

Tex went over to the intern. She stopped talking to an associate and then said to him, "As soon as I saw Dr. Lambert with that big smile, I *knew* something was up..."

As soon as some pleasantries were exchanged, she started talking "shop" and Tex left and found his friend outside the labs talking to another student. He approached them and said, "Kip Gleeson, that was an interesting ending."

"They usually are. I don't think we'll have any more interns that are set for graduation. That was the last one. Let's go to Nick's and I'll buy. Thanks for doing this."

"Hey, it was a fun thing to do. So, what shakes for you over this Christmas break? Are you still planning to buy that new stereo tuner? I guess you'll be seeing Becky during the break?"

"So, Tex, I was thinking I might take the new tuner over to her house and spend a few days with her. Her roommate is leaving for Fort Wayne and won't be there. She has good speakers, so I'll hook them up and use them."

"So, I'll have the house to myself? I wanted to look at getting an Afghan dog. So, I could stay home and see if we're compatible. You won't mind if I bring a dog home for a while?"

"Tex, we need a *dog*. I'm getting a Golden as soon as I graduate. And by the way, I have an interview coming up for an internship, but it's in D.C., so I'll probably have to move there. You can stay home, play guitar, and bond with it. It's got a name?"

"It is an Afghan name. The lady says its name is Kop Su Rhett. I get my new guitar this week. I just need my paycheck, and I can get it out of lay-away."

College towns empty out very soon after Fall terms are over and everyone heads out for Christmas, usually a two-week affair. The town gets quiet, streets clear out, and hardly any activity goes on. As planned, Kip got his brand-new stereo tuner, and they enjoyed it at home until he left for his girlfriend's apartment. The Afghan dog was a wonderful pet and he and Tex bonded right off. Tex even took him to a big park and let him off his leash and he ran away at the speed of a greyhound to the other end and then ran full steam back to Tex. He could've lost that dog in an instant. Kip came by to see the dog, change clothes, and go back to Becky's apartment.

Tex had a heated waterbed on the floor and the dog liked it but would go to another room and sleep on the rug, sometimes. Staying up and playing his new guitar till very late, Tex was sleeping hard the next morning. Sleeping any harder would probably have killed him.

Kop jumped into the waterbed and began barking and jumping in and out of the waterbed. It sloshed and waves of water held by the bed careened around and tossed Tex awake. From the deepest sleep he registered and inhaled smoke into his lungs, his eyes opening to black surging clouds just above his head that prevented him from seeing the ceiling. The dog continued to frantically jump and run to seek shelter from the choking smoke.

Dressing frantically and gaining a sense of priority and staying low from the impervious black as he looked into the next room, he saw flames beginning to shoot from the lower wall and climb up the side into the ceiling. He watched it alight, then travel on the smoke, consuming the room as it rushed to all corners of the living room. At that moment, the large living room plate glass window exploded, and Tex knew that burst of fresh air into the front room would push the fire through the door and he would be trapped, with no escape from the bedroom.

Along the bedroom wall was a sealed off door covered by a rug. Knowing that trying to crash through a window would take too long a time to get out, with an adrenaline surge, he grabbed for his boots to protect his feet, and tore off the rug and pulled the locked door open, breaking the latch apart as it came free and rolled into the yard, trying to get his boots on as protection from the flames. He heard the screams of his dog still inside. He crawled on his knees with fire shooting out the door over his head and saw Kop frozen on the floor at the other end of the bedroom, which was fully enflamed. He yelled for the dog to come, and Kop went through a tunnel of fire and raced into Tex's arms as they crawled away from the flames.

There may have been a chance to grab something, but he ran across the street to a neighbor's house and pushed in their front door and put the dog down yelling at the occupants to protect his dog, call the fire department, and he would try to go back and see if he could rescue any belongings.

He started back across the street and then stopped midway. The house only had two walls standing, and then they came down. He went back inside the neighbor's house and used the phone to call Kip and tell him that the house was on fire, and they would lose everything. He yelled all of this into the answering machine and hung up as the firetrucks pulled up and began spraying water.

Kip and his girlfriend Becky arrived an hour later and were stunned. They thought that Tex had been kidding them, that it was a prank. The only things Kip had left were the clothes he had on his back, and some clothes and his new stereo that he had taken to Becky's house.

One of the firefighters talked to Tex and told him that he almost flipped out when he went inside to fight the flames and stepped on the waterbed. He thought it was a dead person who'd never made it out. The bed never ruptured. In saying goodbye to the house afterwards, Tex took his pocketknife and slit it open.

Later, he picked through the rubble and recovered a couple of old church pews and his two parachutes that had been covered with wallpaper that was blown off the wall by the fireman's hose and saved from the flames. His truck, a 1949 Chevrolet Panel truck, was his new home. He slept on various couches and in basements until he found a farmhouse at the county reservoir to rent until he graduated.

With that concluded and his bachelor's degree in hand, he moved to Michigan to teach school for a year in the Grand Rapids Zoo and then went to Vincennes University in southern Indiana, teaching adult education in churches, community centers, libraries, school cafeterias, and county jails.

Kip did well, got that internship and went to live in Annapolis, Maryland, and work for the Department of Justice, earning his Ph.D. along the way. He landed a swell assignment in Washington, D.C., as a psychiatric physician for the federal penitentiary system.

The two of them kept up communications with each other and they shared the goings-on of their careers and the building of their families. Both were married and had kids. Kip still lived in Annapolis and was able to buy himself a nice sailboat and frequently sailed the Chesapeake and went on weekend cruises with his wife and kid.

Tex and his wife were visiting the in-laws in Forest Hills in New York City, and they borrowed the car and drove down to Annapolis to visit Kip and his family. They reminisced about the old college days and re-hashed the story of the house fire. Looking back, they each sensed they had gained something from those memories.

"Things we had and things we lost," Kip said. "Some things we were just not meant to have, Tex."

"Well, I still feel a pang of loss from back then, still. *My brand-new guitar! A new 10-speed bike and especially my dog!* All the books in my theater library, those are the books I really wanted to keep. And then your stereo, thank God, that was saved."

"You can certainly have them, that doesn't mean you can *keep* them."

Kip said, "I'm heading to Bloomington this summer to do some work. What about you?"

"Surprise! I'll be there to finish some final classes for my master's. So, we'll have to hit Nick's, our favorite watering hole at Indiana University!"

Their plans were made, summer arrived, and they arranged a time to meet and get beers and strombolis at Nick's. Kip was standing by the door of the tavern, talking to a raggedy old man, and it looked like he was being panhandled. As Tex approached, Kip saw him, stopped their conversation, and introduced the old man to him.

"Tex, I want you to meet a man I know. This is Thaddaeus Balch. He was here at the campus to see me for some 'meetings' years ago." Kip turned back to him and asked him what he was doing in Bloomington. Thaddaeus seemed a bit hesitant to answer and Tex picked up the manner and beckoned the two men to come inside.

"Let's get a beer." He mentally guessed the whiskered old man was at least in his mid-70s.

"I can't stay long," he said. "I'm meeting someone right here and I'm headed out to California."

"Okay?" asked Kip.

"I got in a tight spot in Vincennes and got locked up. So, I've seen enough of Indiana for now."

"What were you doing in Vincennes? I used to teach down there," Tex told him.

"Not to put too fine a point on it, I'uz mechanicking in a tractor shop and had just drove back from California with a load of parts, and this man come in the shop and told the owner I'd shorted him on the delivery. Basically, calling me a thief! I done no such stuff, so I hit him on the side of his face with a tire iron I'uz holdin' and broke his jaw. He never called me a liar after'n that!" He squinted a little as he said that part.

Kip shook his head from side to side and put on his concerned face and looked at Thaddaeus. "We talked about that temper thing for a bit of time. I'm sure you remember. It's a matter of you getting back to checking your 'good choice' list before you go to swinging. Remember?"

"Yes, I do, but I'uz mad at the get go and didn't have a time to adjust myself, like you told me to do, I'm afraid. I been out of practice, I'm sorry to say. That mess has costed me a year and four months in Pendleton, on top of it all. Then I was 'hot' and failed my P-test and that give me some added time."

"Let's get back to better times. That hit you gave him was not going to get you a misdemeanor. It will be a *felony*. That's not good. I'm only here for a few days so I can't meet with you. What have you been into that I don't know about? You look plum worn out, Thaddaeus. Is that all?"

"Naw, Sir. I moved a couple of autos from place to place and they didn't have license plates on them, so's I got picked up for that."

"I hope you did NOT!"

"The man I done moved 'em for up to Illinois never told me they was stolen. I spent time in Joliet for auto theft and stayed with 'em till the penitentiary was about closed in seventy-two and they transferred me into Pendelton. That's how I got to Indiana."

Tex was sitting there drinking and listening. Kip was right in the middle of it.

"Wasn't there someone of your family that was around to help you out?"

"When I was first in Joliet and I told my kin about getting put in there, they all went to a meeting with other relatives of inmates to go through this program. So, I thought it might be a better shake than what I got in Vincennes.

"They told them to support me through my rehabilitation. You could have one visit a week. I went into this room, and they began their assessments and life skills development. I come out strong on mechanic and diesel mechanic. Hell, I could have just told 'em that!

"I'uz supposed to have positive friends and family who're law abiding to keep in contact while I'm incarcerated. Most of them were arrested themselves, for one thing or another, so that didn't help. After a while no one come to visit."

The three of them sat at the table and ordered beer by the pitcher, instead of by the mug.

"Then there was more troubles. The visitor application forms that was needed to be filled out weren't done right. Some of them—hell, half of them or more—don't know how to read and write very well and so they just left them blank. The ones that knew how to do the forms dwindled down till they stopped coming. And then, they'uz 'sposed to be puttin' some money in my bank, for me to get cigs at the commissary store. That didn't happen.

"That don't mind. I'm headed out to get a new job, so you take care of yourselves, and I'll get on down the road."

A pickup truck pulled up at that moment and he walked out and got in and they drove away. Kip and Tex sat there talking about him until the subject changed. They ate their strombolis and called it a night.

In a few days, they got back together again at Nick's and talked about the old ex-con, Thaddaeus Balch. Tex was fascinated to learn more about him and more about his story.

"How in the world did you ever meet that old man? Or maybe I should say, him meet you? Those old raggedy bib jeans he was wearing, with holes in them— he looked like he just crawled out from under a tractor."

"He probably did, knowing Thaddeus. He was one of my student interviews I did when I was finishing my practicum. He just showed up one day and I worked with him for, I guess, two years. And then he just showed up walking down the street outside Nick's and saw me. I didn't recognize him at first. He's really put some miles on him."

"Can you imagine—if he was in the *penitentiary* in Joliet until it closed, that must have been a rough go, huh? What did he mean when he said he failed his P-test? What is that?"

"I didn't want to ask him too much. He would want to hang on to me, now that he found me. Can you imagine after all these years? And then, he probably would have tried hustling me for some spare change and I'd be tangled up with him. No, no, no.

"And speaking of getting tangled up, you told me you were going into the jails in Vincennes and doing some teaching, you said. Hell, he could have been one of *your* students! How coincidental is that? That P-test he mentioned was what a parole officer or a corrections officer surprises an inmate to see if they're adhering to the terms of their release and not taking drugs."

"Sounds like he got caught."

They both chuckled at the thought of it.

"He knew what he was doing. He just never thought that he would get caught, that's all. He's not a violent sort of person. At least, he wasn't until he told us about smashing that guy's face in with a tire iron. When I knew him, and I would see him, he was pretty laid back."

"He doesn't sound so laid back now."

"When they first arrive at the prison, they go through categorization that sets the risk level a prisoner might pose to the public or national security should they escape, as well as the likelihood of their attempts to do so. He would have been at the lowest level and okay for open conditions, like freedom to walk the yard and all.

"So now his violence level has gone up and now he fails his P-test. He's got stuff going on. He's pretty old, Tex, as you can see, so he's not going to get much heat from other inmates that roam the yard, but he's still locked up for God knows how many years the next time he screws up. Some people come out and hang onto their freedom and some people cannot."

The summer ended and both men and their wives returned to their responsibilities—Tex and wife to Houston, and Kip went back to Annapolis and his work in Washington, D.C. No one wanted to admit it, but they were a bit older themselves, headed to their mid-life crisis years, and working way too many hours. They promised to keep in touch with each other, but it became almost an afterthought. Unless some serendipitous circumstance would bring them together, they resolved to send Christmas cards and made other such hollow promises as they continued to age. They were still counted as middle-class troopers trying to keep pace with the "Jones's."

The phone rang one evening in Texas and Kip's voice from D.C. was a surprise on the other end of the line. A birthday, a divorce, a wedding—the guesses danced about in Tex's head as they began to talk.

Tex asked how things were going up there in D.C. "Everybody all right, I hope? Good to hear from you!" and so on.

"I was just looking for an excuse to call you and reconnect. It made me think about your interest in that old client I had. We had a beer with him during that summer at Nick's, remember? How are you?"

"Dan Balch!"

"Almost got it. His name was Thaddaeus Balch. How you been?"

"I'm working for ITT, doing personnel work. Guess you are still into Department of Justice stuff?"

"Oh, yes, still here. Sailing when I get the chance. I was curious about someone. Actually, I should say, Thaddaeus Balch. I got a story for you if you've got the time. Well, from the time Thaddaeus left us at Nick's, I thought he was headed into some major trouble. Seems like what we thought about his situation was accurate."

Kip told Tex about what he was able to dig up through the Department of Justice's resources. The story unfolded, with Thaddaeus stealing a German shepherd dog and being apprehended two days later when a neighbor reported a dog's continual barking. It was noise complaint that got him.

"Thaddaeus was in the back yard with the dog and having a beer, a few beers if one counts. He had trouble trying to get out of his lawn chair because of the beer or because of his age or both. Because of his slurred speech and him trying to be aggressive with the officers who responded, they decided to enter his house through the back door and investigate further. There was a Pinkerton uniform hanging from the doorway and a holstered firearm and belt laying on the couch in the adjoining room.

"The officers questioned him to see if he had been on duty, and how long ago, suspecting he may have been drinking on the job. He told them he had not and became agitated during questioning, so he was handcuffed for his own safety.

"Returning to the house to look around further, they discovered that the firearm in the holster did not have a hammer, and so it would not be able to shoot a bullet. Questioned, he admitted he did not have a license for it and said he didn't need one. They became increasingly suspicious when he refused to produce his badge. In their search, they did find a badge attached to the uniform, but it was a fireman's badge.

"While one officer searched, the other continued to question the man about his dog and the suspect gave him two different names for the animal. The dog was wearing a harness that had a hard-handled grip attached to it. It was not a service harness used by and for security work. The harness that was attached was the type of harness used by seeing impaired or blind people. *It was a seeing-eye dog!* A call to the station confirmed that a report of a stolen shepherd did occur two days ago. Thaddaeus then admitted he stole the dog but would not say why.

"He was transported to the station and further interrogated and additional information came out. A search warrant was issued for the suspect's premises and upon their search, they pieced together what they believed really occurred and he was going to be arrested for bank robbery."

Tex was all agog at this news.

"Entering his bedroom, under his bed, officers found a newly painted sign with directions for how to make after hours deposits into the bank's deposit drawer, which was temporarily closed and located on an outside wall.

"The Pinkerton 'Officer' and his dog had been standing by the money chute in the evenings after hours and taking business transactions and currency from those businesses who drove up 'to deposit and protect their assets.' He was using a canvas bag and held it open for the depositors to use, until the repairs on the drawer were completed in a day or so."

The intrigue following the story continued to confound them. On the one hand, Tex had a ton of questions to ask Kip, since he was involved in penitentiary matters. The more Kip explained things, the deeper the story went.

Once the law enforcement investigators thought they had got things sorted out, more information kept coming out. So, the story continued for them.

The Statement of Charges or sometimes called the Court Charging Documents came next in the sequence of order that would be followed in processing this case. These are the pleadings that initiated the criminal charges against Thaddaeus Balch. The arrest documents and reports were used to build the case, and he was formally notified in his holding cell.

Charges can change, depending upon changing circumstances of other evidence coming to light. However, the opening move on the defendant's part is almost always to plead innocent, whether he is or is not.

In *medias res*, Thaddaeus had to obtain legal counsel as soon as possible after the charges were posted. In his case, he couldn't wait. Without money for a defense, he had to rely on a court-appointed lawyer. He chose Hiram Rudasill, a rather colorful and theatric ambulance-chaser, who years ago had been a prominent figure in a bank robbery but had since then fallen into obscurity—though Rudasill's former station with that case was emphasized to Thaddaeus when they met.

The opposing counsel for prosecution was Bicollani Nestor, who had recently joined the prosecutor's staff with a promotion from the court clerk's office. This meant that he had limited courtroom experience as the lead prosecutor. This was only his fourth case to prosecute in his new position.

The court charging document was presented.

THEFT. The manner of the crime: The theft was carried out by unlawful entry and trespass onto the property of Betrice Luhor, whose seeing-eye dog, Topper, was leashed and led away.

GRAND THEFT. Petty theft charges were upgraded to Grand Theft, due to the cost of animal replacement which would exceed $5,000, plus $3,000 in equipment, consisting mainly of harnesses. A felony conviction carries up to three years in county jail.

BANK ROBBERY. Entering any building with the intent to commit a felony or theft, crime, upgraded to Felony, Class 1.

ARMED ROBBERY. Committing an armed offense while using or brandishing a weapon or firearm.

FALSE PRETENSES. Any person who knowingly and designedly, by any false or fraudulent representation or pretense, defrauds any other person of money, labor, or property, whether real or personal, or who causes or procures others to report falsely.

ROBBERY. In California, robbery is the act of taking personal property of another, accomplished by force or fear. Charged under Penal Code 211pc [1] robbery is a crime of violence against a person and is therefore subject to California Three Strikes Laws.

WOBBLER LAWS: (To be argued) The defendant's criminal history would affect the decision and could cause a misdemeanor to be converted into a felony.

Kip read the charging documents over the phone to Tex, and they were both astounded by Thaddaeus's behavior. The first thing that put both of them in a spin was to find out that Thaddaeus *stole a seeing-eye dog from a blind person! What the hell?! A three-year felony for armed robbery? Bank robbery?!*

He never was in a bank, according to the charging document! What serious stuff was Kip seeing at the end of the document that made it worse? Would he be able to plea bargain later? Would he be able to have a bail hearing? More questions than answers.

One thing was certain. Kip wasn't able to get transcripts, only the summaries of the court proceedings. He told Tex to hang on. At last, he got on the computer and got the charging documents. Kip was currently involved in traveling to a couple of prisons to work and didn't have a set date when he would be finished. He might not be able to get more transcripts, just summaries.

Again, he told Tex to hang on. He had grave reservations about the outcome, and he said he would talk about that later.

Tex heard the bells of foreboding ringing in Kip's responses. He would have to wait. Now he started thinking about Thaddaeus's lawyer, Hiram Rudasill. Fingers crossed.

What was indicated in the newspapers about the trial and the jurors presiding was uneventful. Seven women and five men. No sense of any pros or cons. Average. Boring. Forgettable.

You could read the charging document and get the gist of the path of the trial. In the opening statements of Prosecutor Nestor, he went directly at Thaddaeus Balch and said he would highlight his actions and trace his steps throughout the two days he spent on the run before he was apprehended. He would also highlight his lack of remorse, his violent nature, and his violent past. He told the jury that he would seek the maximum sentence on each and every count of the indictment. The newspaper story for that opening day said that the prosecutor never blinked an eye. It was as Thaddaeus said, "Balls to the wall."

During this time, Hiram Rudasill watched quietly as the prosecutor laid out his case, made a note or two on his pad, and seemed indifferent to most of the opening day. "He was low key," quoted Thaddeus.

At the pre-trial hearing with Judge Ignacio Scardino presiding, Attorney Rudasill requested and presented a motion to dismiss, based on flaws present in the charging documents that were vague, non-specific, and patently untrue.

"Your Honor, it is full of inconsistencies. First, it's Robbery, then it's upgraded to Armed Robbery, then it's back to Robbery. You must have a person in front of you to rob them. In that case, Sir, it would be B.U.R.G.L.A.R.Y.

"Secondly, there is no proof that my client took any such dog from any property. If he finds that dog, or any dog wandering around and not on their own property, he was only being a good Samaritan by leading that dog to safety and then trying to locate the owner. The intent of the prosecutor was to unethically boost the charge against my client to a felony, when the misdemeanor, in itself, was excessive and I ask for dismissal.

"Thirdly, your Honor, armed robbery has not occurred and cannot occur if the perpetrator did not have a firearm that was used in the commission of the crime. A 'supposedly' weapon cannot be admitted into this courtroom. My client did not have it in his possession, did not brandish any such apparatus, and thusly, was not able to menace or threaten anybody. No such statements have been taken. No witnesses to the use of such a device by my client is hearsay. The object in question does not possess a firing pen, so by definition, it is not a firearm. My client is protected under the *habeas corpus* law and must be released immediately, your Honor."

Judge Scardino addressed each assertion of Defense Attorney Rudasill's pleadings.

"Testimony and evidence for each assertion and charge will be addressed at trial. That is what we are here for. There is scheduled testimony to decide the first and second count's validity or dismissal, so on Counts One and Two, motion to dismiss is denied.

"Counts Three through Six are interrelated and evidence was presented prior to this hearing and an arrest warrant was issued. Sufficient evidence was presented at the time of issuance to bind the defendant over for trial. Motion denied.

"Prior arrests consisting of two felony convictions deny defendant bail on remand. Gentlemen, let's go to trial."

They returned to the courtroom and the bailiff called the proceedings to order. "All rise. The Court is in session. The Honorable Ignacio Scardino is presiding. Please be seated."

Thaddaeus watched his counsel sit down, as he gave a muffled "Sorry, it's no" to his client.

The prosecutor simply restated his intent to convict Thaddaeus Balch on each and every count. He was joined at his table by two assistant district attorneys.

Defense Attorney Hiram Rudasill again restated what he tried to state in the judge's office. Thaddaeus was instructed by his lawyer not to speak, but to instead write down anything he wanted to say to him on a yellow pad. He tapped the side of his nose with his index finger as a signal that they were going to play it really "smart." Other than that, Thaddaeus was confused and just sat there.

"Oh, hell," Thaddaeus said under his breath as the first witness entered the room. It was the seeing-eye dog bringing in the blind woman, Betrice Luhor, and she took the stand. The jurors came to attention as she entered. How was she going to identify the defendant if she's blind?

She didn't have to. The prosecutor brought a mechanism that was mounted to a display board and asked her what it was. She put it in her hands and told him it was the mechanism that locked and unlocked her back gate.

"What is the significance of this lock?"

"It's a two-step lock that opens and closes my back gate. It locks magnetically. My dog would not be able to operate it. It takes a human hand to do it."

"Do you have a key for it?"

"No, Sir, that's precisely why I have it. My fingers don't work too well. I can use it from the alley side, and I never worry about losing a key. Any person can use it. It's a two-step lock."

There was no cross examination. She started to leave the courtroom, but the prosecutor asked her to return to the stand, pretending it was an afterthought. The jurors watched how the dog moved and how she handled it. Their sympathies were clearly with Ms. Luhor.

Grand Theft Count Two. She was asked about the harnesses she used with the dog, and she presented documentation as to how much they were worth. She had her Braille copy converted into type for the courtroom and the prosecutor entered it as evidence. It was submitted and she left. Again, there was no cross examination.

Bank Robbery was next. The prosecutor had the teller's sign with the erroneous information on it submitted for evidence. He then began explaining the scheme used to get after-hour payroll checks and monies by giving them to the "Pinkerton guard" and "his" dog "for deposit" because "the money chute was being repaired."

The defense pointed out that the deposit chute *was* in disrepair. However, they also pointed out that, although the defendant posted a sign and had a bag to receive the funds, no one "deposited" their funds with him.

Next, the prosecution brought out the Pinkerton uniform, the leather belt with holster, and added it to the evidence pile. At one point, the prosecution returned an item to the evidence pile, after talking about it, and it all slipped and went to the floor, simply making the unspoken assertion that the evidence is piling up. Then they placed the shiny badge atop it all.

Armed Robbery was next. Defense stated that upon inspection it was clear the firearm did not have a hammer and could not fire a bullet. Prosecution showed by reading the statute that the gun did not need to be able to fire. Having it in sight was enough to convince a reasonable person that a firearm was present and potentially lethal.

The prosecution restated the statute: In California, robbery is the act of taking personal property of another, accomplished by force or fear. In other words, the robbery does not have to occur; the law is enacted because of the *threat* of robbery, and that is all that the state needed to prove.

The worst blow was now delivered to Thaddaeus.

Charged under Penal Code 211pc[1], robbery was a crime of violence against a person and was therefore subject to California's "Three Strikes" laws.

The prosecution and the defense rested, and the jury left the courtroom to deliberate, to bring back a verdict of innocent or guilty.

Thaddaeus and his lawyer adjourned to a restaurant across the street, to wait for the verdict to come in. All their talk was casual and inconsequential. Thaddaeus said he was very tired of this trial and wanted to go back to his hotel and lay down. "I'm tired of not getting it and tired of not getting them breaks, like I used to could. I never had thought that I would get so jammed up, out here in California. Both of my other convictions came in Indiana."

"We'll wait for the next stone to turn over and see what we do, I guess," his attorney said, as an aside, not speaking directly to anyone or to someone specifically.

It was mid-afternoon on day three when the jury came back, after going home late on the second day. Verdict days were always subdued in courtrooms. Thaddaeus had seen enough to know that.

He didn't know too much about Wobbler Laws. He had heard they were some kind of special laws where a person's verdict could be enhanced if the trial had a bad outcome. "Pile on something else when you get someone beat down," he said. He had six counts. That was the most he had ever had in his life.

Everyone went back to the courtroom to hear the verdict read.

"I been to prison twice before," Thaddeus began telling his lawyer. "I'm guessin' that we ain't settin' too good, right at this point. I seen you just ever so slowly nod your head from time to time and it's side-to-side movin' and not up and down. What gives?"

"Thaddaeus, California's got some hellacious laws out here and Indiana got the same kind of laws there. The jam you're in will bring them to the fore and after the verdict is read, we'll get another crack at them, but that'll be at the sentencing.

"We don't have hardly any room unless you can catch a break. If the jury doesn't come back unanimously, we'll catch us a good trick, that's what I say."

"All rise, the Court of Judge Ignacio Scardino is back in session. Please be seated. Bailiff, bring in the jury. All rise."

It was the only time that Thaddaeus showed a grin, and he smiled to his lawyer as they watched them come into the courtroom. There was no sense in trying to read the jury. They were going to tell the whole verdict within a minute or two, anyway.

The judge asked the jury foreman if they had reached a verdict, and it was handed to the judge. He took a minute to read it and called for Thaddaeus to stand. He then read the six-count indictment, and he was found guilty on all six charges.

Things became blurry and disjointed for Thaddaeus. All he could hear was "*something, something*" and then he was led away. It was to be another six days before the sentencing hearing commenced and there were a few preparations needed.

The negotiations part of plea bargaining would be expedited, due to the prosecution's stipulations that the Three Strikes Laws would be sought and attached.

For the prosecution, their job was essentially over. They were appearing because of formality. The judge's clerks would prepare the documents and all he would do is read it. Any additional explanations that needed to be given to Thaddaeus would be explained by his counsel.

The Wobbler Laws had the ability to enhance or possibly reduce the sentence's impact on the guilty. It was a way to apply some sense of balance for extenuating circumstances. However, the "Three Strikes and You're Out" application negated any use of adjustment.

Indiana had the Three Strikes Law since 1994, as did California. Felonies committed in Indiana counted the same and were recognized by California. How it was supposed to work is by having the second felony conviction's sentence length be doubled upon the second conviction. Thaddaeus knew that. He served that sentence in Indiana.

Three Strikes Laws vary from state to state. However, California laws were very strict. Longer sentences made the third felony sentence mandatory with life without parole. Thaddaeus's felony theft could have gone either way, but this was a repeat offense, and one other offense was a second felony and now Thaddaeus Balch gathered six additional convictions.

Life without parole.

Jon Bunn

Reunion Until Death

Surreptitiously, a few small alabaster fingers eased over the edge of the ebony marble-topped bureau and hesitated, cautiously feeling the air for contact with the small objects it sought. Soon they were joined by other fingers, and then other ones appeared on the opposite side of the marble and encroached upon its opposites, searching for the same pieces.

Atop the flat surface were a few wheat pennies, Indian head nickels, Mercury dimes, and two or three Walking Liberty silvers. Some wadded gum wrappers lay close by, and the many fingers moved about like the legs of hunting centipedes crossing over the coinage and moving on to capture the gum wrappers with small jolts forward, and quickly retreating and crouching under the table, the murmurs of success rising from below. A small black velvet pinch purse was touched but left on the stand.

The clomping steps of women's thick-heeled shoes came closer and closer, and a mother's hands reached under and corralled the vagrants to complete their dressing in preparation for the Sunday school and church service at the Methodist Church a few blocks away. With the errant energies the kids displayed, it was decided that loading them in a car for the trip was preferable to having them walk down the hill to the church.

Boys got the hairbrush treatment, a scraping rake across the scalp with several strokes each that felt like they were being hit on the head to keep them still and quiet, before the tugs through the hair quit. The Sunday clothes came from nowhere and they were scratchy. The shoes were like clogs—they were not broken in and didn't bend like a regular shoe. They had to be tied into them.

The girls had shoes with straps, and they got to buckle their own. They would then go on the porch to play jacks. That was unfair to the boys, but the boys couldn't manage to get dressed in time to go play marbles. They had to just sit on the porch swing and wait for the grownups, so they could all go as one delegation.

It was church day. The morning for shuffling, clomping, squeaking, and creeping had begun. As everyone came inside the church, the double doors were flung open, and everyone proceeded. The sounds of many feet shuffling made unique noise—the wooden-heeled square-toed shoes struck the wooden floorboards and echoed like a timpani drum and blended with the cacophony of the eager congregants. The staccato of canes could be discerned. The crescendo of drumming feet and rustling skirts and murmurs of those attending began to ebb as folks sought their places and settled into the pews and choir risers.

The kids were led down the hallway and put into classrooms with little chairs. They had to listen to someone tell them stories about Jesus. They sang songs and had to pick out Jesus in the picture coloring books. They got to grow beans in Dixie cups and see them grow. Jesus was always in the center of the crowd and His hair always glowed. This was the easy part.

The tough part was to go to the church where the upright piano would play loudly, and everyone was always standing up and then sitting down. The wooden floor gave its responses. No kids could sing out of the hymn book, as they weren't old enough to read. So, they sat on the benches and swung their feet back and forth until it was time to stand up again.

When kids started getting fussy, the black velvet pinch purse would come out and each kid got some of the pennies or maybe an Indian head nickel to put into the basket plate that was passed around, and they would be rewarded with a little stick of Dentyne gum from Grandma. That little pinch purse always held their attention. They all got at least one penny from that purse to put in the plate. Always! But they never got to keep their pennies.

When Clyde was very young, about five years old, he got enough money together to buy his own pinch purse. They were sold at the drugstore for about four bits, and he could buy one with his own money. The trouble was his brothers and sisters would look around to find out where he hid his money. They planned to take it and divide it up between them. Clyde was very small for his age, but he was also nimble. In the front yard, close to where the family house was built, next to the freshwater well, grew a large and imposing sweetgum tree all the kids played on, and the chickens roosted in at nightfall.

Because Clyde was so small, he could climb up to the very top of it and nobody could catch him or get him, either. So, he took a tin can up into the tree to the farthest twig and stuck his can up there and that's where he hid his money, where no one else could get to it. He finally saved up enough pennies to buy that pinch purse and, beaming with pride, he rode his horse to town to the mercantile and went inside and bought him his own pinch purse. He stuck it inside his pocket and climbed to the top of the sweetgum to put his new pinch purse inside his tin can. Then, when he came back down to the ground, he began to cry. He was asked why he was crying. After all, he got his pinch purse and that was what he wanted, right? After the tears dried and went to sniffles, he explained to his brothers and sisters he was crying because he spent all his money on his pinch purse and had no money to put in it, not even a stick of gum.

Grandma Bunn had a hand fan she used to cool herself off, or to fan a toddler asleep beside her during church. The fan had a picture of Jesus on it and a picture of a funeral home on the other side. What was *that* message? Was Jesus going to die and then go to that funeral home? Old women and men sitting ahead in the front pews would glance back to see that the infants were sleeping and then flash a quick smile that the service might end.

Lots of people would show up at the family reunions and everybody would bring pictures. They would take them out of their pockets and show them around to each other and talk about them while they waited for the food to be set out.

How one learned about relatives was by these pictures. And the stories.

However, the grandkids were young, and no one was interested in a shoebox of black-and-white photos. They were mostly all dead people and those left behind were at the reunion. In the pictures, though, you could see what they looked like before they got old, grew chicken necks, and shriveled up.

It was an ordeal to have an uncle, aunt, or grandparent grab a young one and haul them into a crowd of people, where a speaker tried to keep his audience entertained with a story they liked to tell about that very young 'un. They would carry on until the victim wiggled out or the tale was finished, and they were let go. The kids were judged about how hot they were by someone looking at their dirt necklaces and by how much they dripped sweat on any elders that had the notion to grab and capture one or a few.

When they were finished with the kid, they would say something like, "Get yourself some iced tea and go sit yonder in the shade and cool off." Kids hated to be told to drink iced tea, even though it was in clay crocks in the shade, with large blocks of ice in them. Most of the grownups drank tea, but the kids did not because they hated drinking tea that was not full of sugar.

"Just go play."

And play they did. The Paine homestead was in the deepest part of East Texas, in Douglas, somewhere between Cushing and Mount Enterprise, in Nacogdoches County. Cushing was usually just shy of a hundred people on the census. It was a stop for a rail line that was put in to carry pine log timber and pulp wood. All the surrounding area was pasture for a few beef herds in good times and seed ticks in the timber stands. The Bunn farm was close to the switchyard about a half mile away from the town of Cushing. It had only one caution light flashing at the top of a hill.

When it was reunion time, everyone brought their favorite toys or games to play with. If not, there were always plenty of things to do with lots of cousins. Starting off, when pulling up under some of the shade trees, one of the first signs of community activity was the clanging of folks pitching horseshoes. Big, long jump ropes were used early in the day. Later the ropes were used to have tug-o-wars with. Nets were erected for badminton, dirt was cleared and smoothed down for the marble players—and you better have a few taws in your pocket. The ground that marbles were played on was very big, if one could imagine playing chase over a fifty-foot-wide field. Croquet anyone?

Inside, the house was full of activities for some of the younger kids who might be run over by the bigger ones. A clean and cool wooden floor on a porch invited pickup sticks and jacks, or playing cards, or playing dollies and dress-up. Outside, it could be bows and arrows for the older kids, or maybe slingshots.

Someone usually brought some cane poles to go fishing in the creek, between the deadfalls, if the water was running well. If not, you would need to get permission to walk into the cow pasture and go to the big water, the stock pond. You could at least go into the tall grass and chase grasshoppers for bait. There were rope swings to play on, some with wooden seats and some without. Anybody got an old tire to swing on?

Arm wrestling, hopscotch, hide and seek, tag, singing, playing musical instruments that someone might bring from their school band class back home (saxophone, clarinet, trombone, guitar.)

You might or might not see it at every reunion, but Chinese checkers were always a hit with adults and kids alike. Really old people would even play, as long as their eyesight was not too bad.

While the old pictures were making the rounds, someone went into the house and brought out the stereoscope. Last, but not least, someone came out of the barn on a tall pair of stilts and then the debate started as to which name to call them—stilts or Tom Walkers?

Kids, unbeknownst to them, were always in training. Some youngsters brought baseball gloves, and they played pitch, or they had full-on baseball games with lots of players. Kids some-times joined Little League teams back home, and they would pridefully wear their baseball caps to show off their success.

The kids who showed more endurance to the old people seemed to be the older children. It was a system of teaching the kids to display their better manners while in the company of others, the "Yes, ma'ams" and "No, sirs." Their capture and confinement within the elders were shorter. A saving grace was to have an elder or two, in the throes of feebleness or hard of hearing conditions that abated their restraint, as attention was always diverted to the comfort and feeding of the sages.

One such telling involved the grandkids asking Grandma Bunn about her teeth. It was an awkward encounter for the little ones to come running through the house and passing by the nightstand and seeing an entire mouthful of teeth resting on the table, in a fluted glass of water that magnified the object even further. Cautiously, someone did ask Grandma about how the teeth all got in the water in the first place and why did all her teeth come out at once, as their teeth were being yanked out with a string, one by one? Eat an apple and it will come out. Tie the string to your tooth and tie the other end to a doorknob and slam the door.

She gathered up all the disturbed ones and let them know that her teeth stayed in the glass, on the nightstand, so she could watch them, and they would not run away. Once all their eyes were sufficiently widened, she continued with her explanation and told them about them getting away from her at the church social one Sunday and someone saw them jump down the water well. When the bucket was lowered into the well for the teeth to climb in and come back up, they refused to do so.

"You all know how I like fried chicken, right?" Every moon-eyed kid was nodding with approval as she continued. "I had to catch them somehow. What I did was to get me a fishing pole and I used a fried chicken leg drumstick and lowered it into the well. As soon as they saw the chicken leg, they grabbed onto it and wouldn't let go and I pulled them up and grabbed them back. They like splashing and staying in water, so that's why I keep them in their own glass."

Another story that held traction for decades was the "Little Jonny and the rubber hatchet" story, where Grandma was almost scalped by an excited toddler. It was told without fail at each reunion that the family attended. It may have been told after she died as an homage to her full life.

The adults would sit around, usually congregants of mostly men in their areas and women in theirs. Men's talk was usually about their work, jobs, or hobbies, and the women's circles were more people-oriented issues and riding shotgun on the yearlings. Kids would all come to the reunions dressed in those scratchy church clothes, until they were seen by enough of the other attendees to surmise that they dressed up nicely—and then they were allowed to change clothes and go exploring along the creek or go poking around in the barn. The Paine homestead had a large barn. They had oxen. Someone, at some time mentioned that each oxen had their own name.

"If you fall in the creek, you'd better know how to swim," was the standard thing to hear. Getting muddy was tolerated, but a bit embarrassing to the kids to be stood up at the outside squeaking water well pump and splashed with cold water to get off most of the mud brought back to the people resting in the shade. They were the onlookers. A dipper hung from the well pump for getting a cool dip of water to drink.

The adult wisdom took over and the men and a few boys followed them to the high pasture through the hay field "to look over the place." Then the questions began—"How did you all get so muddy? Who really knows how to swim?"

Then someone said, "I can teach them how to swim. Clyde, I bet you learned how to swim just like the rest of us did." Clyde nodded, "Jonny, come over here, it's time you learned, just like how we learned." And he grabbed Jonny and threw him in the pond, clothes, shoes, and all. They all laughed and thought it was funny and watched him struggle and thrash about. To Jonny, it was like being put at death's door.

Between laughs and guffaws, and "Oh, he's fine. See there, didn't hurt a bit," Jonny's swimming lesson became another story for the reunions yet to come.

They were all men who had come back from World War II. They proved, by coming back, that they were masters of their own fates and were stamped by indelible struggles to persevere as they saw fit. They earned it. Some had external scars, some not. Some had internal scars. How could you see something you couldn't see? Over time, you could.

It started out as "opinion," then "directions," then "orders," "threats," "shoves," "spanked with a hand," "hit," "switched," "a stick," "a belt," "a rope," "a whip," and a fist. The exuberance to embrace that survival, that ordeal, that win back home, energized America to go forward into the future however one wanted. It was "might makes right" and they proved it on the battlefield and then they brought it home. If we were tough, then you'll be tough, was the thinking. That dedication turned into determination. Some left for war with nothing and then came home with nothing and had nothing. That pox passed on to infect others. The divide between the "haves and have nots" widened.

"We will be equal someday, but you're behind me." Separate but equal percolated.

That determination drove many parents to take matters into their own hands and see that their children would benefit from their leadership. No slackers permitted. The British had the saying, "Steady as you go, stiff upper lip." And there was always the adage, "Spare the rod and spoil the child." Corporal punishment was given out and the application was delivered by hand or instrument. "Go outside and stand by that tree, prepare to get your whipping." "You've got it coming ... you *earned* it." "Go cut me a switch ... and if it's not big enough, I'll choose one for you ... and if you run from me, I will give you twice the beating when I catch you." "If I ever see you doing that again, I'll beat you within an inch of your life. I brought you into this world and I can take you out." Such endearment for your kids.

The wife had better go along with the program, too. If not, it may not turn out well for her, as well. "If he drinks whiskey, then you drink whiskey."

That kind of living then brought forward children who were brutalized as they grew up and were indoctrinated with physical and mental pain, having to accept the indoctrination as acknowledgement for survival. The trouble was, they grew up and the scars you could not see, you would then see. It leaked out.

"My dad whupped up on me as a kid and I was better for it. I grew up just fine. Look at me now! Look at what I have become." It was an expressed fealty given by false submission.

"I am the head of my household and what I say goes. Period."

"If you get into a fight at school, you better win. If you come home after losing a fight and got whipped, you have another whipping coming when you get home."

"If he's bigger than you, hit him harder than he hits you. If he's twice as big, hit him twice as hard."

Teachers and coaches at school were given tacit approval to paddle a student for any real or imagined infraction. Get beat at home or paddled at school. The coaches were especially zealous. They had to win football games, basketball games, and win at track meets. Without those strong results, the coaches would find their job security in jeopardy. Female coaches would be on the same hook to produce those shining wins, or they would be sent back home to return as a domesticated wife, damn the time and energy that was needed in those days to get the training and education to be certified to teach, *for 70% of the pay of male teachers.*

School districts looked to find that "woman teacher" that would get the results they were hired to get and were not hardly worth their salt if they couldn't paddle a girl student and make an example of them, burnishing their reputation. What a delight it was to find a rule infraction that would earn a cheerleader a couple of swats with the "personal paddle" used for special incidents and effects on a promising debutante—with a special "legendary" paddle that was always on the desk or hanging on the wall—for not picking up a towel and throwing it in the clothes bin, inadvertently, and having the gossip mill run amok and told all over the school by the next class period.

Fortunately, a student's fate varied by district and tax bases. A better school costs more in tax dollars to attend those schools. The breaks given to teachers and students favored the well-to-do. Better pay for teachers and expanded learning for students produced better outcomes for both. Graduation rates were higher, and college acceptances improved.

The "Land of the Free" was earned through fighting the bloodiest war in history. However, moms, sisters, and daughters did not buy into that bargain very much, because when it was all over, they were pushed away from the table, lost their jobs, and sent home to "be the little Mrs." It did not benefit the thousands of Black and Brown soldiers who fought and died for the same freedoms, which for them became freedoms denied.

When young, no one paid the slightest bit of attention to the kids. Behind that door was your parents own personal business, until you got older, grew up, maybe had kids, and then tried to find out something about their heritage. It was for grownups. Hidden family secrets might be discovered. In today's world, computers took over the heavy lifting that occurred in trying to look at past papers and documents that once were only gleaned from countless hours and days spent in libraries, old Bibles, photographs, newspapers, and other archives.

Soon afterwards, when the elders began to pass on, those old boxes of photos and memorabilia that seemed to have little value other than emotional attachments became important, vaguely, to a few of the related kin and the curious. Some were put away for "later," but many were thrown away or passed on to Goodwill or the Church. It was the original beginning of the data dump.

The creation of Ancestry.com aided in the illumination of lost and forgotten sources. How did your parents grow up? Where did the family originate? How did your granddaddy raise them? And then how did they raise you and your brothers and sisters? Is that why you turned out the way you did? Attending the family reunions was a chance to ask those questions and more, but it was a major hurdle to seek enough information to find out when any ancestors came to America and where they came from, where they went to, and where they settled. Where were they buried?

The pictures that were always taken out of the pockets and purses and passed around were fine clues to have. However, the person who knew anything about the persons, places, or animals in the snapshot had to be alive and also possess good faculties.

This was the beginning of the times that the Family Bible was brought out and select people were allowed to hold it and look at the family trees filled in with all the people you never knew anything about and them about you. Who knew that there was *even* a Family Bible? The center of the ancestorial family resided within the caretakers of that Bible. When was it that you were handed that Bible to hold for the first time?

They will arise from that beckoning and may allow you to seek forth.

"Take care of what you seek," someone always says. These people, however, will already be dead, okay? Alright.

The "dark" secrets that resided in obscurity may then be "remembered" and light shed on distant and perhaps dismal events. Things you never were told. Things that maybe you didn't want to know. Vestigial remnants meant to stay buried. But now that "they" are long dead, the secrets can be revealed, brought back into the light, rediscovered, and once again perhaps, later they will submerge back into the ocean of obscurity like Captain Ahab's white whale. Medical matters created interest in ancestry in later years. Ancestry connects and re-ties lost ties more and more these days.

John Marshall Bunn and Bina Electra Paine were our favorite grandparents, whom we loved since our births. They were married in Nacogdoches County in Texas and settled in the small town of Cushing, within walking distance to the town square and three blocks to the all-grades public school with the natural iron-rich stone façade. It was located by the neighboring communities of Reklaw and Sacul; their town names intentionally spelled backwards by the people that founded them, the Walkers and the Lucases.

Two major time periods were necessary to learn the story about them. As grandchildren we learned bits and pieces from their pasts but were never curious at that age to learn much more. This is the beginning time, let us say as "Period One."

John Marshall Bunn, born February 4, 1875, came from southern Alabama and Bina Electra Paine Bunn, born February 28, 1885, came from Douglas, Texas, where the Bunn/Paine reunions were held for many years.

The town of Cushing itself was founded in 1902, and by 1904 the Texas and New Orleans Railroad added train and passenger service, and it was known as a railroad town. John Marshall and Bina Electra got married on her birthday, February 28, in 1904, the same year the train came to town. At that time, about 300 to 400 people called Cushing home on a permanent basis; it was about a mile square. Its population profile remained steady at 95% White.

John and Bina were farmers. Bina was active in the church social activities, was in a quilt sewing circle, and worked alongside John as much as she could. He plowed his land, about three acres right outside the back door, and worked as a butcher when someone brought over animals to be butchered and dressed. His other plot of three acres was just up the road from the house, a quarter of a mile or so. It was always plowed by hand.

Here was a man who never owned any car, gas tractor, mower, or other contraption, like a gasoline washing machine, at least until electricity came up the road and the house was later wired for it. He walked and worked on his land every day, except Sundays.

He wore striped suspenders, cut a chew from a brick of Bull of the Woods with his pocketknife, and liked to take the evening air sitting in an old ladderback cow leather seated chair under a very large sweetgum tree after the day's work had ended.

The last horse that pulled a plow on his land was named Bob. Bob was also the only transportation to get back and forth to and from the town, which was down the hill.

My grandfather would hitch up Bob and go to town for shopping and to get his mail from the very small post office in his little metal mailbox, that had little dials on the front to dial the combination that opened the little door. Mounted into the little door was a small, beveled glass window with a number painted on it so that you could see if you had a piece of mail, so you didn't have to open that little bitty door to see if you had any little bitty mail.

The feed store, the barber, the grocery store, and the butcher shop were all next to each other and the horse tie-up hitching rails were right outside. A notions store and a drug store/soda fountain were across the street, as well the hardware/tack store. The feed store smelled of molasses oats, alfalfa hay, harness and saddle leather, and manila rope, and these smells were always in the air. This was where you went to pick up your cardboard boxes full of chicken biddies, as the post office could not accept them when they were mailed; the lobby was only big enough for four people to stand inside.

John Marshall and Bina had five kids—Marshall, Wanda, Hilda, Jon Clyde, and Charles.

Grandmother did have a sixth child that was a boy who died on Valentine's Day. Where this bit of information was discovered or revealed may have come from burial records or an extra headstone in the graveyard. And the child died before he could be given a name. This was not an unusual event, at the turn of the century, to lose an infant. A home birth was a regular event in East Texas.

A whistle-stop community would hardly hold a doctor to live in the town. A circuit doctor was the norm. A home birth or death, this was the hidden bit of family history that was never shared.

It was a shocking discovery, but let's go on now with the end of the story after the hidden tragedy was found and everyone in the family got the shock of their life to hear about the "forgotten" death of grandma's child.

Jon Clyde used to ride behind Granddaddy, behind him on the skirt of the saddle when they went to town. Coming down the hill on horseback into town, a small tin building on stilts stood over a small stream and a few old men were always either playing moon or dominoes, and their rattling and stirring up the domino pieces made clicking noises that could be heard a block away. Grandaddy would stop to tip a hat and exchange pleasantries, forecast the weather, and occasionally see his small boy peek around from behind him to look at the idle men. They gave Jon Clyde the moniker "Spook." Their horses were tied to the rail, and they seemed to always present a picture of utter boredom, or being half-asleep, and would hardly crank their necks and turn their heads when he rode up to exchange those pleasantries. Their horses stood around and also looked bored.

Many decades later, it was Spooky's kid that rode into town on a few occasions with his granddaddy to get mail, and like his father before him was seen peeking around from behind Grandpa Sugar, and the men would ask him, "Say, is that Little Spooky you got there?"

On one of those rides to town to get mail, when Grandpa took "Little Spooky" with him, he went into the butcher shop to get some bacon and stew meat. He told his grandson to ask the butcher if he might have a bone he could have for his little dog, Chi Chi, his chihuahua. The butcher and Grandpa were exchanging side glances and smiling at each other.

The butcher smiled back and said he would wrap it in white freezer paper for him to take home for his doggie. The package of meat from the butcher seemed like a lot. When they got home and took off the saddle, fed old Bob and watered him and went into the house, they unwrapped the package. As it turned out, the butcher had given him the knee joint from a cow, and it was as big as the dog itself. Everyone at the kitchen table got a big laugh at the dog bone.

We kids almost did not have a dog at all. When we showed up one evening with the dog in the car at the grandparent's farm, Grandma said the dog would have to sleep outside for the night and could not sleep in the house. And so, when nighttime came, the dog had to be put outside in the ink-black night in a chicken coop and he started barking and crying to be let out. We kids began crying with the dog and would not stop. The ruckus continued until Grandma gave up, relented, and said that the dog could come inside for the night. It made the outside a scary place to go.

The barber shop was next to the butcher shop, and it was where Grandpa took all the young grandsons to get their haircuts. They had to sit on a board seat, which was laid across the arms of the barber chair.

Grandpa was a man of about 5' 7" and he was never upset at anything or anyone. He brought in from the pasture a pie-bald calf to nurse, or attend to in some way, and grandson Jonny—that's me—went to the barn to see the goings-on. The little calf was very small and a few days old. I rubbed and petted on him, and the calf licked me with his pink, raspy tongue, and I bottle fed him. He was as sweet as sugar and then I started calling my granddaddy "Sugar," too, as that was his nickname. I was about four or so years old. To us kids, Granddaddy was Sugar Bunn.

Stepping off the porch and down three steps to the yard put you close to the barbed wire fence where we stepped through, between the four-strand barbed wire and went to pick food: beans, peas, okra, carrots, tomatoes, eggplant, potatoes, and corn. We hulled a lot of peas before we had meals there. Cantaloupes and Black Diamond watermelons. They picked corn when ripe and we got to shuck it and throw the hulls and shucks over the fence for Bob to eat. One year, Grandaddy Sugar planted big watermelons that were lighter green in color, and they had dark stripes going down the sides. Several grandkids stood around and watched Grandaddy go up the steps onto the back screened in porch and get one of those stripey ones, which had been picked that morning and was put in the shade to stay cool from the hot sun for the afternoon feast.

He cut the watermelon long ways with a butcher knife, and everybody was stunned that the watermelon was not the least bit red. It was bright yellow, like a cantaloupe. All the grand-kids were wondering what it would taste like—would it taste like cantaloupes? It was very sweet and tasted like the sweetest watermelon ever. A yellow watermelon!

It was always a delight to get to feed Bob the rinds. He stood at the fence and watched all the little ones and the grownups eating watermelons in the afternoon, under Grandpa's favorite sweetgum tree. Black-eyed pea hulls and other bean hulls would be on his menu, too. Corn on the cob, even.

One day when he was gathering food to cook, Granddaddy went to get fresh corn and stepped through the fence with a basket for the ears—and then he began yelling. He had gotten through the barbed wire and went into the house, holding his arm, rocking back and forth, and yelling loudly, which fright-ened us kids.

He had shucked an ear of corn to see if it was ready to pick, and as he did that, he had grabbed a scorpion with his hand and he was badly stung. We kids were about ready to cry, seeing our Grandaddy Sugar cry. It was frightening to see, and we were afraid. It was the first time I can remember ever seeing or hearing a grown man cry. The memory of it makes me shudder.

He was a peanut farmer extraordinaire. His timber log barn could hold bushels and bushels of dried peanut plants, he would hold in to dry out. He filled the cribs, too, all the stalls, and the hayloft with peanut plants, with the peanuts still on them. After they dried, he would pick off the peanuts to sell and then have peanut hay to feed Bob in the Fall. Inside the barn, the peanut plants would fill the air with a fragrance that was like the smell of a hayloft full of alfalfa, but a little more earthy. He would let us grandkids go to the barn to play, but didn't want us eating lots of drying peanuts, because he said it would make our tummies hurt.

He told all of us to watch for the pretty corn snake that lived in the barn and ate the mice that came into the barn to eat the peanuts. The snake would come around when Granddaddy went to the barn to milk a cow, when she was fresh, and he put out a saucer of milk and the snake would drink it.

Grandaddy Sugar told us kids about him going out to the barn to harness up Bob for plowing and he found him in his stall all lathered up and sweating with foam falling off him and the first thing Sugar said was that Bob would not be plowing today, that he was very tired and would rest for the day. He said that what happened was the witches had come into the barn the previous night and harnessed him up and rode him across the sky and wore him out, and that's why he was all lathered up.

We were all *amazed*, and as proof, he showed where the little witches rode Bob on his back over the moon and showed us where the witches made stirrups to put their feet in from the hair on the withers—they were tied into little loops!

A change occurred to the farmhouse with the addition of a room added onto the back of the house. It was an inside bathroom, complete with a sink that had hot and cold faucets, running water, and a porcelain bathtub. It was the bathtub where we learned about intrigue. Staying at the farmhouse overnights meant that when the nighttime fell, and it was time to go to bed, we would get a "thunder jar" placed under our noisy spring coiled mattress for us to use, instead of us walking through the house on the linoleum floor to the back of the house to go to the restroom.

This was the time for the scorpions to come out on the floor and go hunting for food. We didn't want to get one of our toes, one of our little piggies, caught by mistake and stung, like when it happened to Granddaddy. We were scared to even put our feet on the floor ... at all. The grownups got to have real flashlights on the nightstands, next to their beds. Grandparents also had those waterglasses on their nightstands that held their teeth. It was still a bit spooky.

When the bathroom was built, the walls were built with tongue and groove boards, and in the beginning it was a place where scorpions could hide in the walls and wait till dark to come out. They could crawl around on the walls at night unless they lost their grip and fell to the floor or in your bed.

The solution they thought of was to cover the walls with wallpaper and cover the cracks up. Then the scorpions had to go somewhere else, but they didn't. They stayed. We knew this because Grandma called us to come into the bathroom to show us a scorpion that was trapped in the bathtub. It could crawl around at night with no problem, until it crawled onto the porcelain, and it would lose its footing and slide into the tub and would be trapped. We could see it *really* well! Then we got nervous about taking a bath ... ever. Still, from then on, we always jumped out of bed the first thing in the morning to see how many scorpions we had captured. What an adventure.

One morning it happened that we found one lively one in the tub and we went into the kitchen to tell Grandma, who already had bacon and eggs ready for us to have breakfast. It was then we heard the bathroom door shut and lock, and the water start to draw in the tub. Between bites, we tried to tell her about the big scorpion in the tub and she laughed and said she hoped Granddaddy didn't sit on it, and we could check on it after he finished. We couldn't wait.

As we waited on Grandpa, we could hear his wrinkly butt scooting across the tub as he bathed, and his butt on the porcelain seemed to squeak and chatter as he scooted around. We started laughing and having the greatest time, waiting for him to get out, so we could go in and check for scorpion parts.

When the scorpion story was retold, the conclusion was the grandchildren thought that they would surprise Grandpa Sugar with something special the next day, and so we went into the yard after dark and caught lots of fireflies we put in a jar, and we noticed a partial roll of linoleum standing on end that Grandpa Sugar laid his jeans and shirt over before going to take a bath earlier. We hid the Ball jar down in the roll and took off the jar top and let all the fireflies hide beneath his clothes, so when he got up the next day to dress and go to plow, all the fireflies would rise from the center of the tube and escape, and he would see all the pretty lights coming out and lighting up his day.

John Marshall Bunn passed away in 1964 and Bina Electra Paine Bunn followed several years later in 1975.

There is a time within a duality of searching and learning about one's ancestors where the lack of interest in the past gradually changes and the search for context and meaning of those past lives becomes fulfilling, as the bits of history and family emerge from that shadowy past. It may provide some touchstones that bring context to one's contemporary life. It is reaching out to past loved ones to cherish their memories, if for no other reason than to be a link and expression of love or affection that time does not break, and it brings an inward peace of mind.

Grandpa Sugar was such a person, and he was deserving of his life's mark of respect and family's esteem. He knew about his own beginnings. It was not a secret that had to be gleaned. He knew he grew up and came to Texas as a kid from his birthplace which was in Ashland, Clay County, Alabama. And so, it was a surprise to learn about people in Alabama inviting any Texas descendants of the Bunn ancestors to attend a reunion of Alabama folks.

It was to be held at the family homestead in the middle of the Talladega National Forest, inside the State Park, at the top of the Talladega Mountains. A Bunn relative, who happened to be the town's postman sent us directions for finding the location of the original stone foundation. He said we should ask the Park Ranger at the entrance for help if we needed it.

We went down the park road and when we saw a trail that parted the trees, that would be our entrance. An old sign that was dragged to the opening said, BUNN SAWMILL. That was it. It was down a fire trail. We found people and the cars they drove into the forest parked akimbo. No one from Texas had ever come to Alabama for a reunion since they'd left to go buy land and settle in Texas at the turn before the 19th century. They knew vague bits and pieces of history of the Texas Bunns before the connections dissolved, due to family deaths and other migrations.

We were led into the woods and found a freshwater stream pouring out of the ground, covered with a piece of barn tin that protected it from getting clogged by falling leaves over the years. This was the drinking stream for the ancestors. We drank from that spring and gave prayerful thanks to the Lord for His works.

Inside the forest of parked cars, someone drove in a recreational vehicle and from that vehicle, they brought out the sacred Bunn Family Bible and I was given the nod to hold that sacred book in my lap and I held it carefully, turning the pages, I saw plates of the family trees and the names and dates of distant relatives, long ago passed on.

They knew about the little boy named John Marshall Bunn. Someone told the well-known tale about the day they loaded up and took the train ride to Texas and they said their goodbyes. They almost missed the train because John Marshall, still a child, became scared of the train and all the steam puffing, so that he ran off into the town and hid under the board sidewalk and wouldn't come out. He explained that he saw a man walking on top of the railcars as the train went along and he was afraid that they would make him ride on top, as well.

As old timers are wont to do, some stood in a circle and got out their pocketknives and whittled sticks. Someone else went to the group and showed them something truly rare. It was three or four American chestnuts they found under a tree, in the forest we stood in. The trees are exceedingly rare, and the Bunns were still the protectors and guardians of that secret.

Before we went into the forest to see the ruins of the old family homestead, we spent the night as guests and the postman and his wife drove us to the cemetery and showed us the grave and headstone of Grandpa Sugar's grandpa. It was an obelisk about five feet tall and someone pointed out that the top finial was missing. As a coincidence, they looked about many years' prior and found that it had been taken from his headstone marker and was put on top of another's gravestone. "Borrowed" into eternity, I suppose.

So, the Alabama family had secrets. And the Texans had secrets—the "secret" that was discovered about the death and burial of Infant Bunn on Valentine's Day in 1918. It was tragic in its singularity and as a life's burden. The child's life was always lived as a memory and carried in Bina and John's hearts.

Watching the water flow from the spring, someone asked, "Did you know about the plantations?"

Shine, Mr. Sun

Shine, Mr. Sun. Awaken me in the morning.
Grow this world through another beautiful day.
Lay a cool mist in the valley,
And put in some rabbits that will hop and play.

It's the white rose that grows along the fence line,
And it's so pretty growing through the wagon wheel,
Sharing its beauty all along the pathway
That leads to the gate we must all pass through.

Shine, Mr. Sun. Lead me in the daytime.
Light my path so I don't stumble or fall.
Raise up some flowers, a field of black-eyed Susans,
That sway in the breeze, when evening calls.

GUITAR BREAK

It's the white rose that grows along the fence line.
And it's so pretty growing through the wagon wheel,
Sharing its beauty along the pathway
That leads to the gate we must all walk though.

Shine, Mr. Sun. Send me a ray from heaven,
Where the sky's always blue and there is no grey.
Spin this world around, for a new day's dawning,
And white clouds are floating through another beautiful day.

GUITAR BREAK AND END

Jon Bunn

The Eternity of Time

I relish the day when I go away,
And my bones drift into sand,
That the breeze across my mouth,
Blows the heat to my hand.

The sky is open as I sail away,
Unto a foreign land,
And my consciousness remains with me,
To know that life was grand.

Explode me into the skies above,
Swirl me with the stars,
Make my grains into the constellations,
Glimmer with my au revoirs.

Access me to the galaxies,
That swirl beyond time,
As I thank the Maker of all the stars,
To caress the eternity of time.

Little Spooky

This irony has slipped by me for decades, and it's a small reality that I have recently captured, now that "past" is an "old past" that comes to me when I hear the word "spooky" spoken. From early on, I know it as my dad's childhood moniker, back in the day when Grandpa Sugar sat him behind on the saddle skirt, as they rode Bob the horse to town to buy food and get the mail. They would stop to watch some dominoes or moon being played at the edge of a gully that usually showed signs of moisture.

That ethereal passage of "Spooky" slipped away from him, as Spooky got older, and gained a little more in height. I might say he was the runt of the family and stayed that way. I was not going to be anybody's runt, and certainly not his.

I now know when my visage was established. It was when I was carried to town on Grandpa Sugar's saddle skirt and the domino men saw me and mistook me for him, my father, who was "Spooky" as a child.

It has always been buried in a long-ago distant memory. I never wanted to accept being called "Little Spooky," once I grew some awareness of its attachment to "Big Spooky," my father. I just liked to ride with Grandaddy Sugar on Bob, and I rejected the garbage others may have wanted to attach to me. Back then, I never knew I could do that.

My sister, Kelly, is a mere 4' 10". He was 5' 4". A few years later, I grew to 5'10". Never, I hoped, would I ever be in his shadow again.

Jon Bunn

The Complete Tangiers to Costa Rica Grace Baptist Temple Broken Down Blues Bus

Slipping and sliding through the first few semesters of college was an eye-opener. I took two summer classes before I was allowed to have a full academic load. In the meantime, a clock was ticking for lots of young men, like me, who were graduating high school and staring the military draft down. Either go and get it out of the way or go to college and get a college deferment.

I learned too late the intricacies of registering every semester to get next semester's classes and keep a full-time student deferment status. If you slipped, Welcome Vietnam! I missed by one class, and I watched my deferment status go away. There was a clamor going with the draft system, how it chose "recruits" by taking the eligible ones beginning with the first letter of their last name, starting with A, then move on to B, and so on until you had the military quota filled. My last name with a B would send me to the front lines pronto. A court ruling came that put ALL first letter of last names in and then a random drawing would continue. I drew a #46, maybe good. Oh, wait! It was a #26 … I'm being drafted to go to Vietnam!

I finished my next semester and waited to go to work offshore to work in the Gulf oilfields and make some badly needed tuition money. A high school buddy and I got the idea that we would try and stay state-side and join the National Guard. I wanted to go to the Air Force National Guard. The only unit we could find was in Terre Haute, Indiana a couple of hours away. "We have our quota already, unless you want to stand at the front gate and try and get in that way. You would need to be here and at the gate by 6 a.m."

We left in the middle of the night to make the 3-hour trip. We were at the very front of the gate when it opened. The guard said, "The last spot has just been filled, sorry. The guy that got it was named Dan Quail. Do you know him?" We both drew a blank then and then years later the name came up again, Dan Quayle, Vice President to President George H.W. Bush. Dan Quayle, Mr. "Potatoe" Head himself!

My draft papers were on my desk when I got back to Bloomington. I just counted the days and wondered what kind of life I was about to have. Some of my classmates were already coming back. They were coming home with flags covering their coffins. War is HELL!

I caught the bus that morning on the town square. It looked like a walking funeral. I knew several of the others. And everyone there knew Mable Whorley, the one at the selective service office on the town square in Bloomington, who handed out the draft notices.

The drive to Indianapolis was without comments. Maybe they were thinking, like I was, *Lots of us will never see home again.*

The Drill Sargent met us at the bus when we arrived and started barking orders, "Line up, take your orders, and follow me, single file and no talking."

I wondered how long it would be before they took off all our hair. We stripped and got our examinations. One of the doctors came and pulled me out, saying, "Follow me."

They took me to a small audio room and put headphones on me and said, "When you hear the beep, press the button." I pressed the button and after a few minutes the man told me that his machine might be broken and he held me out from the rest of the induction physical and I had to see an audiologist the next day, so I had to spend the night. I rejoined the other recruits and put my clothes back on, went to another room, and stood at attention, waiting for the sergeant to reenter the room.

He came with an aide who carried thick manila packets and began saying, "As I call your name, you will step forward one step. That step will signify your entrance into the United States Army." He called names, one by one, and everyone stepped forward. He didn't call my name, and I stood in my place and did not step forward. He clearly saw me out of line, so then he got really worked up and asked my name and where was my brown envelope? His aide stepped forward and gave him my folder. He took a glance at it and dismissed me immediately from the room.

As I left the room, I glanced back. All of those young men were standing at attention in line, saluting the flag. In unison, they all took one step forward.

I went to another building and checked in, got a cot, and sat there until supper time. Ate, went to bed. The next morning, I went into an audio box, took another test, and was then interviewed by another doctor. It was my hearing.

"You have a hearing problem. Why is that?"

I then related to him the firecracker explosion I was in, just before I entered the 12th grade, where I was severely burned on my hands. The medical doctor that bandaged me up afterwards sent his paperwork/reports to the Indianapolis doctor. That was it. I was hearing-impaired and the loss was too great to allow me to serve in the U.S. Army. I was sent home, back to Bloomington.

Well, okay then! Now what to do? The school semester had started, all my belongings were stored in a few boxes in a basement. I surprised my buddy when I showed back up, two days after everyone had written me off. He had some feet issues that had stopped his induction as well, and he said to me, "Let's go somewhere, like Europe."

I was thinking that would work. We had to plan this out and get some money together for tickets, for immunizations, and backpacks. We were going to take off and hitchhike around for a couple of months, maybe. Some one of our friends had read *The Drifters*, by James Michener, the novel that follows six young characters who meet and travel parts of Spain, Portugal,

Morocco, and so on. The story got us and so we went to work to get capital and camping gear. Richard and Willie got one model of a backpack, and I chose something different. We had to apply for passports and get them before we could head out.

Who cared that we couldn't speak a lick of any other language except English? Of course, we could speak about ten words of some other language between us. And I'm sure we spoke them while in Europe. Pretty sure, I think.

Willie worked for his family who owned a stone quarry, Richard was a boat mechanic at the local reservoir, and I was a roofing carpenter. We saved our dollars, read Michener, and took off in October. None of us had much money—a few hundred was all each of us had and so, to get to Europe, we went in the middle of the night and flew stand-by. The tickets were $168, round trip to Luxembourg and back.

Everything else was either traveling on our thumbs, the rails, busses, and Eurail passes. We had it all worked out. We'd go everywhere we wanted to go, and just hop on the train, use our Eurail passes, and sleep on the train for free till we got off the next morning! How simple was that?

After a week of hanging around the biergartens in Munich, we met a guy who wanted to join us knocking around. He had been living in an apartment on the Plaza Mayor in Madrid. We just called him Alaska, as that was where he was from, and he hung onto me because I was Tex.

We were trying to find one of our buddies who was stationed on the Army base at Nuremburg. Got on the wrong train, stayed too long on the train, something. We got separated. Alaska was with me; Willie and Richard went poof. The only contact we had for each other, once separated, was to travel to the train station in Madrid seven days away, at noon, to re-hook up. No addresses for any of us, no phones, no mail.

I stayed in a cramped little space on the floor in Barcelona for the week, waiting for noon to come on the seventh day. It was a terrific city. I discovered paella and great seafood!

Nobody told us that there were TWO train stations in Madrid. We never made the connection. I went to one station, and Richard and Willie went to the other, and as I learned later, they went on to the southeast coast of Spain after that and got a villa.

I got stuck with Alaska and I headed to North Africa and stayed for several weeks in Morocco, and then we went to Tenerife and Las Palmas in the Canary Islands. Someone gave me an extra train ticket they weren't going to use, and I took it and traveled to Lisbon and Portugal, and then I flew back to the U.S. via LaGuardia Airport in Queens, New York, and then I hitched from there to Indiana and on to Bloomington.

✳ ✳ ✳

Being out of college and not having earned enough funds to continue was a seesaw, up and down experience. The Whole Theater cadre of people were always in a state of flux and the success of the Haunted House Project gained the attention of an interested few. So, at this time, a person came to us and wanted us to work on a long-term project. It included having a steady income to live on, for one thing.

I'll use the name "Lance" as our fictious project leader for the next Merry Prankster endeavor we embraced. It would be a two-fold project that involved several of us.

First of all, Lance was connected to someone that was connected to a very prominent and monied family that was connected to a pharmaceutical giant, which had a large estate just north of Bloomington in the Indianapolis area, about 50 miles away. Lance took his money from the family to go and make money. At least that's what he said he was up to.

He had heard, through confidential sources, that new cars from America were needed for the market in Costa Rica and if someone were to bring several "new" cars there, they could earn a premium when they were sold. A group of us would be recruited to, by caravan, drive a group of cars to Costa Rica—well, actually just to a transport vessel in New Orleans or Houston to be loaded and sent by water to that country.

Secondly, once we drove all the cars to Houston/New Orleans, we were going to work as a "concert" crew, setting up a large stage, lights, and sound systems for a spiritual teacher and maybe go on the road, setting up stages and so forth in a variety of cities after that. We were to bring our tool chests with carpenter tools, electricals, and lighting equipment. As I was already out of school for a while, I didn't need to withdraw further.

Back to the first part.

We started by going to the mansion of the pharmaceutical giant to get something. I wandered around on the outside porch and noticed that the walls were covered with pictures of race-horses, airplanes, and other exotic stuff. These people lived the dream!

Lance had gone to the car dealerships and bought cars. They were being readied for pick up. As I recall, the vehicles included a white Lincoln Continental, two or maybe three VW busses, and two or three more cars, perhaps a pickup truck or two.

We planned to go as a caravan, all in a row. That didn't work out. Some people got left at stoplights, and some made wrong turns. And so, then everybody pulled off onto the shoulder of the road to wait for the laggards to catch up. We stopped a lot. None of us had any maps, just verbal directions. It was as if Tom Wolfe, a contemporary author, was writing our story and we would be in his next book, after he finished writing *The Kandy-Kolored Tangerine-Flake Streamline Baby*.

The caravan was pre-CB radio days. No cell phones; not invented yet. No way to contact any other person. Flying by the seat of your pants. If you lost site of the persons or cars ahead, you kept driving until you saw one of the big Lincolns and then pulled in. If you could. The first big stop the group had was a rest area close to East Memphis, Tennessee.

I made a half-hearted effort to write a journal of the trip. I was in the men's room at a roadside rest stop and heard some kids chattering outside. It was odd, they spoke English, but talked in rhyme a lot. I thought I was road weary. I wasn't. Others heard their puzzling chatter, and it was later that someone got enough clues to surmise the kids and their adults were a band of traveling gypsies. Quite odd.

Each of us were given a hundred-dollar bill for expenses, if we needed money for anything. I wanted to get to Texas before I spent anything. We picked up a hitchhiker on the side of the road, who looked like he had been there for quite a while. We gave him water and food, and he snuggled down and went to sleep for a while.

Later, we stopped again at a rest stop and the hitchhiker got out "to stretch my legs." I saw him go around to the back of the van and I watched him. OMG, he's a huffer! Before almost anything else happened, we picked up two more hitchhikers. Larry (oops, I meant to say Lance) saw a blue school bus sitting in the yard of a house, close to the edge of the highway with a For Sale sign on it. He stopped, pulled out some dough, and bought it. He had decided he was going to pick up all the hitchhikers we saw and take them with us!

The lettering on the side of the school bus said, "Grace Baptist Temple." The bus looked like it was painted with a paint brush. It was blue. The last two hitchhikers we stopped for went over to ride in the blue bus. One of our crew went over to ride in the blue bus. Bob brought his guitar with him and went over to play, as we jauntily went along.

A huffer is someone that snorts the vapor of something that will get them high. At the next rest stop, our hitchhiker dug into his backpack and pulled out a can of hair spray, then pulled out a box of baggies, sprayed his hairspray into the baggie and huffed it in about two or three drags. He acted like someone had just firmly tapped him on the side of his head with more than just a tap. He came out of his baggie with his eyes crossed.

What kind of roadies were picking up?

We arranged a transfer of our hitchhiker, who we had named Baba Guangee, to the blue bus as soon as we stopped again. Then he was given a new moniker—Alberto Culver G.

We arrived at the state line of Texarkana in the wee hours of the night and stopped at an all-night diner. I was hungry, but not burger stuff. I wanted to get a piece of Texas Pecan Pie. After eating and getting coffeed up and ready to hit the road again, I went to the counter and paid for it with that hundred-dollar bill. I never thought I might be getting into a squeeze with throwing around a C-note, and it was no problem. She let me pay with it and gave me change.

※ ※ ※

Houston was about seven or eight hours away and, now that we'd delivered the cars destined for Costa Rica, we found the area where the festival was going to be held and led by Maharishi Mahesh Yogi, the creator of Transcendental Meditation and leader of the worldwide organization, and a new religious movement. We didn't know who he was till then. First time for everything. This was when we truly knew who we would be building the stages and platforms for. Most of us would have preferred to remain non-religious if we could. Too much of a trip to get so involved so fast. It messes with your psyche and all.

The next morning, Bob came back to our van with his guitar. He was insistent that he play for us a blues rift and song he just wrote. He then wanted to go to see this Guru and be enlightened. He wanted to start learning Hinduism. His enthusiasm was a bit over the top, perhaps because he was consuming lots of "leafy greens" when he was in the other blues bus.

He was going to attend a Satsang, a gathering for devotional activities in the company of good people. Once the activity began, however, he returned to our van. Apparently, he had been told by the Maharishi's followers that his enthusiasm was a bit excessive, and he was asked to leave.

※ ※ ※

"The Road Goes On Forever And The Party Never Ends," would not be written and sung for another two years. I had been on the road for long enough and it was time to get back to academia.

What irony. I started by pointing myself in a new direction and I found another place to live. However, when the next semester ended, my house caught fire while I was in it and burned down to the ground. But I saved my dog!

I guess that qualifies as pointing myself in a new direction.

It Started, Again

We sold all of the horses. We came home one day, and someone had already loaded up our Grandaddy Sugar's horse, Bob, and took him away. He undoubtedly went to be slaughtered or, as they say, "sent to the glue factory." It was the first and the last horse I ever had around long enough to have known about it.

That was the reward for this fine old horse who had pulled a wagon all around, loaded down, and climbed steep hills, carried watermelons to market, ate watermelon rinds we grandkids made for him, ate all the pea and butterbean hulls, and corn cobbs, carried wagonfuls of manure to spread on a three-acre field that adjoined the farm, ate dried peanut plants and hulls, carried each of us grandkids around the front pasture for fun, carried Grampa Sugar back and forth to town to get mail, pulled a Georgia stock plow to break in the ground in the Spring and Fall and in-between times. And for all that, Bob was given less than a pauper's grave as his reward. I cried.

Moving back to town was done in one day. Stuff was loaded into the horse trailer and driven to the house, a five-room. My sister and I noticed that we were going to be living at the edge of "White town." A half a block away was the traffic light that divided the White housing from the Black housing. We were certainly not numbered in the middle-class status by where we were going to live. Early in the mornings and late in the evenings we saw many people walking home to the other side of the traffic light at Park Avenue and 4th Street. There was a line of row houses that lined both sides of the street from there on. It was pretty plain to see.

The parents got the bedroom in the back, then the other bedroom was for sister Kelly. The bathroom was in between. On the other side of the house was the front room, dining room with three doorways, and the kitchen. I got the "dining room," which had three doorways. I had a single bed and jars full of preserved snakes I caught in the swamps.

For a time, I had a crate cage along one of the walls that housed a spider monkey we were going to keep and turn it into a pet. Someone brought it into the bar, and it was traded for something, I don't remember. But we kept it for several weeks before it was finally understood that a spider monkey running throughout the house and swinging from the lampshades and pooping on the curtains was not such a good idea.

A gunrack was on the wall beside my bed, holding five rifles and a quick-draw holster, pistol, and belt that was used for competitions. It was taken in "trade" from someone that swapped his fast draw outfit for a comparable amount of beer in the bar one night. I played with it and did fast draw practice standing on top of my bed. If I dropped it, it would hit the mattress instead of the wooden floor. The other three walls had gun racks loaded with rifles and shotguns. Sixteen to 20 firearms were usually hung in those racks. Handguns were always in drawers.

It was a popular thing to do in wood shop class, make a gun rack and get a good grade. I welded mine together, a four-gun rack because I took metal shop instead. I was voted to be the Safety Shop Steward for our class.

Having a different school and all new students, I was a bit happier and got to know several boys who walked to and from school. The Orange school, with the Bengal Tigers, had sports I could try out for, and I wanted to be on a team. Living in a town for a change was good for Kelly and me.

The first shot I got was during the summer playing Little League and I made the team and played shortstop. I had a .362 batting average, and I was very proud of it. And I had a uniform, too. That felt good. I was proud to see others admire my ball skills. It was a nice feeling. I guess in the back of my mind I wanted to have my dad be proud of me, too. It didn't happen. He never showed much interest in me playing ball.

Instead, he showed his laxity, by never coming to a game—not one—and was dismissive of not only my efforts, but also of my accomplishments. I wanted to be somebody in his eyes, but he never showed anything but indifference.

It happened again. I tried out for band and played the drums, went to all the football games, marched in all the parades, including the Christmas parade. I got nothing from him.

Basketball was next. He never came to a game or saw me throw a ball. Then I went out for track and made Varsity right off. I was a sprinter, and I ran very fast. I was ranked in the top three in my school. I did the 100-yard dash, the 220-yard dash, and finally the 440-yard relays. We ran in a six-school meet, and my 440-yard relay crushed the competition and also broke the county record that had held for many years. Got our picture in the school yearbook and made the city and county-wide newspapers. For what?

What did I have to do to get a thumbs-up? It seemed that whatever I did, I always fell short. I wanted to get a turn for the better and it never seemed to make it to my house. One work-out after another, another set of wind sprints, extra laps added up, and I was getting a little bigger and stronger. Someday!

A few years before this, I saw a black-and-white movie that startled me. It was the 1954 American crime drama starring Marlon Brando, *On the Waterfront*. After all of Marlon Brando's trying to get ahead and getting the short end of everything, he is finally put in the back of a car after throwing a fight and headed for a bad ending.

He looks at the thugs around him, thoroughly dismayed, and says to them, "I wanted to be somebody. I could have been a contender."

The movie ends.

That was me.

It started, again.

My mom's drinking started back up and she was drunk a

lot. Her will seemed to have drained out of her. The town newspaper let her go—she couldn't keep it together long enough to proofread anything. She returned to The Last Frontier to work with Dad and started sneaking drinks from behind the bar. He had to keep her away and took her home. She couldn't drive and we didn't have another car, so she stayed home and laid around drunk. He would come home and beat her, and she didn't seem to have the will to do anything. I had to watch it happen, over and over again.

Both my sister and I were helpless. Our guts were wretched with pain and guilt and the inability to change anything. We suffered. It was not right, and it was so shameful to be involved in and with, but we had nowhere and no one to turn to. Mom went to her room and closed her door, and I stayed away as much as possible with sports.

I walked home and had friends who went the same general direction home to their houses. When we stopped and it was my house we were in front of, I couldn't let them in my house for any reason. They couldn't use my phone, couldn't get a drink of water, couldn't use the bathroom because I couldn't be sure what the scene inside the house would be like if she was drunk and passed out on the couch, floor, or in her bed, or in the bathroom. I wouldn't know if she had any clothes on.

Then, it became the tragedy we must share with the world. If embarrassment and shame could kill, we would be its next victims. Oh, don't you doubt that it can't be taken from you, and you will have nothing else to give up, because it surely can. I felt that if I laid down on the bare ground and died and the Earth could absorb my body—even then, I would be rejected.

An early model 1950 buck-toothed four-holer Buick was parked in front of my house one day when I came home from track practice. The car reminded me of the car Cruella Deville from the *101 Dalmatians* Disney movie drove. I entered the front door and this aged woman in business clothes rose to meet me and her name was Lavatha Lavaca. She explained she was visiting my mom and would be her friend, and they would be going together to attend a group meeting she called Alcoholics Anonymous. I had never heard of it before.

I was startled and grinned. Mom was all dressed. She had brushed her hair, and she had even put lipstick on.

When she came home a couple of hours later, she told me that Lavatha worked at Claybar Funeral Home as an undertaker, and they were going to go to several meetings together. I figured that if you were an undertaker, you had a reason.

What joy and curiosity that provoked. Over the weeks that followed, they attended meetings together and I saw my mother sober for weeks at a time. My sister and I were overjoyed. We began walking to church at night. We didn't go to any daytime Sunday services because we would be seen by all the "good" folks and made fun of or laughed at. Walking at night gave us protection and anonymity.

It was just another sour day I was looking at. As I sat on the front steps of the house, petting my dog Poncho. The way he looked at me, with all the love in his eyes he always had, he was my true and only real friend. I protected him if he ever needed it from very large dogs that sometimes roamed into our yard or ambled down the street. No such things as leash laws in those days. Every dog around always wandered about, looking for a bit of food because their owners didn't care to feed them or they were neglected, got loose, and were strays. Kinda like the way Poncho was when I got him one day at the ranch before we moved to town. He just wandered into the pasture yard and when I called him, he came, as if looking for a friend. I got to keep him!

I actually protected him one night when a large pack of feral dogs were taking their turns with a bitch dog and I took my bullwhip out into the front yard and drove them away, protecting Poncho. We were the best of friends from that point on. He was never tied or chained up and wandered around but stayed close to our house. When we moved to the city, he usually slept under the house and came out to see us off when we walked to school, if it wasn't raining.

Once, I heard a firetruck in the distance and didn't think much about it. But Poncho ran to the half block to bark at it. He ran into the street—and was hit. He rolled over and over several turns before he was free of the firetruck. I screamed for him, but he was instantly gone. Suddenly, my whole world came apart. My neighbor across the street came out and laughed at me for crying like a baby, as onlookers stared.

I was holding Poncho, wrapped in a blanket, when my dad drove up. After leaving me alone to grieve, my father agreed to take me to a great place to go to bury him. We took a drive back towards the swamps to a place we knew called the West Bluff. I picked out the spot and dug the hole and wrapped him in his old off-white woolen blanket, with a double-blue stripe, that he slept on. That dog was the closest one I had to me to give me comfort unconditionally. And now he was gone. It was a terrible day.

On the way back to the house, Dad started talking about Mom going to the AA meetings "with that crazy old drunk undertaker woman over at Claybar's." He said, "She's crazy enough to drink some of that formaldehyde. That's what's probably got her 'buggy'."

I refused to listen to any more of what he had to say. He was slamming my mom. So much for any sympathy. Cruelty had no bounds in his world.

❅ ❅ ❅

The Methodist Church in Cushing, Texas was where we attended when visiting our grandparents, Sugar and Bina. It was the comfort we had that we hardly knew about in those days. It seemed fitting that this church is where I began thinking about my life and where I could possibly go, if I could survive long enough to get out of there. Back home, I asked my minister one evening, in the chapel with very few people in attendance, to be baptized. Except for my sister I asked no one else to attend.

School was about to begin for another year, but as it turned out, after all the ugliness and brutality of how this man treated our mother, he then had her committed for her alcoholism, involuntarily, to the Texas state hospital in Rusk, otherwise known as the Rusk Lunatic Asylum. No goodbyes. No "Best of Luck!" No good wishes. Cold stop. Nothing. We were abruptly sent away to Victoria, Texas to stay with my Uncle Charles and Aunt Mary and their three kids, our cousins.

The Texas State Lunatic Asylum was started in 1856 and by 1961 had grown to nine "insane" or "lunatic" hospitals, including the one in Rusk. According to the Texas Dept. of Health and Human Services, these hospitals "embraced the idea that regimented daily routines, pleasant diversions, rest, and relaxation could cure insanity." It sounds so nice, but in reality, the hospital in Rusk had originally opened as a prison and had a division for the criminally insane until very recently in history.

In fact, Mom was admitted a few years after Ed Guin, who in 1957 was admitted for robbing the local cemetery for female corpses and their skins and so forth. He became known as Leatherface in the movie *The Texas Chainsaw Massacre*. The movie was fiction. The State Hospital was not.

She returned a few months later and we returned from Victoria, Texas, where we had been staying with my aunt and uncle, just in time to pick up the pieces and get on with it, get on with life.

✳ ✳ ✳

There were several sharp knocks at our door in the wee hours after midnight. I heard two people, at least two, talking, and saw flashlight beams waving around. Again, knocking. I got up and opened the door to find three policemen and an ambulance driver standing on the porch and an ambulance with its engine running in front of the house. All I could think of was, *What is going…?!*

"We need to talk to the both of you about an altercation and shooting that has happened at The Last Frontier about an hour ago. Your dad has been shot by a Naval seaman, as he was eating breakfast across the street in the all-night diner."

I heard one of the policemen as he told the story, in which they answered the call and came to the diner and saw both men holding the same gun and nobody wanted to let go and be shot by the other one. They broke it up and got Dad attended to and he went to the hospital in the ambulance. Then they said that unfortunately, our mother was with him, and she appeared drunk and upset and they had to detain her and charge her with public intoxication. They said she would be released later that morning, when Dad was released from the emergency room.

"It seemed to have happened because of an earlier incident," one of the policemen said, "where your dad threw this sailor out of the bar for behavior with a female customer. He apparently went back to the Navy base, got a forty-five and returned. We know your dad carries a revolver, so both of them were involved."

The ambulance driver and a plain clothes officer started questioning us about our living situation. With both of our parents either in the hospital or in jail, they intimated that perhaps it was time for us kids to be removed from our house and taken to an adult supervised place, such as a foster home. We both realized we are very close to being removed and becoming wards of the state.

"We're fine," we both said. The Claybars both wanted us to go to their house for the night. As they owned and operated the morgue and funeral home five blocks away, we had to do a bit of convincing to them that we were self-sufficient and normally didn't see our parents till daylight, when we got up and left for school. Our clothes, schoolbooks, and food were all we needed. We are FINE!

We got up the next morning and went back to "our normal," until we could figure this out. Upon looking around, we each found our 25 cents for lunch money.

By the time we got home from school, Mom was back from jail. I think she found someone to help her open the bar the next evening, while Dad was being tended to. He was put into a plaster chest cast that went around his body and pinned his left arm to his chest. An upper-mummy thing. He would have to wear it for several weeks, then he would need an operation to fix his arm. The bullet entered just off the elbow joint and traveled up his arm, next to the bone and major blood vessel and out through his shoulder blade. He would have to use only his other arm for many weeks.

As it healed, he became more and more demanding on everyone. He tried to push me and my sister around even more than usual. I did my extra push-ups, weightlifting, and the other strength exercises for that One Day that would be coming in the future.

And it came. His arm healed over those next few weeks, and they removed the cast.

It started again.

Looking at my options to physically fight him, pull a gun down and just kill him, cripple him, destroy his arm permanently... Well, there were lots of options and nothing worth doing, because it would only hurt me in the end, and my sister, as well. I looked at him and gauged the fight we would certainly have at any time. I was revulsed thinking about stomping, kicking, and punching him into unconsciousness, but I couldn't see it ending any other way, as my last bit of self-respect and dignity draining away.

I then remembered the conversation I had with my Aunt Jenny when they visited us at the ranch five years earlier. I picked up the telephone and she was mostly silent as I told her at what point I was at. Immediately, she sent me the $35 I needed to buy me a bus ticket, one way, to Bloomington, Indiana, where she lived, and food money for the two-day trip.

He was working offshore and would be gone for ten days. He wouldn't sign any papers for me to join the Navy at 16 years old. I was 15 ½. I was at a dead end and had played my last card. We physically had that fistfight.

I walked into the attendance office at school and told them our family was moving out of state and they gave me my withdrawal papers. From that point forward, I was officially a high school dropout.

I called and said goodbye to my girlfriend, who lived in another town. She gave me a book to read on the way to Indiana—*Black Like Me*. That Greyhound was hauling my ass through a black highway into a tunnel that had no light. I was dazed. I could only sit and gaze out the window and couldn't tell what page in the novel I was reading or where the story was going. It was as if I was in a sailboat with the sails being thrown out and I had no rudder or direction to go. I waited for the gale to overtake me and roil me to oblivion. I had no rope to even hold on to. I felt entirely lost.

However, being lost can be a prelude to finding new paths.

Two aunts … quickly skipping through two temporary homes, trying to find gravity … using a bit of "creative obfuscation" to reground myself into my new high school. And then, having to withdraw from my new track team at the end of the first week of school in order to find shelter, a job. I felt like I was a dried autumn leaf tumbling along the ground on a chilly, sunless, grey day.

❋ ❋ ❋

I am dressed in black pants and a white shirt with an apron to begin my first day waiting tables. Before I learn the menu, I glance outside and know I will be threatened and warned by the cold in the air, something I have not lived through before. I have no real defense against such things.

I take pieces of clothing left by others and wear them. Sort of a strange thing to remember. I tried on the leavings and loss of others that were thrown into the lost and found, which I was not in charge of, in a way not stealing them because they were already lost.

That first feeling I had of finding warmth in someone else's gloves mystified me. Was the glove itself giving out that warmth, and had given someone else that warmth, and now I was the next recipient? I felt as if I was trying on pieces of different people, and then they were part of me as I walked away. Soon, their presence in the gloves was partially driven away by the biting cold, but I was able to tame that feeling as I adjusted to the cold. I became a mixture of many people as I strode. Because I didn't like parts of me, I had to become another person, or other people, to survive. With time, I once again became more of me and less of others.

Jon Bunn

To Be or Not To Be

No one knows with enough gravitas and can talk about where ideas come from, where they go, how much can be remembered, how long ideas stay around, or disappear, or stay away for a period of time and then reemerge in a few hours, days, weeks, or years later.

I had an idea that used me, one that came back, and I gave it enough of a conscience awareness that I began to develop feelings for it. I gave it some memory and it took me.

This is how this thing came about. The TV transmitted the message. Was it an ode? A requiem, perhaps? A colloquy? An omen? It came every Saturday night, very late, around midnight.

"Even a man who is pure in heart and says his prayers by night may become a wolf when the wolfbane blooms and the autumn moon is bright."

It came again, "Good evening, my name is Count Dracula…" It was always at midnight, always in black and white—the most chilling!

I only wanted to be a quiet and gentle man, perhaps in service to others, such as a Renfield, innocent enough, in service to a Count, and so I knocked upon his door.

It was just absurd that those thoughts abandoned me as a juvenile until I became drawn to the legitimate theater stage in high school and then in college. My childhood desire to learn how to build and create monster make-up drove me with determination. I acted the parts on the stage and built and created my own make-ups. Still, it wasn't enough.

The devilry of it was in the details and the techniques. Grease pencils and grease paints. Kleenex tissue and Caro syrup, dabbling with paper towels and liquid latex created skin that could be wrinkled, stretched, torn, and burned. Skin could be omitted all together if need be. Fingers and eyes could be fiddled with in situ, or creatively journeyed across the face or traveled, like teeth, fangs, or throbbing blood vessels, dry or weeping, oozing, bleeding, and gushing. Who needs dialogue when you've got this?

"A touch of powder to set everything, hon, and you are ready for the evening. Shall we take a moment and talk about your hair? What are we gonna do with that mess?"

The first college acting class I took began with orientation and meeting the instructor who came into the room and began. He had a bit of a swagger as he entered. He struck a pose at a quarter turn and established himself thus.

"Welcome. My name is Steve Macht. In German it translates to mean *strength* and *power*."

I swear he stood there, waiting for us to acknowledge him by applause or admiring nods.

"As you can see, this room is full of people"—there were more than 50 in the room—"that I don't have room for, do not want, and will not use. Many of you come here from your high school drama clubs and think this will be fun. It won't be. I'm only looking for one-third of this room to allow into this class, maybe a fourth or less will be chosen. Of the fifty people, plus, standing here, I only want to work with twelve or fourteen, MAX.

"This is my grading system," he continued. "So, pay attention. I don't know you and you don't know me so most of you should leave now, before your feelings get hurt. This is how I grade—an A for God, a B for me, and a C for you if you are lucky. Some of you leave your admit cards and that's it. Class dismissed."

Fire drills took longer than this classroom took to empty. I didn't know what to do and I wasn't going to wimp out, so I stayed. I stayed and learned Stanislavski method acting, was cast in a major production, and earned a B+. Did a short story on PBS, too.

Indiana University has one of the finest opera houses in the United States, with a stage that was only slightly smaller—by one-tenth—than the New York City's Metropolitan Opera's. I worked in the scene shop regularly and on the fly bridge, pulling curtains for rehearsals and ballet performances year-round. After the ballet or opera performances ended their run, we did the loadout, struck the sets, drops, furniture, and loaded them into trucks to go into storage, or reduced and packed to travel on the road to other stages in the Midwest.

I was privileged to be working in the theater and as it was my major. I was most fortunate to be immersed in opera the next building over, as well. In the front of the house, as they say, on one stage, and behind the scenes on the other. There would be a time when I realized my requirements to graduate were being completed. The hole that I needed to fill, I filled by taking an intermediate ballet class. I had zero musical classes, no dance classes, and I couldn't get any credit for playing guitar in a bar, which I did occasionally.

I took a ballet class mid-day (in the opera theater) as an exercise class with the upper-level ballerinas who needed a strong male to practice with. Men were in short supply. It went well. I had to learn some ballet dance positions. I didn't want more "front of the house." I felt flattered that ballerina Marina Svetlova, the director of the ballet department asked me, in person, to come and take her class. I could hardly refuse.

Oh, what was I thinking? I just needed three credits! It was the Spring Ballet. It was *The Firebird*:

"Prince Ivan, the hunter, wanders into a magic wood and captures the Firebird. On her pleading, he frees her, and she rewards him with a magic plume. Kastchei, the evil wizard, has enchanted the Princess and her maids, but with the aid of the Firebird's feather, Prince Ivan rescues the Maidens and marries the Princess amid great rejoicing."

I was a member of the wedding.

Creative people hanging around with other creative people leads to all kinds of things. Some good and some not so good. The open theater stage on the one hand, and the opera stage across the road. The saying is that you cannot serve two masters. So, I followed the advice in the old adage, "If you see a fork in the road, take it!"

Everyone will be drawn to their goal, and it may turn out like a square dance where no one has a partner, but they all want to dance, anyway.

That primal energy for busting through any obstacle drove a lot of us to charge on. Some of my actor friends stayed engaged and took the proscribed steps needed to be successful, following in the footsteps of others who bolstered their commitments. I had friends who took their bachelor's degree work without stopping for summer school or any other gap. And then went right on to get a master's—and continued right through to get a PhD. without a pause. Unheard of for most.

We hippies modified. Many of us gathered together to consolidate our creativity as a group and see what we could do and accomplish. Some of us came from the same high school, same city, and so on. Some of us gathered in the Green Room in the basement of the theater department at I.U. to discuss what we wanted, and how we could form a theater group, beyond the confines of academia, by going into the city to build an independent theater.

At the same time, we had Vietnam protests going on all over campus—sit-ins, and class walk-outs, and blues and folk musicians throwing their anthems at us in Dunn Meadow, where some hustled for money by passing the hat, while listening to Jerry Rubin, anti-war advocate of the "Chicago 7," preaching and teaching.

Some theater troops in Bloomington had their own energies and some pulled energies from others like the Owl Coffeehouse, Vest Pocket Players, The Whole Theater, and my colleagues from the Proscenium Players, our theater group in high school. Other students in the I.U. theater department, including Angel Atwood, and Bill and Emily Harris, went on to form the Symbionese Liberation Army, which kidnapped heiress Patty Hearst.

Some could not wait to graduate. But others of us usually hung out in the Green Room of the theater, running lines for productions we were in or for class assignments, doing homework, waiting for our class to start, or as a meet-up. We bantered around our notions of building our own company and looked to recruit others to join our cause.

We formed our company with people who had an abundance of talent and were excited to get involved. We had actors (that was all of us, I'm afraid), sound and lighting people, costume people, skilled (me, the carpenter) and two electricians, several painters (almost all of us could get it from the can to the canvas), and ad people for newspapers, television, and PR.

I was sitting in the Green Room talking to someone, when Kevin Klein, a classmate who was also majoring in theater, came in and started talking about what he was up to. He said he had made the decision not to take any more time with classes. He was going to quit school and move to New York. Some eyebrows were raised at his audacity.

Kevin had been doing well in the theater department and used to do improv sketches at the Owl Coffee Shop. He had switched from being a music major to theater and from then on, that's all he wanted to do. I suppose he was ready, and shortly after that he did leave I.U. and went to Julliard. Several years later, I was taking a tour of the Metropolitan Opera House in New York City and talking to the guide who mentioned that Kevin was being cast in a movie, *Sophie's Choice*, with Meryl Streep. He did well.

As for me, I became involved in forming a new theater company. We were enthusiastic and soon came up with a plan for a show. The Whole Theater was going to create, build, and run a Monster Mansion for Halloween on October 23-31, citywide! The word was out, and the newspapers and radio stations started promoting and hyping the event.

We needed a building and soon secured a large two-story limestone house at 5th and Madison, which we planned to convert into a haunted house. To get it permitted by the city, it had to be structurally sound. The wiring had to be inspected, and fire escapes had to be functional. We were lucky because the house was sold, and it was scheduled to be demolished. We could do whatever we wanted, as the building would soon be razed. The winding staircase had collapsed and there was no way to get to the second story floor until I built a new one. In planning, laying out, and cutting the stairs, I missed the total length of the stairs and when we installed it, it had this funky forward-leaning staircase, with the treads slanted towards ... the upstairs! You stood on the steps, and they made you lean FORWARD, as if beckoning you to your doom!

Entering the front door, the open foyer to the upstairs revealed an immense spiderweb that encompassed the room, woven by some ambitious hippy macrame devotees. The spider who would inhabit the web would be 10 feet across! It was chilling just to imagine seeing its frightening presence.

The christening of the mansion began with a clean-out of the interior. We figured we needed at least 200 gallons of flat black paint to cover every wall entirely. And let's not forget the floors! All the exterior windows were boarded up and painted black. No light was to invade the haunted mansion. All interior walls then could be painted with appropriate scenes and lit to our satisfaction.

One of our group invented a spiderweb making machine. Inside the foyer, away from the front door, sat a dead man who had died a long, long time ago and his dehydrated body was put in a high-backed chair. Kids were very cautious when they saw him, rotting away like that. They would look at the poor soul from a distance, unsure if he was spring-loaded or something. Someone occasionally would determine that the dead man was just a prop and get next to it and grin. The others would be drawn in. Visually, what they saw was a man inside almost a cocoon of spider webs. Children were then terrified, as he reached over and touched them! How could that happen? He was covered in cobwebs! If he were alive and moving around, he wouldn't have unbroken cobwebs!

"Ah, alas poor Yorick, I knew him well ..."

A table fan, maybe a foot tall, was the machine we built from. A tin cup with a flat lid was mounted from the center of the blades. The lid was attached by a central bolt that held the flat lid in place. The blades were bent to catch more wind, and they moved slower because they were catching lots more wind. Any theatrical supply house will have the magic ingredient, liquid latex! The texture of honey. Equal amounts of liquid latex and gasoline are put into the cup and the lid was held down by a wing nut. When the fan turned on, the latex/gasoline mix was spun to the sides of the cup and once it reached the crack between the cup lid and side, it would be slung out and the wind from the fan blades pushed it forward onto whatever and it would stick. The wind dried it some and it was still elastic. Then, you simply took some talc or white flour and blew it from the palm of your hand, and it stuck to the latex strings. Looked like an old cobweb. It was foolproof!

Did you know that Tide laundry soap is (or was) full of phosphates? Tide put lots of phosphates in their laundry soap and they advertised that your clothes would come out clean and bright. They certainly did. If you turned your black lights on away from your psychedelic posters, you could make the room and your clothes glow!

Each room in the old stone mansion had a theme. The Mummy had its pyramid room, Dracula was next to the Werewolf and the graveyard. Frankenstein had a wonderful laboratory, complete with a tilting table. ("I've done it, I've done it, IT'S ALIVE...IT'S ALIVE!")

I played The Phantom of the Opera and swooned at the lovely maiden who watched me play the organ ... until I turned ... and they saw my face. Oh, the horror of it! And instead of rushing to grab the girl, I leaped past her into the crowd of people who were watching, and pandemonium ensued! God, how I loved it! The organ music was from E. Power Biggs—"Toccata and Fugue in D-minor." ("Listen to them, the children of the night. What music they make! How lonely they seem to be...")

We scrounged and searched around for props to use and found some marvelous things behind the old defunct Showers Brothers Furniture factory. On the back lots people had dumped old metal gears with levers and serrated wheels, real laboratory looking stuff. The old factory warehouse was where the I.U. Opera department stored opera sets and painted scenery.

We performed for nine days from dark till midnight. The "local" ghoul from Indianapolis television—Sammy Terry—came to Bloomington for the inaugural opening of the spook house, which brought us TV coverage and all. Kids came by the hundreds. If you were a little monster, just so high, you got in for 50 cents, or a dollar if you were an adult. As we were a non-profit company, we donated all the proceeds to the Easter Seals Foundation.

We closed the doors and locked them, the windows were all boarded up anyway, and the bulldozer knocked it into rubble.

We did it! And we impressed the city and had tremendous support from the area merchants and organizations—hardware stores, floral shops, pharmacies, furniture stores, jewelers, lumber companies, car dealerships, restaurants, sororities, and scores of individuals aided us in our project. The newspaper described us as Bloomington's multi-arts resource center. That just pumped us up further and we were on a roll. Our PR program flyer listed more than three dozen volunteer workers. It was a huge undertaking.

Then came the BIG part. We went looking for a bricks-and-mortar building. We wanted a permanent home. After all, we needed a physical stage, dressing rooms, a workshop, a costume shop, and myriad other needs that could be solved with a home of our own.

Without hardly beginning the search, a super opportunity stared us in the face. Not a stone's throw from the I.U. campus, right in the heart of the main street leading to downtown, we found a building. It was an unbelievable opportunity.

There was a beautiful limestone church that was being vacated because the owner determined he could make more money with the property by knocking it down and building a large parking garage. It was two blocks from the front gate of the I.U. campus.

I had walked by that church almost daily but didn't really see it until that point. It was built with Indiana limestone, probably at the beginning of the 1900's. From the rear of the auditorium to the front of the elevated stage, the church floor was built with a tilted, descending wooden floor towards the altar. Perfect!

The ceiling was open in the cathedral and huge oaken beams spanned the space. I could visualize the lighting cans already. I could see that the oaken floor underneath the plush carpeting was in excellent shape. A glint of light caught my attention, and I saw three or four coins that must have been dropped from the offering plate and became wedged there, without being retrieved or discovered all these decades. I also found a couple of wheat pennies, an Indian head nickel, and Mercury dimes. I thought that it would be a good omen.

The beginning removal of the interior pews and the unbolting of the seats had not quite begun. Somone had pulled up some of the carpet to inspect the flooring in a few spots. Following them, I looked and found no water damage.

How do we capture this beauty and turn it into a dinner/ theater of sorts? We would have to be able to generate revenue for years to keep it healthy. We needed *money*. We started with the large list of donors from the haunted house. Hat in hand, we personally visited each of our patrons. But, as they say, "the air got let out of our balloon."

We started looking for grant money and approached endowments. Historical building foundations were in our crosshairs. We hit the proverbial wall. Donations and promises to assist were naught.

I'm sure I felt the rejection more than some others. After all, I was actively engaged and working on two stages, two theaters, simultaneously, on in the front of the house, and one in the back, and I could see the potential of this wonderous building for decades to come. I must not have possessed the *je ne sais quoi* to move the needle.

One of our potential benefactors responded that, "It is a great opportunity, and I hope you will get that needed help. I went to that church when I was young, and I would love to see it still standing for a long time.

"The hurdle you are trying to get over may just be too great financially," this potential benefactor added. "The owners of that property can see their return increase with every new floor they pour in concrete. The maintenance on that structure is miniscule. You trying to raise that kind of money may not be sustainable, it probably isn't. Those other two performance venues are already supported by endowments and decades upon decades of alumni giving. They have you beat from the get-go."

The grief at the thought of the eminent loss of this great landmark turned into a parking garage was palpable.

I thought I might have one more last-ditch effort, though I didn't know when or where it would come from. In idle thought, I left the room I rented just down the street and found myself walking by the building one early Sunday morning. Downcast and shuffling along, I only gradually realized I was stepping in glass shards and stone rubble. And then it hit me like a lightning bolt—"our" building had been attacked with a wrecking ball, which had removed parts of a limestone wall. It would probably stand for another day and then the heavy demolition would raze it entirely.

Looking about, I could see the large stained-glass windows still in the sashes, but some panels had come apart and had fallen to the concrete sidewalks below. Some pieces of glass were dangling by the lead strips that had held them together. They were tearing them out, but apparently didn't know how to do it safely and broke several windows in their attempts to salvage something. Stained glass was everywhere.

I became very angry. I had no one to yell at, that early Sunday. In a sense of desperation, I tried to salvage some of the pieces. I had no way to carry anything to my room, just up the street, and stood there looking at this holy wreckage. Some panes I gathered, mostly one-foot sized pieces. The glass held a beauty I had never thought to stop and admire. I turned the panes over in my hands and held them up to the light and noticed how they shined. Looking at them edgewise, I could see layers of colors imbedded. Some were so vibrant, some were pastel. And I knew what I needed to do.

Whoever the hell decided to tear down this church for a parking lot needed to know what he did and to understand what he ruined, destroyed, and defiled? I decided to find out who "he" or "they" were. I would take these beautiful scraps to them. At that moment, I just wanted to get in their face and shame them. This was about all we had left of our dream of having a theater company.

But first, I had to learn something about stained glass. And then I was going to find them. And then they would know what they truly did.

In time, the church was bulldozed, and the lot was leveled. I kept my three or four pieces of stained glass from that beautiful limestone church and stared at them, always wondering about the light and what it would reveal throughout the day.

Interlude to Glass

I found a place to work on my new fascination, stained glass, above the bookstore on the northeast corner of Kirkwood and Walnut street. My window looked across the street at the courthouse on the square.

I found a pamphlet that showed me some basic skills and techniques. I taught myself how to cut glass and how to cut the lead strips that held the pieces together. Then I had to learn how to solder it together. Next, I found a hobby shop that sold colored glass squares I might use. I didn't know what to do with them, yet.

I worked at various jobs during college as a carpenter. Friends of mine bought a large trac of land in Owen County that had a square log pioneer cabin on it from the mid 1800's. The cabin could be salvaged. The logs were all hand-hewn and we were going to have lots of work to do. Plans came together to code each of the logs and stack them for later re-assembly. With a tractor and front-end bucket, a basement was dug, the bottom was graveled, and then a concrete floor was poured. Next came cinderblock walls for the basement. The cabin would be stabilized and above ground.

The original cabin was built by hand. They had dug a root cellar and stacked slanted field stones up until the first run of wooden timbers took over. All the wall timbers were dovetailed and locked together to form the basic square cabin. Then the other sides went up to room height. New framings were replacing rotted wood for doorways, windows, and ceiling joists set, to allow an upstairs to be added.

The open spaces between all of the horizontal wall logs had gaps for the chinking six to eight inches wide. The gaps in the original log home were stuffed with moss gathered and harvested from rocks in streams, small pieces of flat limestone scree, and clay daubs pushed into any cracks they could seal.

The cabins from those times were moist, they leaked, and they were subject to temporary ownership by bugs, bird nests, field mice, and drafts. Summertime sunshine helped dry and bake the mud daubs that worked fairly well in keeping the inside dry. Cooking inside raised the temperature that aided the drying until the Fall weather came, and the rains began to loosen the summer chinkings. Cooking outside in summer was preferred.

We used quick-drying concrete with hardware cloth screening that attached to the timbers. The outside and inside chinking was troweled smooth and gave the cabin a nice look.

The owners knew about me starting to build stained-glass windows and I earned my first commission by building a stained-glass window between two wall beams and building a small window for the front door.

I was always curious about what was in old buildings—I loved looking at old farming implements and digging in old trash heaps. It gave me clues about the people who lived there, what they bought, and what kind of patent medicines they used. I gave the new owners a box of my findings for historical purposes. I also gave them a nanny goat (which I was milking) and one of her kids.

On second thought, it was not the best of gifts. The goat loved to eat spruce seedlings we planted during the preceding summer over the two hundred acres. The goats loved living on the front porch and left their "berries" everywhere. Oops!

❋ ❋ ❋

Essentially, my bachelor's degree was almost completed and I needed to complete student teaching to have my teaching certification from Indiana. I was given a year's assignment to teach school at the John Ball Zoo School in Grand Rapids, Michigan. It was an alternative school, housed at the city zoo. It was envisioned to be an outdoor, year-round school that encompassed the educational fundamentals established by the state and integrated into the subjects we taught such as Pioneer Living, Plant and Tree Identification, Camping, Cooking and

Food Preservation, Early American History, Folklore, Independent Learning, Art, Animal Study, First Aid, and other subjects. It was a full-time, accredited, five days a week school.

We used the classrooms inside the zoo and had two portable school classrooms in the parking lot. Hot or cold, rain or shine, snow, or wind, we went to school. We wrote our own textbooks. This was the second year the school had been in existence.

For me, it was a non-renewable assignment for a full-time teaching position for one-half the pay of a regular certified teacher. The experience was wonderful—teaching in the city zoo, taking students on wilderness excursions and camping trips. It was incredible. But yes, the pay was sub-livable.

I was able to keep my head above water by finding an extra weekend job as a skydiving Jumpmaster at the local airport. I always prayed for clear weather, cold weather be damned, but high winds kept me and the airplane on the ground.

When time allowed me to be away from teaching, camping, cross-country skiing, and skydiving, I was at my drawing board, working on stained-glass designs. I didn't have glass work or tools for that year but kept making blueprints and drawings as I went along.

The Zoo School's culminating event was the end-of-year camping trip. The year before, about 25 students did a week-long campout in Isle Royale National Park, an island in the upper reaches of Lake Michigan next to Canada. It was a camping and backpacking event that we learned about and studied for throughout the year.

This was going to be a bit different, though. The camping trip required lots of equipment—tents, backpacks, stoves, water containers, sleeping bags, etc. Local merchants and others donated or greatly reduced the costs of the gear that was needed. Some of the chaperones already had their own outdoor camping gear.

A "dry run" was needed to teach the kids how to set up tents, use sleeping bags, make fires, cook, wash dishes, keep ponchos at the ready, and so on. The first-year kids' experience was a five-day campout. The second-year students had our "dry run," and it went very well. Everyone was excited—students and teachers, and the chaperones. We had contests for who could cook the perfect pancake. I always lost.

And then … the school expanded student capacity for the second year's program because the first year was so successful. We now had 56 students!

The final week of school was just going to be a review of what we covered and learned throughout the year. The weather was very nice, and all the kids were dispersed throughout the zoo, looking at their study animal and talking about the trip.

I got the call very late Thursday at midnight. My mother had fallen backwards down the stairs leading to the basement, hit a concrete floor, and died of a cerebral hemorrhage. I was in Grand Rapids, and she was in Beech Grove, a suburb of Indianapolis, six hours away.

I had an old Rambler with second and third gears, but no first gear and no reverse. I had incomplete directions, so I just drove as close as I knew how, and then called and got specific directions from there.

Aunts and uncles were there, and funeral arrangements were almost completed. I attended the Saturday service and then I was going to get a few hours of sleep before I drove back. I had felt joyful for a moment and then was weeping the next. I had seen my mother two or three times before I moved out of state. Visits, as I remember it now, were eight or nine years apart. I seemed to always have meager resources for traveling—little money in the bank, and few reasons for visiting.

My hope for my mother had always been that she would somehow beat alcoholism, but at the funeral my uncle told me the reason she fell down the basement steps and died was because she had been drinking. He asked me to promise not to tell my sister, Kelly, about Mom's condition and circumstances.

It is a promise I now cannot keep. Promises are for the living, but truth is for eternity.

I started driving back to Michigan very early the next morning. Upon quiet reflection on the road back, I contemplated Mom's journey and surrender to alcohol. Without a working car radio for distraction, I looped the memories again and again, as I drove away and counted 26 years of failure in her battle.

Twenty-six years.

It felt like I made it to the parking lot of the Grand Rapids Zoo within minutes of departure.

It was a tumultuous time. All the kids knew about my mother's passing and, on the one hand, were very sad when they looked at me, but could help but be jubilant about the prospect of heading into the wilderness. They had worked towards this week for an entire year. I could not let them down, and so I shifted gears to jump in and make their final event as memorable as possible. I needed them as much if not more than they needed me. I'll call it even. The camping trip went off without a hitch.

My one-year non-renewable teaching assignment was fulfilled. I said goodbye to Grand Rapids and returned home to Bloomington, but only for a short while. The Indiana Teacher Certification License would be mailed soon. I began looking for teaching positions that would begin to be posted for the fall and I knew a person who was starting an Adult Education Program at Vincennes University. She lived across the street from me when we were both still in college, prior to our graduations. She told me about the program she was developing, which was scheduled to start immediately. I just happened to be free, and so she hired me.

She directed a program to teach adults who wanted or needed further education, an extra class, in preparation for taking their GED or for applying to a two-year or four-year college degree program. If they were adults and had not been in school for a while, my job would be to get them ready to acclimate to school again and make the most of their classes and studying.

This was quite a shift from my previous position. I would be going from teaching gifted and talented fifth and sixth graders, to adults of all ages who couldn't read information on their feed sacks, and barely knew how to sign their name.

Vincennes University had an extensive outreach to the rural community and this program expanded academia for them. I would be the resource teacher, and I would be visiting them by van with an assistant. We started with testing and evaluating current skill levels, so that we could develop an individualized program that gave each of them specific materials to aid them in reaching their goals. I continued setting up meeting locations, and we established program locations in high school gyms and libraries, community centers, churches, lunch counters, and the city and county jails. A sign on the van said, "A B E Adult Basic Education." Essentially, I became a circuit teacher!

The community far east of Vincennes was very close to NAD Crane (National Ammunition Depot), which is responsible for conventional ammunition manufacturing, storage and depot operations. This was a very rural area. I found a farmhouse I rented in the Amish community near Odon, Indiana. I had Amish and Mennonite neighbors, and also farmers who worked their land with gasoline tractors. I did have electricity and running water, but no phone. I drove a Land Rover back and forth about 50-60 miles each way, daily. I butchered a hog for a lady on her farm and she gave me a Nubian goat for payment, which I milked daily. She went to a friend's land, though he didn't want to milk it. The kid went, too.

I played my guitar and retrieved my easel from storage and continued with drawing stained-glass patterns. Several churches in these rural communities had classrooms and it was nice to have a space to spread out my school resource materials and plenty of room to seat everyone who came to study.

I couldn't help but wander into the local churches to look at their stained-glass windows. Beautiful examples of craftsmanship were abundant in so many churches. They seemed to rely on a gothic motif and that didactic sense that came from the heavy hand of the glass painters, the ones who painted so many elements of the Christian story. These types of glass were fired in an oven to set the illustration, then assembled into window units and installed. The tableaus were dominant throughout rural and urban churches and throughout most of Indiana and the Midwest, even nationally. The bulldozed church that was lost in Bloomington displayed those examples.

The struggle I had between remaining in a rural setting or getting to an urban location that would allow me to develop as an artist was a back-and-forth battle. I decided that I needed to move forward and headed south to Texas. Do you think college loans had anything to do with it? I had crammed seven years into my four-year degree.

I returned to the small town of Orange, Texas, where I came from prior to moving to Indiana. I tested out for my Journeyman's card and joined the United Brotherhood of Carpenters and Joiners of America as a Journeyman Carpenter.

The three general areas of work on the Gulf Coast were divided into residential, commercial, and heavy construction. Any combination of work I could be assigned and called out of the local union hall; I took it. I built houses, did remodeling of offices, built hotel rooms for Holiday Inn, worked in chemical plants, and was building scaffolding in refineries and power plants. I worked *way* up there in the sky!

I had a long-term assignment on a jobsite that was building a power plant on the edge of a swamp in Bridge City, Texas. I was building scaffoldings up the sides of the superstructure, hundreds of feet in the air, for welders, pipefitters, and electricians. I worked every day when it didn't rain and the union pay gave us two different types of wages: regular pay, and "show up money," for days we were rained out, but we had showed up.

And then came what I had waited for, for many years. I found a vacant retail building, rented it, and established my first stained-glass business. I worked during the day pounding nails and grew my business, Looking Glass Studios, at nights, weekends, and days when it rained enough to call off union carpenters from working.

I exhibited two agate stone-centered windows in a citywide art contest and took home a ribbon. Shortly after that, the president of the local bank bought a Tiffany-copy lampshade from me. He had seen it in an article about me in the local paper. That was several hundred dollars I put in my ledger.

With a few radio spots on the local radio, I advertised I would be starting teaching stained-glass classes, twice a week. I certainly got more than I bargained for. I had to teach two-week night classes. They needed stained glass. I had it. They needed solder and irons, etc. I had it. They needed patterns, I had it. They needed carbon paper, I had it. I had it!

Every student who came into the shop wanted to build a window. That was a good thing. I did *not* teach any sort of trinket-making, such as sun-catchers. I had four wooden tables to use for classes. One table was just mine. Many students wanted to come back and do a second, more detailed window.

I was at my shop every night till very late, working on pieces I built for art shows, and I was approaching businesses and galleries. There was a problem I wrestled with. There were no art galleries within 25 miles or more. I needed more exposure and tried to solve it with contacts and art suppliers in Houston, which was almost 100 miles away. I reassured myself that it would work itself out. I was sure.

The Orange Art League wanted to sponsor a juried show for Orange County in conjunction with the inaugural opening of The Brown Center, a very prestigious horse ranch, which was part of a gift to Lamar University. I was chosen to exhibit one of my best windows during the cocktail reception.

The window I displayed in the foyer was a swamp scene of a great white egret, standing in a bayou, secluded in a marsh grass cover. I spent perhaps six weeks drawing, cutting, and constructing the 45" x 45" work. Cutting and grinding and fitting pieces of glass topped six hundred pieces. Years later, the egret window went touring to various galleries and shows throughout the U.S. It currently resides with me, the artist.

Quite by surprise, I was contacted by The Longview Museum of Fine Art in Longview, Texas and invited to display and present some of my recent glassworks as one of ten Texas artists who were chosen throughout Texas in various mediums and being recognized for their achievements. Apparently, members of the Orange Art League were instrumental in forwarding my name for consideration.

Soon afterwards, a large window was commissioned by a client who was building a new home. The client asked me to design and build a window for the gable end of their house. A large deposit was taken, the drawings and colored glasses were agreed on, and I began the work.

The window was in three sections, and it was very large. The three panels measured 3' x 4', 3' x 5', and 3' x 6'. It would be installed by a commercial glass company that had the equipment, skills, and workforce to set the three in place. The remainder of the money was due to me upon possession of the window by the client.

Something seemed out of sorts. Suddenly, the client would not return my calls. A period of time passed and when the client finally responded, he told me that he would not take possession of the window because he had filed for bankruptcy and was going to lose his house. Maybe to look on the bright side, I still have the finished windows in my possession, so I didn't lose them. And they were made from mouth-blown glass shipped from Germany to the United States in a container with thousands of feet of other stained-glasses.

A brief time later, someone did a drive-by past my glass-fronted store and took a few shots at these pieces, which were displayed in the front of my store. Two shots were taken, and the placement of the shooter was determined from the bullet holes in the back wall. However, the three-paneled glass window was completely missed in the attack. The frames that held them had 12 to 14 inches of space between each panel, and the bullets must have traveled through these spaces. A neighbor, walking their dog early, discovered the crime. I had these pieces for decades and they never sold. Finally, I donated them to the Academy of Texas Music, of which I am a member.

I needed to drive to Houston to buy materials for the business: glass, lead, hand tools, and the list seemed full enough to make a 200-mile round trip. I was in the middle of buying and was told about a new warehouse being stocked that would have sheet glass I could buy at wholesale. They were looking to hire someone. Go see, they said.

I go.

I stop.

I look.

It is a warehouse, all right.

I must have seen 75 or 100 more *cases* of stained-glass sheets by the crate full!

I was knocked over.

Someone came over and I got out my little scrap of paper with a few glasses that were on my list.

Very quickly, I started asking questions about the warehouse and mentioned that I also heard that they might have a job opening. "Doing what?" I asked.

The manager began telling me about their company, Bienenfeld Industries.

"This warehouse has just opened up and we're a glass wholesaler that sells stained glass directly from the glass factories in the U.S. and factories that are located throughout England and Europe. We are looking to find a person willing to travel over a multi-state territory to go to the stained-glass businesses and represent our glass factories and get them to buy our glasses. Would you like to see our glasses and the warehouse?

"It is a new position. We'll have four or five people out in the stained-glass marketplace and so, we'll divide the U.S. into four territories. Do you know anything about glass and have any experience?"

I told them about my glass studio and about my recent invitation from the Longview Museum of Fine Art to display some of my work and to give a short talk about it. He seemed impressed and satisfied.

We toured the warehouse, and I was feeling like I was going to pass out. I was so excited!

"Take me into my warehouse," the manager said, "and pretend I'm wanting to buy some glass and sell me some."

I do it and he said, "You did fine."

The timeframe they wanted was to have someone on board in three weeks; that went for all U.S. positions. The first week, the new hires would go to New York City for training. The U.S. was divided into four territories and the fifth one was to take all of Canada.

I was hired. I closed my shop, and I was given moving expenses to move to Houston. I got an apartment within 15 minutes from the warehouse, and we left for New York City. The money offered was just slightly above what I was earning pounding nails, getting rained out, and teaching glass classes four nights a week.

What a whirlwind!

As a working glass artist, I came with skills, a healthy desire to learn and travel, and it was nice having two degrees and a teaching certification. The next thing up was to get some business suits and a nice briefcase. Oh, yes, and then go to New York City! All of it on the boss's credit card. Then we were issued our own American Express cards. Hot damn!

I set up business calls and rented cars at the airports and went to see who was doing stained-glass work. I must have had a dozen states, and I went to just about everyone who did serious glasswork, above hobby craft.

Little did I know just how unique my position was. I observed what was being produced, met countless artists, and saw some renowned artists and works. It didn't hurt that I was still doing glasswork on the side. It certainly helped me become a better artist and I gained lots of artistic friends. I became a valuable resource for them. I helped artists find unique glasses that fit their needs. I was representing the finest glass factories in the world and the finest glasses being produced in the world.

I was a member of the Stained Glass Association of America and attended the annual events and met countless other artists from around the country. I traveled, then I traveled some more. The schedule my company wanted to put me on the road Monday through Friday, three weeks in a row, and the fourth week I stayed at the warehouse for the week in Houston. If it wasn't for the fact that I was still young and strong, I would never have been able to keep up with the contacts. Three or four business visits a day!

This was before cell phones. Perhaps a pager. Too bad, frequent flyer miles were not invented yet, either. In and out of airports and rental cars. We didn't have Google maps to tell us where we were going. Directions scribbled on scraps of paper! Since some appointments had to be rescheduled or cancelled, I took out my airline flight schedule book and rebooked myself, although I did have a travel agent that set the week up for me if I gave to her a day or so ahead. No ad hoc help.

It was the glass! As I was always poking around the warehouse when I was in Houston for the week. I got to look at all the glasses that were shipped in from various places and kept track of what glasses went out and to whom. I could always put away a special sheet, here and there. What did we have and what did I show and carry to glass shops? Lots of unique, one-of-a-kind glasses produced by factories that produced signature glasses for many, many decades.

Glasses came over from England. I had glasses that came from France, and I had glasses that came from Germany. I had glasses that came from Korea, the West Coast, Oklahoma, Portland, and small batch glasses from wherever someone was trying to get artists' attention to sell to. I had glasses from West Virginia that were in bowling ball-sized chunks that were then melted in furnaces for glass blowing.

How do you learn about colors? Roy G Biv—red, orange, yellow, green, blue, indigo, and violet. Some of you remember this was the way to remember the primary colors when you looked into your box of Crayolas.

Roy G. Biv works well for what is known as cathedral glasses. They come in uniform sizes, like windowpanes, and a blue glass was uniform in color throughout. The glass probably had a minor texture, a granite pattern, or some such, on it. Very ho-hum for most stained-glass people to use. Very forgiving when cut by someone with the most basic of skills. Cheap. Machine-rolled with different textures available for the most daring!

Some people—not me—use plastic sheeting, which can mimic every one of the glasses. And it can't cut you or shatter if broken, so they are safer, especially if there's children around.

Then the glassmakers found ways to make glasses that were not uniform and boring. We are talking Renaissance era and earlier now. Experimentations were underway to find unique colors and something to make their melted globs be attractive to the artisans that designed, constructed, and used them in building the large windows of the Middle Ages. It started with learning how to make whiteish glass and putting colors in the white glass that flowed and mixed in different pigments and made unique color combinations. Those were the glasses that were rich and vibrant and those glasses, Opalescents, were the chosen ones for church windows, such as the glass pieces that I rescued from the Indiana church demolition.

Glassmakers kept their formulas secret and protected them at all cost. The glassmakers in Italy were so protective, they moved the glassworkers to the island of Murano to live and work there and they weren't allowed to leave the island, lest they share a secret with rival producers who paid them well for their rival's secrets.

An example: Glass furnaces had to run continually, 24-7. Glass furnaces were operated at temperatures in excess of 2,000 degrees. The fire couldn't be left unattended to cool down or go out, or the furnace pot would crack, and glass would pour out, perhaps starting fires that were difficult to put out. Neighborhoods would be lost. This was another reason to keep glassmakers on an island, in addition to keeping the process secret.

Another example. Glass needed to be as free of contaminants and as clear as could be. The smallest pebbles and stones that got into the molten glass would bring a defect into the batch that later, when cooled, could break a glass pane, and destroy a window years later.

Glasses had "character," and each factory made their glass different than other glass producers. A guarded secret: how to put tiny, even bubbles into a piece of glass and cool it and use it, because tiny bubbles in a clear piece of glass gave it a glitter-like-sparkle by the sun's rays. The secret finally escaped from Murano and spread among other glassmakers.

Potatoes! It was potatoes that were thrown into a molten batch of glass, steamed up, and then poured into sheets that contained and captured the tiny bubbles. Glassblowers today know them as "seeds."

When the cathedral of Notre Dame burned in April 2019, the world gasped at the tragedy they witnessed throughout the day and night as it burned. But the famous 13th century Rose Windows—opalescent glasses—were spared, and suddenly a great segment of humanity realized what a treasure had been spared. Multitudes sought to know more about the windows and the stone works that now had to be repaired. Experts expected it would take from ten to 40 years to make the cathedral whole again.

As was mentioned before, there were other glasses that were being used and worked by glass artisans, once the Second World War ended. Synagogues and churches still needed new windows for new construction, and it was a chance for glass artists to look in new directions. Glass factories, here and abroad, answered that craving with glasses that answered that need. Their palettes were expanded upon, and once new glasses were introduced and made available, the race was on.

The glass revival meant that glass could be mouth-blown from the end of a blowpipe, poured through dual power rollers, and dipped with a ladle, mixed with other colors, and pressed into sheets.

The different factories created wonderful sheets of glass. It did seem that every sheet produced had characteristics that mimicked the previous sheet but was different. So, glasses had colors that were strong on one side of the sheet and faded away as the color went to the other side.

Some French glasses had smoky whisps that faded away and left a trace of seedy clear that was as delicate as lace upon the wind. Some German glasses looked like someone poured clear syrup that flattened out and the pattern froze before reaching the edge. Reamey glasses. An ox eye, a bubble captured in time the size of a baseball, thicker in places that became magnified and moved as you shifted your gaze.

One of my favorites were made by a man holding a blowpipe and gathering molten glass larger than a basketball, probably the size of a blow-up beach ball, on the end of a fifteen- to twenty-pound blowpipe. He blew a large cylinder that stretched, as the pendulum swung it into a pit he stood over, until it reached a certain size and was hardened enough to swing it to a table where he cut both ends away and tonged it open to form a sheet. He then put that sheet into a furnace to anneal it, then it went down an assembly-line belt, where it cooled and was then put into a crate for shipping to the U.S. or to another country.

Another favorite: A gather of light-colored amber glass was pendulum swung into the pit and the large bubble was then suddenly encased and sprayed with water, which made the whole bubble craze with spidery cracks all over the entire cylinder, and then it was quickly put into a fiery glory hole that resealed the cylinder's crazes. Once again, both ends were cut away, the bubble was softening and beginning to sag when the tongs were used to flip it and open it to lay flat on the assembly line, relieving the stress. And then it was annealed and put on its way to the awaiting crate for shipment. Alligator crackle glass. It came in cherry red, too!

Specialty glasses, although not a dominant glass for the U.S. markets, still had their place. Any glass that was unusual in color or texture filled a niche here and there, with the idea of being used sparingly. Too much use of something unusual might gain attention; it would just scream gaudy and amateur-ish. There were glasses that waited patiently in their bins for just such a special occasion. Most of us kept those glasses away from prying eyes. I had many.

I had two German opal glass sheets that mixed a tint of purple with a pastel blue that I wanted to keep and someday build the eponymous wisteria trellis window. I had the glass for over 40 years. A couple of decades passed, and I heard the factory had closed up and was out of business. It seemed that some of the chemicals used in the manufacture of some of their glasses were so caustic to the environment, it was killing the nearby foliage.

I designed and created a jolly landscape window, full of bright, light greenery that was celebrating a beautiful day, the emergence of Spring or something, and I needed to create a panorama view for the back yard. I had seen a translucent milk background glass that had little flecks of transparent colors sprinkled over the surface that melted in. The little multi-colored frit was about the size and shape of saltine cracker crumbs, and it wasn't a distraction to the tableau. It was delicate in its creation at the factory and an easy glass to cut and fit. It was called "confetti glass." It was indeed.

Another specialty glass that had significant impact within the stained-glass community,, and as much impact on the residential and commercial flat glass industry was the introduction of glue chip glass. Imagine a plain clear windowpane. You look out of them all the time. The Koreans fabricated this glass and shipped it to our warehouses regularly. Here is what it is and how it is done.

Windowpane glass is sandblasted on one side, very lightly, just enough to make it non-transparent. Then "horse glue," as we called it, was thinly sprayed on the glass and it was allowed to dry and "cure." When exposed to the sun, or to a heat lamp, the glue would shrink, and it had enough strength to literally pull off some of the surface of the glass and it mimicked what a frozen window would look like with frozen water ice crystal patterns on a winter's day. If someone didn't want to spend handsomely for stained glass, Korean glue chip glass would be the ticket. It hardly blocked any light coming through. It showed an entire sheet of glass that was "frozen." We shipped it in 600 square foot crates. It would be found in many window and door businesses nationwide.

Sheet glasses could be fabricated many ways and usually consisted of pouring a ladle full of glass that was dipped from the furnace onto a set of double rollers and the rollers pressed it to the right thickness as it came out and rested on a movable steel bed, like a large slab of cookie dough. It traveled away from the rollers at the same rate as the bed moved along, insuring a uniform thickness in the glass as it was laid out and the sheet began to cool and stiffen. The length of each sheet was uniform for that manufacturer, but it varied among the factories. There were no industry standards for the size of glass sheets produced. Floating glass rollers over molten metal beds is known as the Pilkington process. Some glasses floated over inert gas.

As an agent for several factories, domestic and foreign, I had access not only to the products that were being developed and presented in the U.S., but I could hardly keep up with working in my own glass studio during the week I was off the road.

Three friends I knew who were college friends in Portland, Oregon were seriously going to undertake the planning and construction of their own furnaces to make glass. I would see Boyce at national glass shows and meetings and hear about their progress over the years. I was learning about glass characteristics involving expansion and contraction. It was something I needed to know if I was going to be blowing hot glass.

Some glasses would cool differently than some others, and when they were put together, such as when artists were trying to fuse them together, they would simply cool down to a point and then shatter. Bullseye Glass was in the midst of solving that issue. They had gorgeous glasses and were learning about COE's (coefficient of expansion). Solving that would be a major boost to sales. And then they solved it!

I flew to Albuquerque to meet with some customers and then to Las Vegas for a national glass show. I got up and got ready to see customers in and around the city and I was then going to drive over to Santa Fe and then to Taos. I left my hotel room, and my car was parked outside my door, covered in dust. The sidewalk was covered in dust, and the street, too. What gives?

Surprise! Mt. Saint Helens, way west of me in Oregon, had erupted and it was sending giant plumes of smoke and ash into the air. I surmised that it must be a hell of an event to have that smoke and ash travel east and cover the town of Las Vegas. What an event! Are you kidding me? A VOLCANO?

In Las Vegas, I ran across Boyce, and we talked and caught up with each other's lives. I asked about the ash and about the factory if everything was good. Of course, the volcano was front and center. I still get a chuckle about our meeting that day. He said to me that "since we have had sooo much ash everywhere, we might as well start shoveling the ash into our furnaces and make Mt. Saint Helens Glass. What do you think?" We both laughed.

It was at such a time that I was also commissioned to build some of the largest stained-glass windows of my career. I had the tables to draw my large windows out and to cut, grind, and fit the many pieces together without disturbing the work. The commissions I earned went to the materials I needed to acquire to start building.

In a casual conversation with a friend, he mentioned to me that he heard about a benefactor seeking to put a large window into a chapel he was having built, and he was donating both to a foster home as a gift. Boys and Girls Country contacted me shortly afterwards, and I accepted the commission to do the window.

The benefactor's inspiration came from the chapel that was located on the Texas A&M campus in College Station, Texas. The benefactor was giving a wonderful gift to the community in Tomball, Texas. When I solidified the drawing of the pur-posed window, it was going to be 9 feet wide and 15 feet tall and it would face a western exposure. A large radiating circle with rays of emanating beveled glass would be highlighted in the setting sun.

Having had so many glasses at my fingertips over the years, and having looked at so many glasses, I've reflected on the pallet of colors I used over time. What I believe is that I began using more colors over time that were not dense and opaque and were lighter and lighter as I continued to work in glass. Toward the end of my career, I enjoyed working with pastels and glasses that had characteristics in the panes that expressed movement, more so than vibrant colors. At that point when I was asked to describe windows I would be working on, my usual answer would be, "It's basically clear."

I had many glass artist friends I stayed connected with when the distribution warehouse closed. As I was their contact for so long, I was very interested in what many of them were doing and what they were working on. One contact was my friend Becky from Ft. Smith, Arkansas. We were always swapping pictures of our latest commissions, and we tended to motivate each other. She would send me some pictures of a commission she was working on, and I would return pics of my work back to her.

An example of us swapping photos—and this was before the computer age, where you just sent them with a click of the mouse—were some pictures of the chapel window I completed after the installation was done. She sent me back a wonderful window she did of a girl in a meadow joyously dancing in the breeze that used Bullseye glass, described as "catspaw," in the maiden's long dress. The meadow's flowers bloomed at her feet, and I liked the addition of irises, a favorite flower of mine.

I was working on another large window, Come Unto Me, for a funeral home and I copied the style of her irises at Jesus's feet in the Garden of Gethsemane. Then I waited for Becky's comments to get back to me, as I knew she'd see my irises. My window was approximately 9 feet by 15 feet tall.

Oh, what a wonderful picture I got back from Becky! She had completed an arch window of a dragon entwined around the commissioner's last name, Stallone. She'd made a window for Sylvester Stallone.

Well, you could say that was a dichotomy. One of us working on Christ and the other working on the Devil.

With fingers crossed, I applied to *the* glass school for one of the coveted spots and wanted to be immersed in the environment. They worked day and night at several programs and lived at the school. I was elated to find a response from Pilchuck, and I was accepted to attend. However, I realized that traveling from Houston, Texas to Stanwood, Washington would be an expense beyond my resources. It was a huge disappointment that I had to turn this opportunity down.

The Texas Glass Artist Association was given a great opportunity to show off its members and our works in a special showing in San Antonio as a fundraiser to assist a giving program for a national charity. The glass show was (as I remember) installed in the glass atrium lobby of a downtown bank. We were encouraged to bring the best work we had. I remember more than 20 artists exhibited work.

This was my first time exhibiting some of my blown glass. I brought some of my windows and maybe 20 or more vessels. The show ended and 19 pieces were purchased to raise money. Eighteen of the 19 sold were my blown glass vases.

Economics always changes things for artists, and I was no different than any other one. My hot glass shop was closed, and I spent a long time pursuing a career in the business world. I continued to seek and accept commission work. My wife at the time, Elizabeth, was a glass artist, too (a good one), and together we raised two fine daughters until our paths went separate ways.

So, here comes the heavy lifting. I was then going to look for my new home, one with a garage big enough for a home studio—for worktables, glass bins, and the tools needed to continue to work in glass, albeit not at the level I pursued in earlier years.

Once my new wife, Donna, and I looked around our new home, we realized we had more room than we did in our two previous patio homes. We actually had more windows, too, and we started deciding which stained-glass windows we wanted to hang and which windows we didn't want to hang. I was still making a few as commission pieces which were "basically clear."

Donna and I celebrated our blended family of three boys and two girls, and then came an important priority. Each of our five grandkids needed to have their own window, to have, to hold, and to grow up with. So, between an occasional commission, I completed five windows, one for each of them.

That left several windows that were cleaned up and stored on an inside closet wall, a place without a home. Since most of my windows were not small and needed a larger place to hang and show off, they sat around.

Now, people won't be able to buy a window they might like if they can't see it! The windows needed to get out of the closet to begin with. And someone needed to see them. I started looking around for a place where they could be seen. I went to some festivals, juried shows, and set up a tent and Donna and I sat in chairs. All day long we sat in chairs or walked around and then sat in chairs some more. The fun wasn't quite what we had expected.

Plan B.

Galveston, Texas is where the beach is, You can go and eat seafood there, you can fish, you can tour 1900-era mansions that are still standing after the historic hurricane destroyed most of the city and killed an estimated 8,000 people, the largest number of deaths of any natural disaster ever in the United States—The Great Galveston Storm.

My wife and I strolled down the Strand, idling along, looking for a place to eat seafood po' boys and have cold beverages. "Look right there. What is that, an art gallery? It's on the Strand. One block over is the seawall—that's where the cruise ships dock!"

Nice gallery. It carried all kinds of art—jewelry, photography, ceramics, metal sculptures that wave in the wind, paintings, cast iron, linens. But no stained glass and no blown glass. I inquired.

"Can't see you for several days. See us mid-week. Bring a portfolio. Goodbye."

I returned mid-week with three small pieces, all polished up, a portfolio, and hope in my heart. Their commission structure was low, I would have to probably hang my own windows, and if they sold a piece, "How long would it be before we get a replacement?" (Nice problem to have!)

They liked the windows I brought, but had a comment, "This window is fine for a home but, we are right here, one block from where the cruise ships dock, and some may be a bit large. We could try it. What we think will be a good market, if people like your work, is something a bit smaller, something that someone will take under their arm and return to the cruise ship to go home with. Do you think that would work for you?"

I'm thinking, "Like a worm in an apple!"

I hadn't realized what a great opportunity this actually was. Having a cruise ship dump people at the front door of the gallery! How sweet is THAT? I started making sales within two or three weeks, depending upon what ship docked. I went to the studio and started to design and build their replacements. So, here we go. I'm getting regular hits on my small windows and one of the owners wants to buy one of my pieces, too!

That 100-mile round trip was fun to take. Donna smiled, too. However, she was still looking at several large windows I had leaning up, here and there, and we had to do something with them, at some point.

"I know, we'll ask the kids if they want any of them."

These windows were all the orphan babies that had been with me—some, for decades. They were built and then displayed multiple times, some went on tour all over the U.S. and came back home. I did have some other windows that were shipped out and damaged, and I didn't spend time refurbishing the breaks.

As the relationship grew at the Galveston gallery, I was allowed—if the space was available—to increase the number of windows above what I currently hung. I picked up an extra spot occasionally. That was good for business, me, and them.

So, now that Donna and I had a new home, I saw opportunity in the three floor-to-ceiling plate glass windows in the formal dining room. So, from the windows I was building and selling at the gallery, Donna would occasionally take one and put it aside for later hanging in our dining room.

The location of the gallery was a prime selling environment. At the beginning, I hung just two or three windows in the gallery, and that grew to over six or eight within the three years I was in the gallery. Aside from building and selling windows, I was asked on a few occasions by people to come and look at windows they had in their vacation homes that had survived the 1900 hurricane. Matching glasses for repair work was almost insurmountable.

So, Donna got her windows for our dining room, I built more replacements for the ones she picked, and I had eight windows in the gallery to sell. Oh, Happy Day!

On the night of September 13, 2008, the eye of Hurricane Ike approached the Texas coast near Galveston Bay. The winds increased and the two-day prior rainfall totals exceeded 20 inches. Just east of Galveston Bay, water from the storm surge was over the first floors of many houses. Most of those communities were utterly devastated. Wind and waves pounded houses. Even some houses that were elevated on 14-foot pilings were rolled into the water. Surge heights were measured at 16.9 feet.

In Galveston, the day before, the rising storm surge was overtopping the 17-foot seawall. Behind the seawall, the land sloped downward to the lower elevations of Galveston. The Lone Star Flight Museum suffered massive damage, from moderate to severe, to all the aircraft hangers. All the airplanes except one were damaged with about 8 feet of saltwater.

The Galveston Railroad Museum suffered damage throughout. Historical locomotives were scrapped after suffering severe damage. The art gallery I was in was across the street. On the first floor.

My wife and I lived 60 miles to the north of Galveston, and we had our own battles to fight. Our home's first floor was flooded, and we lost power that continued for three weeks. We slept on the second floor and lived during that time in the garage and on the driveway, using my glass work benches to keep some things out of the water. In preparing for the coming hurricane, we filled a couple of garbage cans with water and began eating or cooking everything we had in our freezer.

The winds howled as we tried to sleep. Our roof was incessantly pounded, hour after hour, with falling pinecones, and we had trouble sleeping, always vigilant for any large limbs or trees falling through our roof. We had 80 trees. The neighbor across the street woke up with a 70-foot tree laying atop one of their bedroom's gables.

The portable battery-operated radio was all we had for communication, plus the radio in the car. News was scarce, Galveston was being destroyed. People were wading down the middle of our street, pulling a wagon that carried a large ice chest they filled with BBQ sandwiches they had cooked and made themselves, and were passing out to those in need. I stood mid-calf in the water next to a pile of our furniture, chairs, rugs, and such, declaring that we appreciated their efforts to help us, but there were people a few houses down that really needed a hand and "thanks anyway." The family of four were two adults and two small 1st or 2nd grade girls pulling the wagon through the water and they gave us our sandwiches, which made us smile, we thanked them, as they went on down the street.

From a historical point of view, the radio weather forecaster said that Hurricane Ike followed the path of the Great Galveston Hurricane of 1900.

There was no need to guess the outcome of the gallery situated one block from the seawall and next to the Train Museum. I mentally thought about what the gallery would look like. Utterly destroyed, I was sure. From what we could glean from the reports, two-thirds of Galveston was essentially wiped away. The last punch to the gut would be to remember that the gallery had no insurance on contents. I was sickened to think about so many of the artists that contributed works that were the best they had and now they lost it all. The gallery was probably emersed in saltwater.

It was not hard to imagine it, as painful as it was to recall from memory. My wife and I had been in hurricanes before. For me, this was the fifth one. I would need to tear out all my wooden floors, take out the walls, tear out all the kitchen cabinets, upper and lower, no refrigerator, no dishwasher, no vacuum cleaner, on and on, and on. The only thing left was the carpet that ran up the stairs to the second floor. It was soaked in a foot of standing water until the water receded several days later and it was wicking its way to the second floor. We had to tear that out as well.

It would be months before we would go into Houston, for any reason. The hurricane blew out hundreds and hundreds of skyscraper glass windows and it would be a very long time before they could even "get it in the dry."

In the meantime, the downtown streets were covered in tons of glass shards. Finding building materials and cabinets and sinks, and washer and dryers would be the hurdle for us. We just wore our clothes until we couldn't stand ourselves or each other and we would go into the yard and pile them up for burning. We continued to live on the driveway that was on the north side of the house, and where we were sheltered from most of the winds. We lived that way for weeks without electricity.

The reports from the news channels became more organized and informative—once we had electricity restored, that is. Every structure in Galveston was flooded with water. I expected it would still be a few weeks before any highways would be passible and that would be for the rescue and ambulances taking people out of flooded hospitals, setting up and operating food and medicine depots. Thank God for the Cajun Navy!

A friend of a friend of a fellow Galveston gallery exhibitor left me a message and a phone number to call. They had information for me about the Galveston gallery. One of the gallery's owners knew someone in the National Guard who was attempting to get a ride on a high-water military half-track rescue truck to survey the street where the gallery was, in order to assess the damages and assign resources. No one was permitted to enter the area. They were there to prevent looting, primarily.

The next day I got a call from someone who was relaying a message that the gallery was entered to assess the contents and to figure out who would be allowed entry. But it turned out that he was also allowed to remove some things and had just a few minutes to do so. He loaded things in the back of the half-track, and as it turned out, he recovered some of my stained-glass windows! And he was calling to tell me that someone would contact me to say where they would be so that I could pick them up.

I found them stacked in a pickup and they didn't look so bad—no mud or broken panes, no first-glance damage. They clearly had watermarks on them but not much else. But the more I unwrapped them, the more surprised I was. I was not finding damage! Would I ever be so lucky? Well, I guess this time I would be.

I finally got the mental picture as to how it had happened. It was pretty simple. The gallery's storefront windows never broke during the rising tide that came with the hurricane. The water simply rose up its eight or nine feet inside, the hurricane moved onto higher ground, the water receded and left them hanging to dry.

Duh, they are windows! I built them to be used as windows and I sealed them like you would any other glass window, to go into an opening. They weren't hurt by being submerged for just a short time and then they drip-dried.

We still had too many stained-glass windows at home after all the travails and I decided to keep a smaller group of them. Why? Because I liked some of the survivors. As painful as it was for my ego, I agreed to garage sale some of them. It was like the granny who had so many children, she didn't know what to do.

So, some of them went with the excess things left over from the hurricane at our house and sold in the driveway yard sale.

Imagine, I was building windows that would be galleried in the few hundreds of dollars, up to $1,500. Some people came by to look.

The driveway bargainers would stop and walk over and say, "I can go $35..."

Some friends took a window or two with them after coming for a visit.

I kept a few for the new house we were moving into, once I found the house.

I made a gift to the Methodist Church.

I donated windows to a local charity that sold them and kept the money to aid families in need.

Stained glass windows, historically, were made to present a story to the masses, because they didn't know how to read.

I started out to learn about glass, to teach myself something, so that I could go tell the man that sold and destroyed that church what a mistake he made. On reflection, that beginning was 50 years ago.

Who's Going to Heaven

Who's going to Heaven when the wind starts to blow,
And a crown of thorns is worn by those that stayed
    for the show,
And the water keeps on rising and washes out the road,
Does the screaming wind say, "You're staying,"
    or " You're the next to go."

They stayed too long, and they knew it was wrong,
    a time or two before.
Their excuses used their character, as the storm closed
    the door.
Their hopes were all forgotten as they hugged the
    moving walls.
The tidal surge kept a coming, as the waves broke the floor.

BREAK

Many a times their reasons made a case to stay or go.
It won't be that bad, you know, our pride will help us stay.
Let the grace of God surround us, in this fury in the night,
If we can find a place in this wreckage to kneel down,
    we'd like to pray.

CHORUS

Possessions have no value when they're piled on
    Crystal Beach,
And the Saviors that came to save us are a long time
    in their last sleep,
Let the waves of time remind us when it's time to stay or go,
And who's going to Heaven when the wind starts to blow,
And who's going to Heaven when the wind starts to blow.

C.E.P.

When the teaching day began, it always started with the startling sound of an alarm going off at 5 a.m. It seems I was unable to get used to hearing that ringy dingy. I was working for three school systems as a substitute teacher, going from district to district at the drop of the hat, beginning at that 5 a.m. bell, which was the time the automated computer system in monotone voice would describe the opening slots available for the day. If you wanted the assignment, it would give you the contact person, location, and the subject you would teach, while the regular teacher was away.

Hop to it, Bunkie, the fire drill to get up, get going, and out the door had to take 15 minutes and then the drive to school, in the dark, could be an hour or more.

Some schools were new, clean, had good staff, energetic students, and dedicated teachers. They were a joy to work in and for. Education should be this good everywhere—History, Art, Science, Government, English, Theater, Machine Shop, and Agriculture in the Big Barn next to Welding. Some teachers requested me, specifically, to take their class; art classes were my joy.

Nice schools, meaning that they were clean and kept the graffiti wiped down, were nice. School kids have this vibe to them that was readable as I watched them going to and fro, and their classroom demeanor. Getting hired into a school of *your* choice was a bit tricky. The hiring window was open for just a few weeks and then Teacher Orientation started and hiring windows closed for the year. The best you could do was to do your best in the hopes you could be recognized and be a good fit for the next year. *Year?* Might as well talk about salary and get all the disappointments at the same time out of the way.

There was the time when all the hiring was done, the dust had settled, and everybody went about their lives for another year, but then I learned about a new school that was going to be built for Houston Independent Schools, one of the largest school districts in the U.S. It was going to be an alternative school. That's all right with me, I began my teaching career in an alternative school, in the city zoo in Grand Rapids, Michigan. So, I wanted to learn more about this new school.

The school was going to be a "partnership" school, something between a public and private school. I got directions from the office and drove over to see it. Construction on the building had already begun and the first students would arrive within a week or two! Very fast! What's the catch? Where are the students, now?

The location for the school was in the southwest part of town. That should have been the tipoff, right there. The need for the school was pressing and haste was needed. They had the building they were going to use and the walls and so forth were being installed.

What I drove into was the parking lot of a vacant shopping center, probably a Wal-Mart or something like it. It was large, and the parking lot was large and filled up with machinery. There was scaffolding erected across the front of the building and pallets of sheetrock being driven inside. Crews of men were raising walls and building corridors and walkways. Electrical conduit straps and trays were being installed and electrical grids were being completed.

Two areas had been moved into—the receptionist desk inside the front entry, and one other office that adjoined it. I met with someone in that office. The school director. As I approached the receptionist desk, I looked into one of the classrooms and saw a dozen or so girls, sitting around desks, taking instruction from a female teacher. They all wore school uniforms.

The school director said I had the right public and private school experience, elementary, secondary, and college level teaching experience, and managerial background that would be needed for the Director of Admissions position he wanted me to establish and operate. The school would be growing, as the school had the classrooms built out and were ready to occupy. Teachers and other staff would be added as they were identified, and the needs increased.

So, in a nutshell, I found a school that would be a whirlwind environment to work in. The school was a combined enterprise of using public schools and their per capita money of state education funds and the private industry that would contribute to the "business" and take profit percentages and then would open, after a year or so later, another school campus for HISD (Houston Independent School District).

The location, I mentioned, being in the southwest area of Houston tipped me off and the director confirmed it. The students were coming from one of the major gang activity areas in Houston, which was riddled with crime. Other students would be mixed in with the school's population—those who are chronically truant, had behavior issues, or they were underaged high school dropouts! Texas state law mandated that a person had to attend school until they graduated or turned 18. Like a Wheel of Life sort of thing.

As finished classrooms were built out, we added students that were clustered generally by grades, 7th with 7th, 8th with 8th and so on. Segregated by sex, too. The school continued to take students, and the population gradually grew, to a few hundred. I did all the enrolling and did orientations that lasted a week. Lots of info and lots of "what if's" to get everyone off on the right foot.

Members of different street gangs made my classroom orientations and their participation a challenge. Lots of blow-ups, as they flashed their gang signs and tried to "claim their turf" in my classroom. I had a female assistant and an armed city policeman outside my classroom door. Every week I had a new class of students. A couple of knock-down, drag-out fights a week was the norm. Rival gang members would wind up in my classroom and the room would erupt. Usually, the policeman and a hall monitor or two took control and brought order back to my room. Sheetrock walls were repaired.

Academics were self-paced and either on a computer or by worksheet. Someone could advance quicker with a subject and not wait on the teacher to lecture an hour a day. Progress was certainly accelerated, once the student understood how fast they could advance. The challenge was keeping "the street" out of the classroom.

Some students were able to catch up from when they dropped out of school and hit the streets. Some could start thinking about actually being a high school graduate, instead of a dead-end dropout. Little did they know there was a wolf hidden in my sheep's clothing!

Were there disruptions in the school? Yes. The males on staff were not small folks and the people from the streets were quick to "mix it up." Security was tight. The front lobby receptionist area and my office were the only areas that were not secured. Controlled entrance was required.

Students coming into the school from the streets, the bus, or drop-offs went through metal detectors, plus a pat down, always. Girls were no exception. Long hair and bras were problem areas, hiding places for switchblades, shivs, and knives. Boys on one side with male staff; girls on the other side with female staff.

The structure and implementation of the schools had been presented to the school system and approved before I entered the picture. Some procedures and guidelines were adjusted, I'm sure, but that was not in my pay grade.

Let's get serious, really serious. When students were ordered to attend this school, they defied their parents and refused to attend. Parents then had to bring their truant to a juvenile judge to explain or get a fine from the county. Many parents were working two or more jobs and declared to the court they couldn't control their child. Many times, they admitted they were scared of the child because of the child's angry outbursts.

The school fixed that—they set up a Juvenile Court *in the middle* of the school and had the hearings on campus.

Usually around 6 a.m. or so, two county truant officers would show up at junior's house, get him out of bed in many cases, provide "jewelry" (handcuffs) if the situation warranted, and he would be in my classroom that morning, whether he wanted to be or not.

Another way to look at it is to think we were all trying very hard to make this young person successful—in spite of himself!

9-11

I picked up an American flag today,
I hardly knew what I was doing.
It must have fallen from another car,
And I picked it up from the side of the road.

I know I learned somewhere that the
American flag should not ever touch the ground,
And the only honorable way to lay it to rest,
Is to have it consumed by fire.

I picked up an American flag today,
I hardly knew what I was doing.
The Stars and Stripes looked so vivid today,
It was something that happened, I know.
It wasn't thrown away.

I dusted it off and put it in the seat beside me.
It was a grateful passenger,
As we started on the road again.
The people in the other cars smiled at me as I got back in.
"I know," they must have thought, "you
picked up the flag for you.
But I also see when you picked it, you picked it up for me."

Jon Bunn

Nine-Eleven

September 11, 2001. I left for work that morning and heard on the news the part about an airplane hitting the Twin Towers. On the way in, I saw every kind of vehicle on the street carrying and displaying the American flag. No news report I heard on my car radio mentioned what type of aircraft it was that had collided with the building. I'm thinking someone flying a small Cessna would be the idiot that couldn't see the huge building and ran into it.

Every kind of vehicle on the road that morning sprouted American flags. I couldn't imagine where all of them came from. This was quite a spontaneous reaction. I saw a flag that had fallen from a car that morning and I stopped and picked it up.

Then the second plane hit the Twin Towers. It was a commercial airliner.

Good Lord, what gives? By the time I got to school, the busses were starting to come in, mostly empty. What televisions we had were set up throughout the school and the day became crazy. I kept about a dozen 7th grade boys in my classroom and their reactions were all over the place. Many parents chose to keep their kids at home. It was an ominous morning.

The camera men and women were riveted on the fires burning and they were filming live. As unfortunate as it ever could be, the cameras caught and broadcast people falling and dropping from the sides of the buildings to their deaths, prior to the towers collapsing. It all happened so fast, my young students must not have been able to juxtapose themselves away from such horrors and some started yelling and laughing with glee to see the people tumbling down the side of a building on the way to their death, as if they were being entertained, as if they were watching a studio wrestling show on television.

Within moments of their glee and laughter, I became mad at them, recalling my own memories of standing at the top of the Twin Towers at Windows On The World for my own marriage, years before. These young boys soon read the moods of other students and staff and regretted their outbursts. I was able to understand that the wild excitement and energy coming from the boys was their way of processing a turbulent experience no one had ever been through before. Teachers and staff alike.

My orientation classes continued, and the student population grew from a few hundred students to over a thousand students. High school and middle school dropout enrollments hardly slowed. The second school was built out and they were taking in comparable numbers of students.

Let it be clear. Public/private school organizations or business interests are a complex and tangled affair in so many instances for communities and state education agencies. Many a community has found it to be a political cauldron, and this school was no different. To assuage some of the proposed reformulation of school systems, HISD and the CEP school invited some important voices to tour the school. Our school population was overwhelmingly minority. The staff was minority based. Perhaps it may have been a factor in inviting the son of Dr. Martin Luther King, Jr. and guests to visit.

Some of the teachers, myself included, prepared a short singing program for the attending guests. I played the guitar and 15 or so girls sang a couple of hymnal songs, as well as my choice, "Amazing Grace" to MLK III and accompanying guests. He was delighted that song was chosen and spoke to the girls about the beginnings of the song and how it came about.

I moved from directing enrollments and orientations to becoming a classroom teacher. We were at or near capacity. It was my time to move forward and onward. The school was full of high-risk people in high-risk environments, both at the school and at home. It was high-risk for staff, as well.

❋ ❋ ❋

So, about that time, on a doctor's check-up appointment, he said to me, "Let's look at your arteries in your neck and we'll do a scan to get a better look."

My wife and I went to get the results of the CT-scan.

"Oh, we can fix this easily enough, what's your schedule next week?"

"Just having family in for Thanksgiving…"

"I'll set you up the week after that and we will get you all taken care of, how's that?"

"Okay …. so, now, what are we going to do?"

"My x-rays indicate that you have some blockages we're going to fix. I'm guessing I'll get you in and I'll do a *triple heart bypass!*"

In actuality, it turned out to be a *quadruple* heart bypass. But that's another story for another time.

Ride a Train into Tomorrowland

It's a short rope meant to hang a man,
It's a long rope when it's you that's going to fall.
It's a crazy game that you keep playing,
When you know it's not your name that's called.

Hop on a bus down to Tampa, man,
Better yet, get on a bus to Disneyland.
Quit dragging around what people keep saying,
Put a smile on your face and get a tan.

Ride a train into Tomorrowland,
The future you make can change so fast.
Hop on board the fire-breathing Iron Horse,
Remember to watch the scenes as they go past.

Roll the dice and play with the past,
As a grain of sand in the hourglass.
Like you're falling through the Twilight Zone,
You embrace the Light and you head on home.

About the Author

Iwas born in the far western corner of No Man's Land in Oklahoma's Cimmaron Strip – the Trail of Tears, which is a translation of what the Native Americans called "The place where they cried." I was then raised in Texas from a young age, but much of my childhood also became a trail of tears, which eventually led me to drop out of high school and head to the shelter of relatives in Indiana. I re-enrolled in school there and began carving out a life for myself, including graduating from Indiana University and becoming a teacher.

The 60's was a time filled with British rock 'n' roll and American folk and bluegrass music. I bought myself a 12-string guitar and started playing and learning the latest songs and even performed in a few bars for spare change while finishing school. I studied the works and lyrics of others, and then began to write songs of my own. But sometimes the lyrics weren't enough words for what I was trying to say. And so, I began to realize I wasn't writing a song. I was writing a story. And gradually, I began to realize I was thinking like a writer.

But the only reason I was able to capture these ideas was because I was writing them down. I had a notebook I carried around with me and jotted ideas and random quotes and thoughts in it that sparked my imagination. These jottings are just like change in your pocket, ready to use when a story starts coming into focus.

After publishing my first, and then my second novel, people began asking me how to write a book. My advice is to simply "Start writing!" Get it down on paper—sentences, paragraphs, thoughts—and then go back over it later and read it, re-read it, add to it, or delete it. The seed is the part that grows the tree. For me, one song led to a book. But the main thing is to get it written down, and then improve it later. It's like polishing shoes. Put the polish down on the shoe and then begin the polishing that will make the scuff marks fade and disappear, and make the shoes shine.

Just keep writing. Get your first draft completed, and ignore the spelling mistakes, the verbs in the wrong tense, the fact that maybe everything isn't quite in the right order. You also shouldn't share any part of your first draft with your friends and relatives, even though you may be dazzled by your own literary wizardry. Let it rest before moving on. Give it time to ripen, a few weeks or so. Resist temptation. No peeking! Then you're ready to revise it—your second draft.

There are many, many books that can give an aspiring author guidance. I found Stephen King's *On Writing, A Memoir of the Craft* especially inspiring. I encourage you to read one or a few of these types of books, enough to give you some grounding. This is not to confuse or to discourage you, but to give you some signposts. I *still* read what other writers proffer. They give you so many new ideas to explore and try out, and it makes you feel like you're in good company.

Jon "Tex" Bunn
Spicewood, Texas
September 2024

Jon Bunn has donated a copy of this book to the Bookshare program, part of Benetech.org's global literacy initiative. Bookshare provides eBooks for the blind and others with disabilities around the world. He encourages all authors to donate a copy of their book to this worthwhile program.
To find out how:
www. bookshare.org/CMS/partners/authors
or write to: authordonations@bookshare.org

Jon is also a volunteer author in the Texas Talking Book Program free library service for people who are unable to read standard print due to visual, physical, or reading disabilities. The program serves more than 18,000 visually impaired Texans each year.
For more information:
www.tsl.Texas.gov
1-800-252-9605